Charter Schools and the Law:

Establishing New

Legal Relationships

Charter Schools and the Law:

Establishing New

Legal Relationships

Preston C. Green III and Julie F. Mead

Christopher-Gordon Publishers
Norwood, Massachusetts

Credits

Christopher-Gordon Publishers, Inc.
1502 Providence Highway, Suite #12
Norwood, Massachusetts 02062
800-934-8322
781-762-5577

Printed in the United State of America

10 9 8 7 6 5 4 3 2 1   07 06 05 04

ISBN: 1-929024-66-5
Library of Congress Catalogue Number: 2003109005

This book is dedicated to

Fiona Greaves, Catherine Williams

and

David Mead

Contents

Acknowledgments xiii

Chapter 1. Introduction 1
  Background to the Charter School Movement 1
  Charter Schools and School Law 5
  Format of the Book 8

CHARTER SCHOOL OPERATIONS

Chapter 2. Statutory Provisions and Variations That Define
           Charter Schools 17
  Issues Affecting the Establishment of the
    Charter School 17
  Home Schools and Cyber Schools: Must a Charter
    School Be a Place? 20
  May For-Profit Entities Operate Charter Schools? 24
  May a Charter School Applicant Appeal the Denial of a
    Charter? 26
  May Charter Schools Charge Tuition? 29
  Must Charter Schools Comply with Health and Safety
    Standards? 30
  State Constitutional Challenges to Charter Schools 31
      Are Some Charter Schools Actually Private Schools
        and Therefore Not Deserving of Public Funds? 31
      Are Charter Schools a Constitutional Part of
        a Public School System? 34
    Do Charter Schools Create an Unconstitutional
      Divestment of Authority? 35
  Conclusion 36

Chapter 3. Accountability 43
  State and Federal Accountability Standards 43
  Issues of Contractual Accountability 45
    Standards Guiding Revocation/Renewal Decisions 49
    Charter Schools' Ability to Enforce Charter
      Contracts 54
  Accountability Enforced by Parents 54
  Conclusion 56

Chapter 4. Charter Schools and Finance 59
Overview of Charter School Funding Systems 59
Financial Mismanagement on the Part of Charter Schools 60
Economic Effect of Charter Schools on School Districts 62
    State Constitutional Challenges 63
    Statutory Challenges 64
Protections from Districts' Withholding Funds
    from Charter Schools 66
Discriminatory Treatment of Charter Schools 67
    Equal Protection Clause 67
    State Constitutional Provisions 69
Students with Disabilities 70
At-Risk Students 71
Distribution of Assets upon Closure of Charter School 72
Conclusion 72

Chapter 5. Charter Schools and Employment 77
Teachers' Role in Charter School Development
    and Approval 77
Issues Related to Hiring Employees 78
    Who Is the Employer? 79
    Must Charter Schools Contract with Employees? 81
    May Teachers Receive Leaves of Absence to
        Work in Charter Schools? 82
    Can Teachers Be Assigned to Work in a
        Charter School? 83
    Must Charter School Teachers Be Certified? 84
Issues Related to Working in a Charter School 88
    May Charter School Employees Bargain Collectively? .. 88
    Does Charter School Employment Implicate
        Participation in State Teacher/Employee
        Retirement Funds? 91
    Do Tenure Laws Apply to Charter School Teachers? 92
    Do Charter School Teachers Have Any Rights
        to Return to a Previous Position in a School
        District? 92
    Do Any Provisions Relate to Termination of Charter
        School Teachers? 93
    What Other Provisions of Charter School Statutes
        Relate to Employees? 95
    Is It Fair to Treat Charter School Teachers Differently
        from other Public School Teachers? 95
Conclusion 96

INSTRUCTIONAL DELIVERY IN CHARTER SCHOOLS

Chapter 6. Charter Schools and Race 101
Overview of the Equal Protection Clause 101
Racial Balancing Provisions 102
Non–Racial Preference Admissions Policies 111
Court-Ordered Desegregation Decrees 114
Charter Schools with Curricula That Appeal to
    Particular Racial and Ethnic Groups 117
Conclusion 118

Chapter 7. Charter Schools and Gender 123
Charter Schools and Requirements for Gender Equity 123
Could a Charter School Be Targeted to Serve only
    One Gender? 126
Legal Authority Guiding Single-Sex Education 128
    Principle 1: Exceedingly Persuasive Justification 136
    Principle 2: Substantial Relationship 138
    Principle 3: Comparable Benefits 139
Conclusion 140

**Chapter 8. Charter Schools and Students with
    Disabilities** 145
Section 504/ADA and Charter Schools 146
Charter Schools and the IDEA 150
May a Charter School Serve Only Children with
    Disabilities? 158
Implications for Charter School Authorizers 159
Conclusion 161

Chapter 9. Charter Schools and Religion 165
State and Federal Statutory Provisions That Limit the
    Involvement of Religious Institutions 166
Facial Challenges under the Establishment Clause 169
As-Applied Challenges under the Establishment
    Clause 172
    Charter Schools That Are Operated by
        Religious Institutions 172
    Parochial School Conversions to Charter Schools 176
    Charter Schools That Are Operated by a Majority
        of Members from One Religious Institution 176
    Partnerships for the Provision of Secular Services 177

Leasing Agreements between Charter Schools
and Religious Institutions 177
State Constitutions 178
Equal Protection Clause 179
Practices That Might Face Establishment Clause
Challenges 180
Teaching Ethics and Morality 180
Teaching Creationism 182
Providing Released Time for Religious Instruction 183
Providing After-School Religious Instruction 184
Conclusion... 185

**Chapter 10. Charter Schools and the Rights of Parents and
Students** 189
Mandatory Uniform Policies 189
Free Speech Clause.. 190
Substantive Due Process 191
Hybrid Constitutional Claims 192
Submission to Random Urinalysis as a Condition
of Attendance 194
Parental Involvement Contracts 197
Substantive Due Process 198
Equal Protection Clause—Freedom of Association....... 198
State Constitutions 200
Charter School Discipline Codes 200
Conclusion... 201

Chapter 11. Concluding Thoughts 205

Appendix A
Public Charter Schools Program: Nonregulatory
Guidance (December 2000) 211

Appendix B
Office of Civil Rights: Applying Federal Civil Rights Laws
to Public Charter Schools: Questions and Answers 221

Appendix C
Nonregulatory Guidance: The Impact of the New Title I
Requirements on Charter Schools, Draft Guidance
(March 24, 2003) 239

Appendix D
  Summaries of Selected Cases Involving
  Charter Schools 247

Appendix E
  Charter School Statutes 263

Appendix F
  Charter School Law and Policy Links 267

Index 269

About the Authors 273

Acknowledgments

This book is the culmination of a truly collaborative effort at legal scholarship. Some chapters were first published as academic articles.[1] Others were written for this volume alone. All are the product of numerous hours of reading and re-reading statutes, identifying legal issues, and puzzling over which issues are particular to charter schools and which are not.

We have many people to thank for bringing this project to fruition. Christopher Miller and Judith Risch, graduate students at the University of Wisconsin-Madison, provided considerable help locating and deciphering various statutory provisions. We also thank Fiona Greaves for helping to develop our legal analysis. We further wish to thank the charter school contacts working at state educational agencies for their kindness in graciously answering our questions by both phone and e-mail. For the manuscript reviewers, we greatly appreciate their thoughtful suggestions for improving earlier drafts. We also extend our gratitude to the editors and staff at Christopher Gordon Publishers for their input, support, and patience as the book developed.

We also owe some personal thank-yous. First to our children, Noah Green, and Caitlin, Conor, and Kelly Mead, we are grateful for the truly joyous relationships only children can offer. They are our true accomplishments. Finally, we thank our spouses, Fiona Greaves and David Mead. Without their love, encouragement, and support, we would not have had the courage to embark on this adventure.

Endnotes

1 Portions of Chapter 2 and Chapter 11 come from Julie F. Mead, *Devilish Details: Exploring Features of Charter School Statutes That Blur the Public/Private Distinction*, 40 Harv. J. on Legis. 349 (2003). Portions of Chapter 6 come from Preston C. Green, *Racial Balancing Provisions and Charter Schools: Are Charter Schools Out on a Constitutional Limb?*, 2001 BYU Educ. & L. J. 35 (2001). Portions of Chapter 7 come from Julie F. Mead, *Single-Gender "Innovations": Can Publicly Funded Single-Gender School Choice Options Be Constitutionally Justified?*, 39 Educ. Admin. Quart. 164 (2003). Chapter 8 first appeared as Julie F. Mead, *Determining Charter Schools' Responsibilities for Children with Disabilities: A Guide through the Legal Labyrinth*, 11 B.U. Pub. Int. L. J. 167 (2002). Portions of Chapter 9 come from Preston C. Green, *Commentary: Charter Schools and Religious Institutions: A Match Made in Heaven?*, 158 Educ. L. Rep. 1 (2001).

Chapter 1

Introduction

In the realm of public education, charter schools are a relatively new construct. Appearing first in the 1990s, charter schools are public schools that are formed by a "charter" between a designated chartering authority and those who wish to operate a school. State legislatures grant charter schools autonomy from many laws and regulations that apply to traditional public schools. In exchange for this autonomy, charter schools must achieve the educational goals that are established in the charter. Failure to do so may result in the closing of the school.

This chapter provides a background to the charter school movement and explains why charter schools may be vulnerable to litigation. It concludes with a brief overview of the legal issues that are covered in subsequent chapters.

Background to the Charter School Movement

In 1983, the National Commission of Excellence warned in its influential report, *A Nation at Risk: The Imperative for Educational Reform*, that the public school system was creating a "rising tide of mediocrity that threatens our very future as a Nation and a people."[1] Charter schools were one of several reforms that arose in response to *A Nation at Risk*. In 1988, educational consultant Ray Budde introduced the concept of charter schools in his book *Education by Charter: Restructuring School Districts*. Budde proposed that local school boards give a charter to teams of teachers within a school to develop educationally innovative ideas. Albert Shanker, former president of the American Federation of Teachers, popularized the concept in his weekly news column in the *New York Times*.[2] In 1991, Minnesota became the first state to pass a charter school law. By 2003, this number had increased to 40 states, the District of Columbia, and Puerto Rico (See Figure 1.1).[3] The number of charter schools has also grown steadily during the same decade. The Center for Education Reform reports that as of January 2003, there were nearly 2,700 charter schools serving a total of 684,000 students.[4]

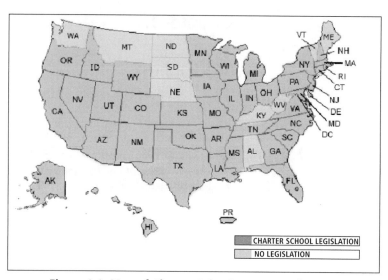

Figure 1.1. Map of Charter School States as of 2003[5]

Proponents assert that charter schools have several benefits. First, these schools create more educational choices for families to find the public school program that is right for them. Second, charter schools provide competition to traditional public schools. Such competition, some argue, will challenge traditional public schools to become more responsive to the needs of parents and students. Third, charter schools serve as a laboratory for the development of educationally innovative ideas. Charter school statutes promote such development by providing autonomy from various laws and regulations. Charter schools also encourage individuals and groups from outside the public school system to implement their own educational visions. Finally, charter schools promote accountability because they face closure if they fail to meet the standards established in the schools' charters.

Within these generalities, however, charter schools vary greatly from state to state. Some states have allowed for broad application of this idea, permitting many entities to authorize charter schools and allowing an unlimited number of charter schools to exist. Other states have instituted far more restrictive charter school programs, limiting both the number of charter schools and those that may authorize them. Accordingly, the specifics regarding how a charter school may be established differ from state to state. Table 1.1 summarizes the wide variety of organizations and officials that enjoy charter-granting authority.

Table 1.1. Organizations and Officials with Charter-Granting Authority

Charitable Organizations	Minnesota
City Council	Wisconsin[6]
County School Districts	California
Intermediate Educational Agencies	Michigan, Minnesota, Ohio
Local School Districts	Alaska, Arizona, California, Colorado, Connecticut,[7] Delaware, District of Columbia, Florida, Georgia, Indiana, Idaho, Illinois, Iowa,[8] Kansas, Louisiana, Michigan, Minnesota,[9] Missouri, New Mexico, Nevada,[10] North Carolina, Ohio, Oklahoma, Oregon, Pennsylvania,[11] South Carolina, Tennessee, Texas, Utah, Virginia, Wisconsin, Wyoming
Mayor of a City	Indiana[12]
State Board of Education	Arkansas, Arizona, Connecticut, Delaware, Hawaii, Idaho, Illinois,[13] Louisiana, Massachusetts, Mississippi, Missouri,[14] North Carolina, New Hampshire, New York,[15] Oregon, Texas, Utah, Virginia
State Board of Charter Schools	Arizona, Puerto Rico[16]
State Commissioner of Education	New Jersey
Vocational School Districts	Oklahoma
Colleges and Universities	Florida,[17] Indiana, Michigan, Minnesota, Missouri, North Carolina, Ohio, Wisconsin[18]

As Table 1.1 indicates, the majority of states grant chartering authority only to the state educational agency and local school districts, independently or in combination with other districts. Colleges and universities also have this authority in eight states. The most unusual chartering authorities occur in Minnesota, Wisconsin, and Indiana. Minnesota has granted authority to charitable organizations.[19] Wisconsin and Indiana have used chartering authority to address concerns of urban education reform by granting chartering authority limited to the city limits to the Common Council of the City of Milwaukee[20] and the mayor of Indianapolis,[21] respectively. Minnesota stands out as the state that has granted this authority to the most entities.[22]

Charter school statutes also vary according to the number of charters that may be granted and the duration of the charter. Tables 1.2 and 1.3 summarize these characteristics.

Table 1.2. Limitations on the Number of Charters That May Be Granted

Unlimited	Arizona, Arkansas, Colorado, Delaware, Georgia, Indiana, Michigan,[23] Minnesota, Missouri,[24] New Jersey, Ohio, Oklahoma,[25] Oregon,[26] Pennsylvania, Puerto Rico, South Carolina, Texas,[27] Wisconsin, Wyoming
Limited to a Statewide Total	Alaska, California,[28] District of Columbia, Hawaii, Idaho, Illinois, Iowa, Kansas, Louisiana, Massachusetts, Mississippi, New Hampshire, New Mexico, New York, North Carolina, Rhode Island,[29] Utah, Texas[30]
Each Charter-Granting Authority Limited to a Certain Number of Charter Schools	Connecticut,[31] Florida,[32] Nevada,[33] Virginia

While Table 1.2 shows that 18 states and Puerto Rico now allow an unlimited number of charter schools to be created, the remaining states put restrictions of one form or another on the number of charter schools. This constraint sometimes takes the form of a statewide limit on the total number of charter schools. Of these, Mississippi has the strictest cap, allowing a total of only six charter schools statewide. In other cases, the only limitation is the number of charter schools one charter-granting authority may sponsor. For example, in Connecticut only two charter schools may exist in any one school district. In addition, even though Missouri and Oklahoma place no statutory limit on the total number of charter schools, a practical limitation does result, however, since these states have granted chartering authority only to districts of a particular size.

Table 1.3. Maximum Length of the Charter Term

3 years	Arkansas, Delaware,[34] Florida, Kansas, Minnesota, Oklahoma, South Carolina, Utah, Virginia
4 years	Mississippi, New Jersey[35]
5 years	Alaska, California, Colorado, Connecticut, Georgia, Idaho, Illinois, Massachusetts, Louisiana, New Hampshire,[36] New Mexico, New York, North Carolina, Ohio, Oregon, Pennsylvania, Puerto Rico, Rhode Island, Wisconsin, Wyoming
6 years	Nevada
10 years	Michigan, Missouri
15 years	Arizona, District of Columbia, Florida[37]
Not Specified	Hawaii, Indiana,[38] Iowa,[39] Texas

As Table 1.3 shows, variation also occurs with respect to length of the charter term. Although the most common term length is 5

years as specified in 19 states and Puerto Rico, terms range from a low of 3 years to a high of 15 years. Renewal terms are of similar length although Delaware, New Jersey, and New Hampshire allow longer terms upon renewal of the initial charter. Some states have not specified a charter contract length, thus leaving the matter for contract negotiation.

Despite this variability, charter schools have several characteristics in common. First, states relieve charter schools of certain state laws and regulations in exchange for the schools' commitment to achieve educational outcomes that are delineated in the charter. Sometimes, that relief is granted in the form of a blanket exception to state laws or regulations pertaining to education. In other cases, charter schools must specifically request waiver from those portions of the state education code from which they seek relief. Second, proposals must undergo a review process that scrutinizes their educational mission and curricular focus. Third, schools must bind themselves to specific provisions of a charter or contract negotiated with the charter-granting authority. State statutes uniformly define required provisions for charter school contracts. Although the contents of the charter vary, the school has no authority to exist without its development. In addition to the statutory requirements for charter contract provisions, the parties may include any negotiated provision, and these discretionary provisions, too, become binding on the school. Finally, if the school fails to achieve the educational outcomes set out in the charter, it is put on notice and given a chance to correct its problems. However, if the school continues to perform under expectations, its charter can be revoked or not renewed at the end of its term.

Charter Schools and School Law

The study of law is the study of relationships. Law considers what authority a government has over its citizens and the limitations that constrain that authority. School law is the study of the relationships a school has with the state, the community, its school board, its staff, its students, and its parents. Federal and state constitutional guarantees and numerous statutory and regulatory provisions at both levels govern these relationships. In addition, case law has evolved to instruct schools about the application of legal principles in the public educational environment. Until the advent of charter schools, that environment was characterized by state constitutions that mandated legislatures to create systems of public schools. Most state legislatures responded by delegating authority to state educational agencies and/or to local educational agencies. These agencies, in turn, created the regulations that govern traditional public schools. However, charter schools, by definition, have different relationships with state and local authorities from traditional public schools. These relationships are defined by the specific authorizing statutes in each state and by the particular provisions of an individual school's contract with its sponsoring authority.

As an illustrative example, Figures 1.2 and 1.3 depict the delegation of authority for education in the state of Wisconsin before and after the enactment of charter school legislation. Note that not only has the Wisconsin legislature added new institutions to whom authority has been granted, it has also granted existing local educational authorities (school districts) the license to create three types of educational options for its students: traditional public schools, charter schools where the school district employs all staff (instrumentality charter schools), and more independent charter schools where the school district does not employ any staff (non-instrumentality charter schools). Note, too, that the state legislature has defined the role of its state agency with respect to charter schools differently depending on the chartering authority and the type of charter school (instrumentality or non-instrumentality) created. Each state that adopts charter school legislation creates before-and-after pictures such as those depicted here, although the precise parameters vary from state to state.

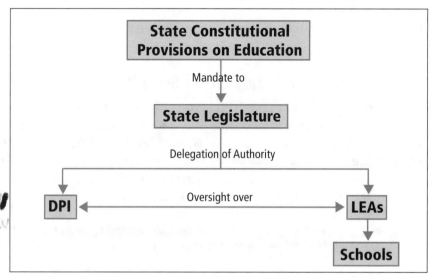

Figure 1.2. Traditional Delegation of Authority over Education in Wisconsin
DPI: Department of Public Instruction; LEAs: Local Education Agencies

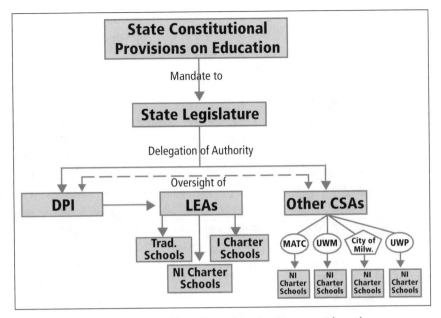

**Figure 1.3. New Delegation of Authority over Education
in Wisconsin with Charter Schools**

DPI: Department of Public Instruction; LEAs: Local Education Agences; CSAs: Charter School
Authorizers; MATC: Milwaukee Area Technical College; UWM: University of Wisconsin-Milwaukee;
UWP: University of Wisconsin-Parkside; Trad.: Traditional; I: Instrumentality; NI: Non-Instrumentality

Whatever structures are created by charter school legislation, these new relationships create legal issues not present in more traditional public school settings. For example, what effect does the introduction of specific contract performance standards have on relationships between schools and the state or between schools and their parents? Complicating the issue further is the fact that charter schools may be relieved from state laws and rules, but remain bound by federal statutory and regulatory requirements. Also, some of the educational benefits identified in the previous section may subject the charter school movement to litigation. Many families have exercised their power of choice by attending charter schools that are disproportionately one-race. This phenomenon may violate federal constitutional and statutory provisions. Legislatures have taken several steps to counter this problem, including implementing racial balancing provisions that require charter schools to reflect the racial composition of the surrounding school districts. But these actions also raise legal questions.

Moreover, the element of competition may also make charter school statutes susceptible to litigation. School districts have argued that charter schools take away educational funding. Consequently, several school districts have asserted that they cannot satisfy their constitutional duty to provide an adequate education. Charter schools have countered that states violate their statutory and constitutional rights by failing to provide them with equitable or adequate funding. May statutes allow charter school funding to be a matter of contract negotiation or does "equal educational opportunity" demand that charter school students enjoy an equivalent amount of state and/or local school dollars spent on their behalf?

Furthermore, the element of educational innovation might bring on litigation. First, plaintiffs have claimed that the autonomy granted to charter schools places them outside constitutional understandings of what constitutes a public school. Specifically, they have argued that charter schools are too autonomous either to be considered "public" or to be part of a constitutional system of public schools. Second, the charter school movement has sparked the interest of religious institutions, whose participation might raise constitutional concerns. What federal and state constitutional prohibitions related to the separation of church and state apply, or do not apply, to the establishment of charter schools? A third consideration stemming from educational innovation may be what, if any, liability may be owed to students and their parents if an educational innovation fails to produce the desired achievement for its students. Finally, charter schools have tried ideas, such as parent involvement contracts and mandatory dress codes, that implicate the rights of parents and students.

These issues and others form the basis of exploration in this book. Now that states have created a new kind of public school known as a charter school, a new question must be examined: What legal issues particular to the charter school context should be understood by policymakers, charter-granting authorities, charter school operators, and parents considering charter school attendance for their children? Examining this question necessitates investigation of the statutory requirements associated with charter schools; issues of equal educational opportunity based on race, gender, and disability; student and employee rights; and separation of church and state. In short, addressing this question requires an examination of the relationships charter schools have with each of their constituencies.

Format of the Book

The following chapters address each of those issues and specific questions related to them. In addition, the chapters consider guidelines for policymakers and practitioners about avoiding lawsuits relating to the various issues identified. Chapters 2, 3, 4, and 5 all consider legal issues related to school operations. Chapter 2 explores the statutory variations of states' charter school laws and the varying requirements they place on charter schools. It examines a number of questions, including the following:

- May existing public or private schools convert to charter school status?
- May "home schools" become charter schools?
- May charter schools exist in cyberspace without a physical location for students to attend?
- May charter schools charge tuition?
- May for-profit educational management companies operate charter schools?
- To what standards of health and safety are charter schools held?

Chapter 3 analyzes one of the charter school movement's defining characteristics, accountability. Questions addressed in chapter 3 include the following:

- How are charter schools held accountable through state systems of assessment?
- How do the accountability provisions of the No Child Left Behind Act of 2001 apply to charter schools?
- How do charter contracts define accountability?
- What is the role of charter school authorizers in charter school accountability?
- What cause must exist to justify revocation or nonrenewal of a school's charter?
- Are charter schools vulnerable to educational malpractice challenges?

Chapter 4 considers the legal issues surrounding funding for charter schools. It explores such questions as:

- How are charter schools funded?
- What statutory provisions are designed to prevent fiscal mismanagement on the part of charter schools?
- What issues arise regarding the economic impact of charter schools on school districts?
- What happens if school districts withhold funds from charter schools?
- Can charter school statutes provide less funding to charter schools than to non–charter schools?

- Can chartering authorities subject charter schools to more stringent accountability measures than non–charter schools?
- Are state school finance systems vulnerable to challenges from charter schools that serve large populations of students with disabilities and at-risk students?
- What issues arise surrounding the distribution of assets upon the closing of a charter school?

Chapter 5 focuses on issues related to charter schools and employment. Questions under study include the following:

- Must charter schools hire state-certified teachers?
- Do federal statutes prohibiting employment discrimination apply to charter schools?
- May charter school employees unionize?
- Does charter school employment implicate employee retirement benefits?

The next section of the book is divided into five chapters that discuss legal issues related to instructional delivery in charter schools. Chapters 6, 7, and 8 all consider equal educational opportunity in charter schools. Chapter 6 examines issues of race in charter schools. The questions addressed include:

- Do charter school racial balancing provisions violate the Equal Protection Clause?
- Must charter schools comply with court-ordered desegregation decrees?
- Do charter schools with curricula that appeal to a particular racial group violate the Equal Protection Clause?

In like manner, Chapter 7 examines issues of gender in charter schools by considering:

- How does Title IX apply in the charter school context?
- Do single-sex charter schools violate the Equal Protection Clause or Title IX?

Chapter 8 addresses charter school's obligations for students with disabilities by examining the following questions:

- How do Section 504 of the Rehabilitation Act and the Americans with Disabilities Act (ADA) apply to charter schools?
- How must charter schools serve children with disabilities in compliance with the Individuals with Disabilities Education Act (IDEA)?
- What are the implications of section 504/ADA and IDEA for charter school program development?

- Are charter schools created to serve only children with disabilities consistent with federal disability law?
- What are the implications of section 504/ADA and IDEA for charter school sponsors?

Chapter 9 analyzes legal questions that may arise regarding religion. Those questions include the following:

- May charter schools be located on church grounds?
- May charter schools teach religion in the classroom?
- May religious organizations operate charter schools?
- May charter school statutes prohibit religious organizations from operating charter schools?

Chapter 10 explores the legal questions that surface related to the rights of students and parents in charter schools by addressing the following:

- May charter schools have mandatory uniform policies?
- May charter schools that serve chemically dependent or incarcerated youth condition admission on a student's agreement to submit to random urinalysis?
- May charter schools require parents to sign parental involvement contracts as a condition of admission?

Finally, Chapter 11 provides some concluding remarks based on the earlier analysis.

As will become clear, the legal terrain on which charter schools operate is complex. Many of the issues described here have already been argued in courts of law. Others are just beginning to surface. Still others require a careful examination of the interplay between state, federal, and contract law in order to fully understand how legal principles are given expression in charter schools. All demonstrate that by authorizing the creation of charter schools, state policymakers are truly establishing new legal relationships between schools and the public they serve.

Endnotes

[1] David P. Gardner. et al., *A Nation at Risk: The Imperative for Educational Reform. An Open Letter to the American people. A Report to the Nation and the Secretary of Education* 5 (1983).

[2] Albert Shanker, *Where We Stand*, N.Y. Times, July 10, 1988, at E7.

[3] As this book went to press, Maryland became the 40th state to enact charter school legislation. It is not included in the analysis of state statutes that follows.

[4] Center for Ed. Reform, *Charter School Highlights and Statistics,* available at http://www.edreform.com/pubs/chglance.htm (visited Mar. 5, 2003).

[5] Map taken from U.S. Charter Schools, web site operated by the U.S. Department of Education at http://www.uscharterschools.org/pub/uscs_docs/gi/state_ map.htm (visited Sept. 10, 2003).

[6] Wis. Stat. § 118.40(2r)(b). Only the Common Council of the City of Milwaukee has this authority.

[7] Local charter schools are approved first by local boards of education and then by the state board of education. Conn. Stat. §10-66bb(e).

[8] Local charter schools are approved first by local boards of education and then by the state board of education. Iowa Code Ann. § 256F.3(3).

[9] Educational districts may grant charters. Education districts are partnerships among at least five school districts. Minn. Stat. § 124D.10(3).

[10] Local school districts need the approval of the state board of education. Nev. Rev. Stat. 386.515.

[11] A regional charter school may be chartered by a group of local school districts. Pa. Stat. Ann. tit. 24 § 17-1703-A

[12] Only the Mayor of Indianapolis has this authority. Ind. Code § 20-5.5-1-15.

[13] State board of education may grant charter on appeal of local school board's decision or if charter is approved by referendum. Ill. Comp. Stat. 5/27A-6.

[14] State Board of Ed. may only grant charters on appeal. Mo. Rev. Stat. § 160.405.(2)(3).

[15] Charters may also be submitted to local school districts or board of trustees of state universities. State board of education is the only entity authorized to issue a charter. N.Y. Educ. Law § 2851(3).

[16] The charter school organization is known as the Educational Reform Institute. 111 P.R. Laws Ann. § 18.

[17] State universities may develop research schools. Fla. Stat. § 228.056 (4)(e).

[18] Only the University of Wisconsin–Milwaukee, the Milwaukee Area Technical College and the University of Wisconsin–Parkside enjoy this authority limited to the geographical limits related to the institution. Wis. Stat. § 118.40(2r).

[19] Minn. Stat. § 124D.10(3).

[20] Wis. Stat. § 118.40(2r).

[21] Ind. Code § 20-5.5-1-15.

[22] Minn. Stat. § 124D.10(3).

[23] Universities are limited to a statewide total of 150 by the year 1999.

[24] Chartering authority limited to urban districts, but no limits within those districts.

[25] Chartering authority limited to school districts with 5,000 or more pupils, but no limits within those districts.

[26] No more than 10 percent of students may be enrolled in charter schools in any given district.

[27] There are no limits on the number of district-sponsored charter schools.

[28] The statute limits the number to a yearly statewide total that increases as the years progress.

[29] Charter schools are also limited to serving 4 percent of the state's school-age population.

[30] State-sponsored open enrollment charter schools are limited to 100 statewide.

[31] No more than 2 charter schools per school district.

[32] Limits based on district size.

[33] Limits based on the size of the county.

[34] Initial term is 3 years, but may be renewed for terms of 5 years thereafter.

[35] Initial term is 4 years, but may be renewed for terms of 5 years thereafter.

[36] Initial term is 5 years, but may be renewed for terms of 7 years thereafter.

[37] Only Florida charter schools operated by a municipality or other public entity are eligible for terms of 15 years.

[38] Indiana's statute does not list a maximum length of a charter contract, but does specify that the minimum length of a term must be 3 years.

[39] Iowa's statute does not list a maximum length of a charter contract, but does specify that the minimum length of a term must be 4 years.

Charter

School

Operations

Chapter 2

Statutory Provisions and Variations That Define Charter Schools

This chapter explores the statutory variations of states' charter school laws. These issues affect both how schools are created and how schools operate. These issues all revolve around characteristics that each state has used to define charter schools in its jurisdiction. These special statutory characteristics have sparked litigation in several jurisdictions and may have the potential to do so in others.

First, issues affecting the establishment and operation of charter schools are explored, including such topics as conversion of private schools to charter schools, home schools and cyber schools, the involvement of for-profit management companies, whether the decisions made by charter-granting authorities can be appealed, whether charter schools may charge tuition, and the application of health and safety standards. Next, the chapter examines various challenges to charter schools from a state constitutional perspective. It includes discussion of three topics: (1) Are charter schools too private? (2) Are charter schools part of a constitutional system of public schools? and (3) Do charter school statutes unconstitutionally divest authority from state and local boards of education?

Issues Affecting the Establishment of the Charter School

Charter schools can be developed in one of three ways. A charter school may be a new educational program, not in existence before being granted the authority to charter. Second, a charter school may be created when a traditional public school is converted to charter school status. Third, a private school or program may be converted to a public charter school. All three types of charter schools currently operate in the United States. Depending on the wording of the authorizing statute, states may allow one, two, or all three types of charter schools.

Of all the ways that charter schools are created, the conversion of an existing public school to charter school status may be the least controversial. Conversions of traditional public schools or public school programs are allowed in all charter school states. In fact, Mississippi limits charter schools to this category, expressly prohibiting the development of "new" charter schools and the conversion of private schools to public charter schools.[1] All other charter school states allow the creation of new schools as charter schools, although Iowa allows only the creation of "a new school within an existing public school."[2]

Even the conversion of public schools may not completely escape controversy, however. One interesting case is *International High School: A Charter School at LaGuardia Community College v. Mills*, which involved two public alternative high schools in New York.[3] Both had been designated "twenty-first century schools"[4] and therefore enjoyed some waivers from New York education statutes, including an exemption from participation in the state's Regents examinations. After converting to charter school status, the schools requested an extension of this waiver, which the state denied. The schools filed a judicial appeal, and the court determined that New York's charter school statute clearly contemplated that charter school students would sit for the examinations and that, upon conversion to charter school status, the schools effectively surrendered the variances they had received earlier.[5] This case serves as a caution to those considering conversion, to make certain that they understand not only what they can gain from charter school status, but also what they might lose from the conversion.

Another New York case, challenging the development of a new charter school, illustrates the political interests that may become involved in granting a school's charter. In *Board of Education of Roosevelt Union Free School District v. Board of Trustees of the State University of New York*, a school district and a group of district parents and students challenged the grant of a charter to a proposed school that was to be developed within the district's boundaries.[6] The plaintiffs complained that the Board of Trustees, as the charter-granting authority, failed to follow proper procedures for granting the charter. The court agreed, ruling that New York's charter school law required, as a prerequisite to granting any charter, that a charter-granting authority make explicit findings that a proposed charter school would improve student learning and achievement in the geographic area to be served. Because the Board of Trustees had failed to make such findings, the court remanded to the Board of Trustees for further consideration.[7] In addition to the unambiguous reminder that procedures established in charter school statutes must be carefully observed, this case also highlights the tension that may arise when charter school authorizers other than school districts exercise their authority. Here, the local school district forcefully opposed the actions of the university authorizer in creating a new public school option in the same locality.

The conversion of private schools into public charter schools produces far more variability from state to state. As depicted in Table 2.1, only 9 states and the District of Columbia currently allow these conversions, while 27 states expressly prohibit it. Of the states that allow private school conversion, Wisconsin and Utah restrict conversion to nonsectarian private schools. Wisconsin also requires school districts considering private school conversions to first hold a hearing to "consider the level of employee and parental support for the establishment of the charter school and the fiscal impact of the establishment of the charter school on the school district."[8]

[handwritten marginalia: Why do private schools convert to charter to [get?] money?]

Table 2.1. Private School Conversion to Charter Schools

Private School Conversions Allowed	Arizona, District of Columbia, Michigan, Missouri, Oregon,[9] Pennsylvania, South Carolina, Texas, Utah,[10] Wisconsin[11]
Private School Conversions Prohibited	Arkansas, California, Colorado, Connecticut, Delaware, Florida, Georgia, Hawaii, Idaho, Illinois, Iowa, Louisiana, Massachusetts, Mississippi, Nevada, New Hampshire, New Jersey, New Mexico, New York, North Carolina, Ohio, Oklahoma, Rhode Island, South Carolina, Tennessee, Virginia, Wyoming
Statute Does Not Address This Issue	Alaska, Indiana, Kansas, Minnesota, Nevada, Puerto Rico

It is often difficult to discern when a structural change to a private school truly becomes a conversion to a new public status and all that it entails. Drawing these lines may also raise legal issues. For example, most states require that charter schools admit students on a random basis if applicants outnumber available seats. Random selection is also a requirement under federal law in order for charter schools to be eligible for federal monies offered through the federal charter schools program.[12] Accordingly, the Michigan Department of Education scrutinizes conversion charters to ensure that former students of the private school receive no preference in the enrollment process. Its regulations state, "if over 75% of students had previously attended [the] non-public school this would be taken as evidence that good-faith advertising was not done and [the] charter school would have to defend its advertising efforts to receive state aid."[13] Similarly, states that prohibit conversion from private to charter school may define conversion with recognition that a new charter school may wish to inhabit premises formerly occupied by a private school. Determining whether a school has converted or whether a new school has occupied an old building may be confusing. For example, New York's statute expressly prohibits the conversion of existing private schools to public school status.[14] It considers factors such as shared location and whether "the charter school would have the same or substantially the same board of trustees and/or officers as an existing private school" to help discern whether a charter school application is, in fact, a petition to convert.[15]

As these two examples illustrate, even when a statute contains clear provisions prohibiting the conversion of private schools, there remain difficulties and ambiguities in determining whether a proposed charter school is a "new" school or a "conversion" school. In such a statutory context, whenever a private school closes and a charter school opens in the same physical space, the charter school should be prepared to demonstrate its independence from the previous entity or risk denial of its application. It may also be necessary to show that all area students, not just those previously enrolled, had genuine and equal access to the charter school program.

Home Schools and Cyber Schools: Must a Charter School Be a Place?

The use of charter schools to permit home schooling is another statutory variation that has sparked considerable controversy. Twenty-five states expressly prohibit the use of charter school laws to provide funding for the support of home schooling. For example, Oklahoma's statute reads, "[a] charter school shall not be used as a method of generating revenue for students who are being home schooled and are not being educated at an organized charter school site."[16] Table 2.2 lists the states with similar prohibitions. The remaining states' statutes are silent on the issue, allowing the inference that in those states a charter school could be used to support the education of students who never congregate at a place called "school" but instead remain at home.

Virtual schools are chartered

Table 2.2. Charter Schools as Home Schools

Charter Schools as Home Schools Permitted	Alaska, Arizona, Arkansas, California, District of Columbia, Hawaii, Idaho, Massachusetts, Michigan, Missouri, New Jersey, New York, Ohio, Puerto Rico, Texas, Wisconsin
Charter Schools as Home Schools Prohibited	Colorado, Connecticut, Delaware, Florida, Georgia, Illinois, Indiana, Iowa, Kansas, Louisiana, Minnesota, Mississippi, New Hampshire, New Mexico, North Carolina, Nevada, Oklahoma, Oregon, Pennsylvania,[17] Rhode Island, South Carolina, Tennessee, Utah, Virginia, Wyoming

Even among states in which statutory language prevents charter schools from supporting traditional home schooling, charter schools may serve children who receive instruction through the Internet at home in so-called cyber schools.[18] In order to justify cyber charter schools, their proponents have drawn a distinction between "home schooling" and instruction that occurs in the home.[19] Although the term "home schooling" is apparently reserved for parental instruction of children in the home, instruction delivered in the home via the computer is described as a school that links teachers and students by means of the Internet in a virtual educational community; and creates a different type of school from "home schools," in that they may fall under a different statutory category.[20]

In Pennsylvania, the question of whether this distinction marks a substantive rather than a semantic difference has already spawned litigation.[21] Pennsylvania's charter school law contains a provision expressly stating that it is not to be used to provide funds to home schoolers.[22] Nevertheless, Pennsylvania school districts have chartered a total of nine cyber charter schools.[23] Four lawsuits have been brought challenging the existence of these special charter schools or seeking to prevent them from enrolling students from across the state who were not residents of the sponsoring school district.[24] The legal challengers asserted that these cyber charter schools directly violated the statutory prohibition against home schooling and a number of other statutory provisions.[25] In response, the sponsoring school districts argued that their programs were neither home schools nor the conversion of home schools to charter status. Rather, they suggested that the programs were best considered nontraditional home-based instruction. The Commonwealth Court of Pennsylvania first refused the Pennsylvania School Boards Association's (PSBA) request for a statewide preliminary injunction on the issue and interpreted Pennsylvania's charter school law as permitting cyber charters.[26] The court rejected PSBA's arguments that the charter statute required schools to have specific premises, finding no explicit language to prohibit cyber charters and referencing instead various passages in the state charter school law that indicated legislative intent to use charter schools as a means to provide innovative environments for both students and teachers. The court also determined that "cyber education" satisfied compulsory attendance requirements.[27] Thus, the court determined that cyber charter schools were consistent with statutory requirements.

The Pennsylvania Legislature settled the argument in June 2002 with the enactment of House Bill 4.[28] The new provisions revised the state charter school statute by vesting the Pennsylvania Department of Education (PDE) with exclusive authority to grant and oversee charters for cyber charter schools. The provisions create additional requirements applicable only to cyber charter schools, requiring them to provide the state with details about their operation; to maintain administrative offices and records physically within the state; to provide students with all necessary equipment; and to disclose relevant information about the school, its staff, and its operations to parents. In addition, upon the expiration of their current contracts, existing cyber charter schools must seek charter renewal directly from the PDE. School districts are precluded from renewing those charters. Finally, existing cyber charter schools must submit documents to the PDE to enable it to determine whether the school is in compliance with statutory requirements. As of August 14, 2002, three of the nine existing cyber charters were determined to be out of compliance with the statute.[29] The PDE has the authority to revoke the charters of cyber charter schools that fail to come into compliance.

Cyber charters have also generated controversy in two other states. In California, as in Pennsylvania, the state legislature instituted provisions to regulate cyber charter schools.[30] Nothing in California's charter statute explicitly or implicitly precludes the use of home-based instruction as a method of education delivery. Although no litigation has challenged this status quo, statutory provisions enacted in 2001 require that charter schools providing less than 80 percent of student instruction at a physical school site fulfill further requirements in order to be eligible for state funding. Moreover, non–classroom-based schools must complete a funding audit form to demonstrate that at least 50 percent of the funds they receive are spent on student instruction. If that funding level is not met, the California State Board of Education is authorized to impose funding reductions of up to 10 percent during the first year of noncompliance, with increasing penalties in subsequent years. Finally, a charter school providing non–classroom-based instruction is also prohibited from receiving any funding unless an audit form is properly filed with the state.

In Wisconsin, as in California, nothing in the state charter school statute expressly precludes state funding for a charter school that serves home-schooled children and their families or delivers instruction via the Internet, yet a cyber charter school has drawn legal attack, nonetheless. The Wisconsin Education Association Council (WEAC)[31] recently filed suit against the Appleton School District challenging the operation of its cyber charter school, Wisconsin Connections Academy, as a violation of state law.[32] The school enrolls non-residents of the school district through the statewide open enrollment program in addition to district residents.[33] WEAC maintained that the state legislature did not intend the charter school statute to allow virtual education or to allow the statewide open enrollment program to be used to allow students to attend school in nontraditional virtual settings.[34] The court disagreed, finding that the cyber charter school "operates within the parameters" of the charter school law and that nonresident students "have correctly enrolled" in the cyber charter from other districts.[35]

In addition, public debate about cyber charter schools in Wisconsin has raised further objections by groups that represent home-schoolers: the question of whether the acceptance of cyber charter schools will subject home schooling to regulatory control. One such group, the Wisconsin Parents' Association (WPA), fears that "'with money comes strings.'"[36] According to one WPA member, "'Home-schoolers have opted out of government schools for one reason or another. Now here's something that will bring the government right into people's homes.'"[37] Statutory provisions requiring charter schools to satisfy all health and safety regulations applicable to traditional public schools and subjecting charter school students to periodic state academic examinations are of predominant concern to this group.[38] The WPA has succeeded in finding a sponsoring state assemblyman to propose a bill amending the open enrollment program to preclude the participation of any "pupil [in] a school or program in which the pupil will receive less than 50 percent of his or her instruction from a licensed teacher who is present in the same room as the pupil,"[39] which, if enacted, would effectively prevent students from enrolling for a complete education in cyber charters under the open enrollment program.

As these three states demonstrate, cyber charter schools may raise unique legal issues that require examination of the intersection of a state's charter school law with its laws governing compulsory education, home schooling, statewide open enrollment, and school funding, in order to determine the legality of cyber charter schools in a given state. In addition, the manner in which states resolve these questions has the potential to radically alter traditional conceptions of public schools as places where communities send their children for collective instruction and social interaction. The experiences of these three states also suggest that policymakers will be called upon to weigh the relative merits of cyberspace approaches to instructional delivery.

May For-Profit Entities Operate Charter Schools?

The question of whether for-profit management companies may obtain charters has also invited controversy. Most states require charter schools to operate as nonprofit entities.[40] Five states (Arizona, Colorado, New York, Virginia, and Wisconsin) have enacted statutes that contain no language requiring charter schools to operate as nonprofit entities. Presumably, then, each of these states permits charter-granting authorities to grant a charter directly to a for-profit entity. In all other states, schools must operate as nonprofit organizations, but they may still elect to contract with a for-profit company for management of the school. When those situations arise, the relationship between the nonprofit operators of the charter school and the for-profit contractors may come under scrutiny.

Questions about the relationship between for-profit contractors and charter schools in this type of partnership motivated four Pennsylvania lawsuits. In the first two cases, *West Chester Area School District v. Collegium Charter School*[41] and *Brackbill v. Ron Brown Charter School*,[42] the local school districts had denied charter applications due to concerns about the closeness of the school's relationship with its contractor. In both cases, courts examined whether each school's proposed board of trustees was sufficiently independent of the for-profit company, Mosaica, Incorporated, that was contracted to operate both schools. Mosaica had prepared each charter school's application, raising the question of whether the schools had been properly "established" by nonprofit companies.[43] In both cases, the court rejected the challengers' argument and allowed the grant of charters to the schools.[44] In its *Brackbill* holding, the court provided a list of factors to determine whether a charter school properly respects the non-profit requirements of Pennsylvania statutes:

> [T]he Charter School's articles of incorporation state that the school is organized as a non-profit corporation under Pennsylvania law. The Charter School's bylaws and the revised application both state that the Board of Trustees has full authority to operate the school, including determining general academic, financial, personnel, and other policies as outlined in the CSL [Charter School Law]. Additionally, the agreement makes clear that the Board of Trustees is independent of Mosaica and that Mosaica can exercise no authority which may not be delegated under the School Code and other applicable laws and resolutions. There is nothing in the record to indicate that any member of the board is employed by Mosaica or has any financial interest in the company.[45]

By contrast, the relationship between a nonprofit charter school operator and its for-profit vendor may trigger a violation of Pennsylvania's statutory not-for-profit rule if it appears to lack the requisite independence.[46] For example, in *Butler Area School District v. Einstein Academy*, the fact that the nonprofit Einstein Academy Charter School and its for-profit vendor, Tutorbots, Incorporated, were owned and operated by the same two individuals raised the question of whether the nonprofit was simply a front for the operator.[47] In fact, in a related petition in a separate case requesting declaratory judgment from the state's Commonwealth Court on its role in the oversight of Einstein Academy, the PDE noted that "[d]ocuments provided by Einstein to the PDE do not evidence any independent fiscal oversight or any other independent entity of Einstein's operations or of the contract between Einstein or Tutorbots."[48]

Another Pennsylvania case, *School District of the City of York v. Lincoln-Edison Charter School*,[49] established that determining the relationship between the nonprofit charter applicant and its for-profit management company depends on a complete assessment of the final agreement between the parties.[50] In *Lincoln-Edison*, the school district had denied an application for the conversion of an existing public school to a charter school, which was to be operated by a for-profit company, Edison Schools, Incorporated. The district pointed to "the questionable relationship between the applicant and Edison Schools, [Incorporated]" as one of its reasons for denying the charter.[51] The charter applicant appealed to the Charter School Appeal Board (CAB), which overturned the denial and ordered the school district to grant the charter even though no agreement had been finalized between the proposed charter school and Edison, Incorporated. On appeal, the Commonwealth Court determined that the CAB had erred in ordering the school district to grant the charter in the absence of a finalized management agreement.

All these cases examining the relationship between nonprofit charter holders and their for-profit vendors suggest that when states require charters to be held by nonprofit entities, disputes may arise concerning the contracts with for-profit management companies. Resolving these cases requires the careful examination of the application, bylaws, and management contract; a determination of how and by whom decisions are made for the school; and the investigation of the relationships between the for-profit entity and those involved in the school's governance.

May a Charter School Applicant Appeal the Denial of a Charter?

Charter school applicants may or may not be able to appeal the denial of a charter school petition. Fourteen states and Puerto Rico have elected not to create an appeals process (see Table 2.3). In fact, some statutes may even preclude appeals altogether. For example, Delaware has determined that "[i]f application is made to the Department or a local board as an approving authority and the charter application is not approved, such decision shall be final and not subject to judicial review."[52] Notwithstanding the absence of appeals procedures, one might argue that states that have multiple charter-granting authorities with overlapping jurisdictions actually have a *de facto* appeals process, because an applicant denied by one authority can simply petition another charter-granting authority for approval.

As Table 2.3 shows, 25 chartering states and the District of Columbia have created some type of appeals process to challenge the denial of a charter application. As depicted, appeals may be directed to a variety of reviewing bodies. The most common appeals route, allowed in nineteen states, is to the State Board of Education. Five other states allow appeals to some other state agency or official, including two states (Indiana and Pennsylvania) that have created special boards specifically authorized to hear charter school appeals. Two more unusual processes occur in Michigan, which allows voters to decide appeals through a ballot initiative process, and Oklahoma, which permits dissatisfied applicants to submit the issue to mediation or arbitration. Finally, seven states and the District of Columbia have statutory provisions expressly granting judicial appeal, either directly or after exhaustion of an administrative review process.

Table 2.3. Appeals Processes

No appeals process described in statutes	Alaska, Arizona, Arkansas, Connecticut, Delaware, Hawaii, Kansas, Massachusetts, New York, Ohio, Puerto Rico, Rhode Island, Texas, Utah, Virginia
Appeals allowed to: State Board of Education	California, Colorado, Florida, Georgia, Idaho, Illinois, Iowa, Louisiana, Mississippi, Missouri, Nevada, New Hampshire, New Jersey, New Mexico, North Carolina, Oregon, South Carolina, Tennessee,[53] Wyoming
State Educational Agency	Wisconsin[54]
State Superintendent	Idaho, Minnesota
Special Charter Appeals Board	Indiana, Pennsylvania
Mediation/arbitration	Oklahoma
Voter initiative	Michigan
Court of law	District of Columbia,[55] Florida, Illinois, Missouri, New Hampshire, Oregon, Pennsylvania, South Carolina

States that have created administrative appellate procedures sometimes grant the reviewing decision-maker the authority to grant directly a charter denied by another charter-granting authority, while in other states the matter is remanded to the initial charter-granting authority with an order to grant the charter. Still other states limit the appellate decision-maker to issuing recommendations, which the charter-granting authority must consider upon a rehearing of the charter application.

At least one court has ruled that denials of charter school applications must include specific findings of fact in order to ensure adequate judicial review. In *Shelby School v. Arizona State Board of Education*, the court determined that specific findings were necessary to document "the precise basis for the Board's decision" in order for a reviewing court to ascertain whether the decision was reasonable.[56] The court also determined that the state board could consider creditworthiness of applicants and the relationship of the charter school directors to a church, given the charter school statute's requirements that schools demonstrate a plan for financial soundness and operate in a nonsectarian manner. The court also rejected the school's contention that it had a constitutional property interest under the Fourteenth Amendment to the grant of a charter once the state board determined that its application satisfied all the requisite elements. The court found that a determination that an application is satisfactory is but one step in the process and no protected property interest exists until a charter is actually issued.

The Supreme Court of South Carolina in *Beaufort County Board of Education v. Lighthouse Charter School Committee* first determined that the state board of education should not reverse the denial of charter school application by a local school board unless the findings made by the local school board were "clearly erroneous."[57] Likewise, any reviewing court should apply the same standard. In this instance, the court held that a school board's denial of a charter on the grounds that the proposed charter school failed to satisfy health and safety requirements, and the racial composition requirements under state law, was supported by the evidence. In another case, an Illinois appellate court, which also applied a "clearly erroneous" standard of review, determined that the reversal of a charter school application conditioned on the submission of a viable facility plan was within the school board's authority.[58]

A series of seven Pennsylvania cases have established several guiding principles related to charter school appeals in that state.[59] *West Chester Area School District v. Collegium Charter School*[60] established the leading precedent determining that the CAB has the statutory authority to conduct a *de novo* review of any charter school application and can substitute its judgment for that of the denying local school district if the CAB determines such action to be proper. Subsequent cases established that:

1. The CAB enjoys the authority to grant charters on a conditional basis,[61] but a finalized contract between any charter school and a for-profit management company is necessary for a decision on any appeal where questions have been raised about the nonprofit status of the charter applicant.[62]

2. Petitions establishing community support for a proposed charter school need not be verified[63] or include the addresses of those signing the petition,[64] and only need to be collected in the district or districts in which the charter school seeks to operate.[65]

3. The 75-day limit for school districts to either grant or deny a charter is mandatory and the act by an applicant of filing an appeal after the expiration of that period transfers jurisdiction for the application from the school district to the CAB.[66]

4. Failure of a charter school applicant to include all requisite elements in its application provides sufficient grounds for the denial of a charter.[67]

5. A charter school must exhaust available administrative remedies prior to asserting a judicial claim.[68]

May Charter Schools Charge Tuition?

People may consider tuition as one obvious distinction between public and private schools. All but three states (Alaska, Connecticut, and Georgia) have explicit statutory language prohibiting charter schools from charging tuition. Three other jurisdictions (the District of Columbia, New Jersey, and Tennessee) allow schools to charge tuition under the same conditions as traditional public schools, such as when a student who resides outside the school district's boundaries seeks to attend the school.

Federal charter school legislation also addresses the issue of tuition. First enacted as the Charter Schools Expansion Act and now incorporated as part of the recent reauthorization of the Elementary and Secondary Education Act, known as the No Child Left Behind Act of 2001,[69] federal law defines a charter school as one that "does not charge tuition."[70] Therefore, in order for a charter school to be eligible for federal planning and implementation grants or participation in the credit enhancement program,[71] a charter school must abide by the prohibition on charging tuition.[72]

One would think that these prohibitions and the condition prohibiting tuition in order to receive federal funds would prevent the question of whether charter schools may charge tuition from even arising. Nonetheless, the Common Council of Milwaukee has raised this very issue. In its ordinance[73] and in its charter school contracts, the City of Milwaukee—as a charter-granting authority under Wisconsin statutes—declares that its charter schools may accept students on a tuition basis, except those students authorized to attend under the charter statute.[74] Wisconsin statutes prohibit charter schools from charging tuition.[75] In part, the City's challenge derives from the state's limitation on students eligible for City charter school attendance to resident Milwaukee students who were previously (1) enrolled in Milwaukee Public Schools; (2) enrolled in the Milwaukee Parental Choice Program (MPCP);[76] (3) enrolled in grades K–3 in Milwaukee private schools not participating in the MPCP; (4) not enrolled in school; or (5) enrolled in another charter school.[77] The provisions in the City's ordinance and the City charter contracts, however, allow schools to accept students on a tuition basis who do not fit any of these five categories.[78] Thus, the City's position appears to conflict directly with the Wisconsin statute's clear prohibition on students' paying tuition.[79] The Wisconsin Department of Instruction (DPI), however, has taken no direct action on this issue.[80] The Legislative Audit Bureau recommended that "the Legislature amend statutes to allow charter schools established by the City of Milwaukee, [the University of Wisconsin-Milwaukee], and Milwaukee Area Technical College to charge tuition to noncharter school students or to enroll students at all grade levels in the charter school program, even if the students did not participate in the Milwaukee Parental Choice Program."[81] The Wisconsin legislature has not acted on this recommendation as of yet, and there have been no changes to this portion of the statute.

Must Charter Schools Comply with Health and Safety Standards?

Charter school statutes uniformly hold charter schools to the same health and safety standards as traditional public schools. Federal law, too, defines a charter school as one that adheres to "all applicable Federal, State and local health and safety requirements."[82] Such compliance, then, is a necessary condition to participate in federal programs providing support to charter schools.

The imposition of health and safety standards may be especially complicated for a cyber charter school because there may be no clear "school" that must meet these standards. The school could be the offices where the teachers work, or, as the Wisconsin Parents Association fears, the rooms in the homes where the children learn. In the absence of statutory definitions, no clear answers to these questions exist. If it were determined that homes where children learn must comply with the standards, a wide range of questions would arise as to how a cyber charter school or its charter-granting authority would ensure such standards were being met. For example, one concern is whether parents would have to open their homes to inspection. Furthermore, if it were determined that the homes did not meet the standards, it is unclear whether parents or school authorities would be responsible for making the necessary changes.

Health and safety requirements were an issue in the *Beaufort* case. The school district requested additional information from a charter school applicant regarding how the school's proposed facility would satisfy the health and safety requirements "applied to public schools operating in the same school district,"[83] as required by South Carolina's charter school law.[84] The school responded only with assurances that its standards would be comparable to public schools, but provided no information concerning how the requirements would be satisfied. The school district subsequently denied the charter, in part on the ground that the school did not satisfy the health and safety requirements of the application process. The Supreme Court of South Carolina determined that the school district's finding in this regard was based on sufficient evidence and was not clearly erroneous. Unfortunately, given that acquisition of facilities may be difficult, especially at the application phase of the charter process, some applicants may find it difficult to provide more than assurances that health and safety codes will be honored.

State Constitutional Challenges to Charter Schools

The first section of this chapter explored the variety of ways legislatures have defined their charter schools. The litigation reported here has examined charter schools from a state constitutional perspective. In other words, the challengers questioned whether legislators had overstepped their discretion in creating charter schools as a public school option.

Are Some Charter Schools Actually Private Schools and Therefore Not Deserving of Public Funds?

Charter school statutes have been subjected to challenges that their autonomy from state rules and regulations makes them too "private" to receive state funding. In fact, charter schools have been variously described as "quasi-public,"[85] "other non-public,"[86] and "hybrid public schools."[87] As Table 2.4 shows, the constitutions of a number of charter school states contain provisions that might prohibit funding to private schools. Five states prohibit funding of private schools. Eleven states permit funding of only public schools. Three states permit funding only to schools that are under the exclusive control of the state.

**Table 2.4. Charter School States with Constitutions
That Might Prohibit Funding to Private Schools**

Prohibit Funding of Private Schools	Alaska, Hawaii, Michigan, South Carolina, New Mexico
Permit Funding of Only Public Schools	Connecticut, Delaware, Florida, Indiana, Missouri, New Jersey, North Carolina, Oklahoma, Rhode Island, Texas, Wyoming
Permit Funding Only to Schools That Are under the Exclusive Control of State	California, Massachusetts, New Mexico

The first decision to address whether charter schools were public schools deserving of state funding was *Council of Organizations about Parochiaid v. Governor*.[88] The Michigan Supreme Court answered this question in the affirmative. Although the high court ruled that the state constitution did not require public schools to be under the exclusive control of the state, it went on to find that Michigan's charter schools would have satisfied this requirement. The state exercised control over charter schools through the authorizing bodies' power to approve and revoke charters. The state also exercised control through its funding of charter schools. Moreover, the legislature intended that the other sections of the school code applied to charter schools. No specific provisions of the charter school statute limited the power of the state. Furthermore, when the legislature revised the school code, it specifically included charter schools within the code's provisions.

The Michigan Supreme Court also rejected the claim that the state's charter schools were not public schools because they were run by a private board of directors, and the authorizing body had no means to select members of the board. The legislature exercised control over the board by prescribing the method for choosing school officers. The state also maintained control of charter schools through the authorizing bodies, whose boards were publicly elected or appointed by public bodies.

Since *Council of Organizations*, two other state appellate courts have examined whether charter schools are public schools. In *Wilson v. State Board of Education*,[89] the California Court of Appeal held that the state's delegation of certain educational functions (such as control over curriculum, textbooks, educational themes, teaching approaches and operations of charter schools) to parents and teachers who write charters and to the grantees who operate the schools did not violate a constitutional provision requiring the legislature to provide for a system of common schools. The court reached this conclusion in part because the legislature retained control over charter schools. As the court explained: "Where the Legislature delegates the local functioning of the school system to local boards, districts or municipalities, it does so, always, with its constitutional power and responsibility for ultimate control for the common welfare in reserve."[90]

The court also rejected the claim that the charter schools violated a state constitutional provision requiring public schools to be under the exclusive control of officers of public schools. First, the legislature declared that charter schools were public schools under the exclusive control of public school officers and directed the courts to interpret the statute liberally to effectuate this conclusion. Second, the court interpreted the "exclusive control" language of the constitution to mean that the legislature could not fund schools that were in opposition to the public school system. Charter schools were clearly not opposed to the public school system because "an overarching purpose of the charter school approach is to infuse the public school system with competition in order to stimulate continuous improvement in *all* its schools."[91]

Third, the court wondered "what level of control could be more complete than where, as here, the very destiny of charter schools lies solely in the hands of public agencies and offices, from the local to the state level."[92] Chartering authorities exercised control through their application approval and revocation powers. Chartering authorities were also authorized to inspect any part of the charter school at any time. The state board of education exercised control through its authority to promulgate implementing regulations. Funding of charter schools rested in the hands of the state superintendent of schools.

Fourth, even schools that were operated by nonprofit public benefit corporations, as permitted by the California charter school statute "could never stray from under the wings of the chartering authority, the Board, and the Superintendent."[93] Fifth, chartering authorities exercised control over educational functions, such as curriculum, through their power to deny charters. Finally, the court rejected the argument that charter grantees were not officers of public schools. The constitution authorized the legislature to provide for the incorporation and organization of school districts. The legislature acted within this constitutional grant of authority by deeming charter schools to be school districts.

In *In re Grant of Charter School Application of Englewood on Palisades Charter School*, a New Jersey appellate court also held that charter schools did not violate a constitutional provision requiring public money to be used only for public purposes.[94] The court reached this conclusion because the enabling statute stipulated that charter schools were part of the public school system and were in the best interests of its students. Also, the statute declared that charter schools were public schools and their governing boards were public agents. Moreover, the court observed that the state commissioner of education could revoke a charter at any time, and that the district board determined the amount of a charter school's budget.[95]

The *Council of Organizations, Wilson,* and *Palisades Charter School* cases suggest that charter schools in other states would withstand challenges that they are too private to be considered public schools. Other courts may defer to legislative findings that charter schools are public schools and hold that states exercise sufficient control over charter schools through the approval, budgeting, and revocation processes.

Are Charter Schools a Constitutional Part of a Public School System?

Charter schools may also be vulnerable to claims that they are too different from other public schools to be considered a constitutional part of a public school system. Table 2.5 identifies charter school states with constitutional provisions that might limit the variability of public schools. Thirteen constitutions require the state to provide a system of public schools. A number of state constitutions contain language that might further limit the variability of charter schools. For instance, seven state constitutions contain provisions that require states to provide for an "efficient" system of public schools. Plaintiffs might claim that charter schools fail to comply with constitutional understandings of efficient systems. Because many charter schools provide unique instruction, their students may have a difficult time transferring to other public schools.[96] Additionally, ten states have constitutional provisions that require a "uniform" system of public schools. Charter schools may be vulnerable to constitutionality claims based on such provisions because they imply that all public schools should have substantially the same educational programming and administrative structure.[97]

Table 2.5. Constitutional Provisions That Might Limit the Variability of Charter Schools

System of Public Schools	Alaska, Arizona, California, Hawaii, Louisiana, Michigan, New York, Ohio, Oklahoma, South Carolina, Tennessee, Utah, Virginia
Efficient System of Public Schools	Arkansas, Delaware, Illinois, New Jersey, Pennsylvania, Texas, Wisconsin
Uniform System of Public Schools	Arizona, Colorado, Idaho, Indiana, Nevada, New Mexico, North Carolina, Oregon, Wisconsin, Wyoming
Uniform and Efficient System of Public Schools	Florida, Minnesota

In *Wilson*, the California Court of Appeal ruled that charter schools did not violate a constitutional provision requiring the state to provide for a system of common schools. The court found that the term "system" had come to mean a "unity of purpose, as well as an entirety of operation; and the direction to the legislature to provide 'a' system of common schools means *one* system, which shall be applicable to all the common schools within the state."[98] This meant that the educational system "must be uniform in terms of the prescribed course of study and educational progression from grade to grade."[99]

The court then concluded that charter schools were part of a single system of common schools. It deferred to the legislature's finding that charter schools were (1) part of the school system; (2) under its authority; and (3) entitled to full funding. The court also held that the statute placed charter schools firmly within a system of common schools. Charter school teachers had to satisfy the same minimum requirements as other public school teachers. The educational programs of charter schools had to meet the same requirements as other public schools. Student progress was measured by the same assessments applicable to all public school students. Finally, charter schools received funding comparable to public schools, and the statute protected against funds flowing outside of the system.

Do Charter Schools Create an Unconstitutional Divestment of Authority?

Finally, charter school statutes may be vulnerable to claims that they unconstitutionally divest authority from entities that are authorized to supervise public school systems—such as state and local boards of education—by granting chartering authority to independent public agencies, such as public universities.[100] Three state high courts have analyzed this issue; all have upheld the constitutionality of their charter school statutes.

In *Council of Organizations*, the Michigan Supreme Court ruled that the state's charter school statute did not unconstitutionally divest the state board of education of its constitutional duty to provide "leadership and general supervision" over public education.[101] Because the statute declared that charter schools were public schools, the court found that the legislature had subjected charter schools to the same degree of board of education supervision as other public schools. The court also rejected the assertion that the state's charter school statute unconstitutionally divested control over the public schools from the voters in a school district. A review of the history of Michigan's education clause revealed that the framers of the state constitution intended public education to be under the control of the legislature, which was under the control of the entire state electorate.

In *Utah School Boards Association v. Utah State Board of Education*,[102] the Utah Supreme Court ruled that the state's charter school statute did not unconstitutionally divest "general control and supervision of the public educational system" from the state board of education.[103] The court rejected the claim that the state constitution did not authorize the state board to manage charter schools in a manner different from other parts of the public school system. Such an interpretation would have been unreasonable because it was beyond question that the state board of education could operate separate types of schools in a different manner. For instance, the state board's accreditation rules for junior high and middle schools were different from those for high schools and special schools.

In *Board of Education of School District No. 1 v. Booth*,[104] the Colorado Supreme Court held that the state charter school statute's second-appeal provision did not unconstitutionally divest "control of instruction in the public schools" from local boards of education.[105] Individuals or groups that wished to open a charter school applied to the local board in the district where the school would be located. Any interested party could contest a local board's decision to deny a charter by appealing to the state board of education. On the first appeal, the state board could either affirm the local board's decision or remand with specific recommendations for reconsideration. If, on remand, the local board again denied the application, a charter school applicant could make a second appeal to the state board. On the second appeal, the state board could remand a decision to the local board with instructions to approve the charter application if doing so would be in the best interests of pupils, school district, or community. The Colorado Supreme Court upheld the second-appeal provision because it did not constitute a final contract between the local school board and the charter school applicants. Instead, the second-appeal provision merely required the local school board to make a good faith effort to resolve any issues that might prevent the opening of a charter school.

Conclusion

As the discussion in this chapter has demonstrated, the specific statutory provisions of state charter school law raise a number of interesting legal issues that span the life of a charter school from establishment, to operation, to revocation. To varying degrees, charter schools, their sponsors, and state policymakers have turned to the judiciary to help define more clearly the relationships that exist between each of the parties in the charter school movement. In so doing, each state has engaged in a complex process of defining what "charter school" means in its public educational system.

State constitutional litigation involving charter schools has come in several forms. So far, courts have upheld the constitutionality of charter schools against these challenges. Courts have deferred to the legislature, and looked to the statutory text to conclude that charter schools are not so different from traditional public schools as to be unconstitutional.

Endnotes

[1] Miss. Code Ann. § 37-28-5.

[2] Iowa Code Ann. § 256F.2(4A).

[3] 715 N.Y.S.2d 490 (App. Div. 2000).

[4] "Twenty-first century schools," a category of schools separate and distinct from charter schools, are defined by state statute as "schools which are implementing approved . . . five-year plan[s] to enable all students to achieve levels of educational achievement that are competitive with high international standards through implementation of innovative instructional strategies and restructuring of school management and programs." N.Y. Educ. Law § 309-a(1).

[5] *International High Sch.*, #15 N.Y.S. 2d at 493. The court found no basis for overturning the state's decision as arbitrary or capricious.

[6] 731 N.Y.S.2d 524, 527 (Ap. D. 2001).

[7] *But see* Board of Educ. of Riverhead Central School District v. Board of Regents of the University of the State of New York, 754 N.Y.S.2d 437 (A.D.3 Dept. 2003) (a court considering a similar challenge to the grant of a charter found that the charter granting authority had made the requisite findings prior to issuing the charter).

[8] Wis. Stat. § 118.40(2m)(am).

[9] Conversions are only allowed in the case of alternative schools. Or. Rev. Stat. § 338.035(6) (2002). Oregon statutes define an "alternative education program" as "a school or separate class group designed to best serve students' educational needs and interests and assist students in achieving the academic standards of the school district and the state." Or. Rev. Stat. § 336.615. These schools may be public or private. Or. Rev. Stat. § 336.631.

[10] Only nonsectarian private schools are eligible for conversion. Utah Code Ann. § 53A-1a-504(3).

[11] Only nonsectarian private schools are eligible for conversion. Wis. Stat. § 118.40(4)(2) (2002).

[12] 20 U.S.C.A. § 722li.

[13] Wayne Jennings et al., *A Comparison of Charter School Legislation: Thirty-three States and the District of Columbia Incorporating Legislative Changes through October, 1998,* 37 (1998).

[14] N.Y. Educ. Law § 2852(3).

[15] *Id.* The statute lists additional factors:

In determining whether an application involves the conversion of an existing private school, the charter entity and the board of regents shall consider such factors as: (a) whether the charter school would have the same or substantially the same board of trustees and/or officers as an existing private school; (b) whether a substantial proportion of employees of the charter school would be drawn from such existing private school; (c) whether a substantial portion of the assets and property of such existing private school would be transferred to the charter school; (d) whether the charter school would be located at the same site as such existing private school.

[16] Okla. Stat. Ann. tit. 70, § 3-136(A)(9) (*Id.*).

[17] Pennsylvania law permits cyber charter schools but provides that the state's home schooling regulations, Pa. Stat. Ann. tit. 24, § 13-1327.1 are not applicable to these cyber charter schools. Pa. Stat. Ann. tit. 24, § 17-1745-A(a).

[18] *See generally* Christian F. Rhodes, *Razing the Schoolhouse: Whether Cyber Schools Can Overcome Statutory Restrictions*, 167 Educ. L. Rep. 561 (2002).

[19] *See* Defendant's Proposed Findings of Fact at para. 63, Fairfield Area Sch. Dist. v. National Org. for Children, Inc. (Com. Pl. of Adams County, Pa. Dec. 11, 2001) (No. 01-S-1008).

[20] Rhodes, *supra* note 18, at 567.

[21] Pennsylvania Sch. Bds. Ass'n v. Zogby, 802 A.2d 6 (Pa. Commw. Ct. 2002); Butler Area Sch. Dist. v. Einstein Acad., No. 2001-50031 (Pa. Com. Pl. Sept. 10, 2001); Fairfield Area Sch. Dist. v. Einstein Acad., No. 01-S-1008 (Pa. Com. Pl. Dec. 11, 2001), *rev'd*, 804 A.2d 762 (Pa. Commw. Ct. 2002); Department of Educ. v. Einstein Acad. Charter Sch., No. 51 M.D. 2002 (Pa. Commw. Ct. filed Feb. 8, 2002).

[22] Pa. Stat. Ann. tit. 24, § 17-1717-A(a).

[23] Pa. Dep't of Educ., *Charter Schools Legislation*, at http://www.pde.state.pa.us/charter_schools/cwp/view.asp?a=146&Q=61834&charter_schoolsNav=|572|&charter_schoolsNav=| (last visited Mar. 3, 2003).

[24] *Zogby*, 802 A.2d at 6; *Butler Area Sch. Dist.*, No. 2001-50031 (Pa. Com. Pl.); *Fairfield Area Sch. Dist.*, No. 01-S-1008 (Pa. Com. Pl.); *Einstein Acad. Charter Sch.*, No. 51 M.D. 2002 (Pa. Commw. Ct. filed Feb. 8, 2002).

[25] *Zogby*, 802 A.2d at 6; *Butler Area Sch. Dist.*, No. 2001-50031 (Pa. Com. Pl.); *Fairfield Area Sch. Dist.*, No. 01-S-1008 (Pa. Com. Pl.); *Einstein Acad. Charter Sch.*, No. 51 M.D. 2002 (Pa. Commw. Ct. filed Feb. 8, 2002); Brief for Petitioners, *Einstein Acad. Charter Sch.*, No. 51 M.D. 2002 (Pa. Commw. Ct. filed Feb. 8, 2002). For example, the Pennsylvania School Boards Association (PSBA) asserted that "virtual attendance" did not satisfy compulsory school attendance laws; that cyber schools were the functional equivalent of home schools, which were impermissible under the charter school statute; and that cyber schools violated school staff certification requirements. Pennsylvania School Boards Association, White Paper on Cyber Schools 27 (Oct. 2001) (on file with author).

[26] Pennsylvania Sch. Bds. Ass'n v. Zogby, No. 213 M.D. 2001 (Memorandum Opinion 2001), *vacated by* 802 A.2d 6 (Pa. Commw. Ct. 2002).

[27] *Id.* at 12.

[28] H.R. 4, 186th Gen. Assem., Reg. Sess. (Pa. 2002).

[29] The three schools are Commonwealth Cyber Charter School, Einstein Academy Charter School, and Pennsylvania Learners Online Regional Charter School. As required by statute, Pa. Stat. Ann. tit. 24, § 17-1750-A(c), letters for each of the nine cyber charter schools are available at http://www.pde. state.pa.us/

charter_schools/cwp/view.asp?a=146&Q=61834&charter_schools Nav= I 572 I &charter_schoolsNav= I (last visited March 3, 2003).

[30] Cal. Educ. Code §§ 47605, 47612.5, 47614.5, 47616.7, 47634.2.

[31] WEAC is the Wisconsin affiliate of the National Education Association and represents the interests of the majority of public school teachers in Wisconsin. *See* Wisconsin Educ. Ass'n. Council, *About WEAC*, available at http://www.weac.org (last visited Mar. 20, 2003).

[32] Johnson v. Wisconsin Dep't. of Pub. Instruction, No. 2002CV002943, (Dane County, Wis., May 15, 2003).

[33] Wis. Stat. Ann. § 118.51.

[34] Notice of Plantiffs' Complaint, Jul. 18, 2002, *Johnson*, No. 2002CV002943 (Dane County, Wis.). The petitioner's complaint sought to prevent the charter school from providing on-line schooling to nonresident students and sought a judicial declaration that Wisconsin statutes do not permit virtual charter schools. *Id.* at 3.

[35] Johnson v. Wisconsin Dep't. of Pub. Instruction, No. 2002CV002943, (Dane County, Wis., May 15, 2003) at 16.

[36] Marc Eisen, *The Next Big Thing, Publicly funded cyber-schools could serve home-schoolers*, Isthmus, p. 6, March 15, 2002 at 6.

[37] *Id.*

[38] *Id.*

[39] Bill proposed to the Wisconsin General Assembly by Assemblyman John Lehman.

[40] *See e.g.*, Mass. Gen. Laws Ann. ch. 71, § 89(e) (West 2003); Pa. Stat. Ann. tit. 24, § 17-1703-A.

[41] 760 A.2d 452 (Pa. Commw. Ct. 2000).

[42] 777 A.2d 131 (Pa. Commw. Ct. 2001).

[43] *West Chester Area Sch. Dist.*, 760 A.2d at 469; *Brackbill*, 777 A.2d at 137.

[44] *West Chester Area Sch. Dist.*, 760 A.2d at 473; *Brackbill*, 777 A.2d at 139.

[45] *Brackbill*, 777 A.2d at 137.

[46] Butler Area Sch. Dist. v. Einstein Acad. No. E.Q. No. 2001-50031 (Pa. Com. Pl. Sept. 10, 2001).

[47] *Id.* at para. 8-9. The court granted the plaintiffs' motion for an injunction, concluding that plaintiffs had demonstrated "a clear right to relief on the issue of whether Einstein was validly chartered by [its sponsor]." *Id.* at para 20.

[48] Brief for Petioners, Department of Educ. v. Einstein Acad. Charter Sch. at para. 29, No. 51 M.D. 2002 (Pa. Commw. filed Feb. 8, 2002).

[49] 772 A.2d 1045 (Pa. Commw. Ct. 2001).

[50] *Id.* at 1050.

[51] *Id.* at 1047.

[52] Del. Code Ann. tit. 14, § 511(k).

[53] Appeals are only available to schools seeking conversion to charter school status after failing to make adequate yearly progress. *See* Tenn. Code Ann. § 49-13-108.

[54] Wis. Stat. § 118.40(2)(c). In general, no appeals process is available. Only those charters denied by the school board of the MPS may appeal to the Department of Public Instruction. *Id.*

[55] Appeals are also allowed to the District of Columbia Council. D.C. Code Ann. § 38-1702.01(c).

[56] 962 P.2d 230, 244 (Ariz. Ct. App. 1998).

[57] 516 S.E.2d 655, 660 (S.C. 1999).

[58] Board of Educ. of Community Consol. Sch. Dist. No. 59 v. Illinois State Bd. of Educ., 740 N.E.2d 428, 434–435 (Ill. App. Ct. 2000).

[57] *See* West Chester Area Sch. Dist. v. Collegium Charter School, 760 A.2d 452 (Pa. Commw. Ct. 2000) (establishing standards for the propriety of management contracts with for-profit management companies); Souderton Area Sch. Dist. v. Souderton Charter Sch. Collaborative, 764 A.2d 688, 697–698 (Pa. Commw. Ct. 2000) (holding that the CAB may grant charters on a conditional basis); Shenango Valley Regional Charter Sch. v. Hermitage Sch. Dist. 756 A.2d 1191 (Pa. Commw. Ct. 2000); School Dist. of the City of York v. Lincoln-Edison Charter Sch., 772 A.2d. 1045 (Pa. Commw. Ct. 2001) (holding that a finalized contract between any charter school and a for-profit management company is necessary for a decision on any appeal where questions have been raised about the nonprofit status of the charter applicant); *School Dist. of* Philadelphia v. Independence Charter Sch., 774 A.2d 798 (Pa. Commw. Ct. 2001) (holding that a 75-day limit for school districts to either grant or deny a charter was mandatory, and the act by an applicant of filing an appeal after the expiration of that period transfers jurisdiction for the application from the school district to the CAB); Brackbill v. Ron Brown Charter Sch., 777 A.2d 131 (Pa. Commw. Ct. 2001)(ruling that failure of a school district to act on an appeal within the specified timeframe effectively transferred jurisdiction to the CAB); Montessori Regional Charter School v. Millcreek Township School District, 810 A.2d 718 (Pa. Cmwlth. 2002) (holding that regardless of the number of original applications filed with authorizers, a charter school applicant is only required to obtain the signatures in support of the appeal from those districts in which the school wishes to operate).

[60] 760 A.2d 452, 460 (Pa. Commw. Ct. 2000).

[61] *Brackbill* 777,A.2d at 131; *Souderton*, 764 A.2d at 688.

[62] *Lincoln-Edison*, 772 A.2d at 1045 (Pa. Commw. 2001).

[63] *Id.*

[64] *Id.*

[65] Montessori Regional Charter Sch. v. Millcreek Township Sch. Dist., 810 A.2d 718 (Pa. Cmwlth. 2002).

[66] *Independence Charter School*,774 A.2d at 798.

[67] *Shenango*, 756 A. 2d at 1191.

[68] *See* Village Charter Sch. v. Chester Upland Sch. Dist., 813 A.2d 20, 24 (Pa. Commw. Ct. 2001).

[69] No Child Left Behind Act of 2001, 20 U.S.C. § 6301.

[70] *Id.* § 7221i.

[71] The credit enhancement provision of the No Child Left Behind Act provides federal funds to be used as collateral to facilitate the ability of charter schools to borrow funds "to address the cost of acquiring, constructing, and renovating facilities." *Id.* § 7223.

[72] *Id.* § 7221i.

[73] Milwaukee, Wis. Code, § 330-7(1).

[74] The City allows schools to charge tuition to students "who are attending [the] Charter School, but who are not doing so under sec. 118.40(2r)[the charter school statute]." Contract between the City of Milwaukee and the Downtown Montessori Academy 7 (Aug. 31, 1998) (on file with author).

[75] Wis. Stat. § 118.40(4)(b)(1).

[76] The MPCP allows low-income Milwaukee students to use a publicly funded voucher to attend any participating private school in the city. *See* Wis. Stat. § 119.23.

[77] *See* Wis. Stat. § 118.40 (2r)(c).

[78] *See* Milwaukee, Wis. Code, § 330-7(1); *see also* Montessori Contract, *supra* note 74. For example, some students may be in grades four through twelve and have neither participated in the MPCP nor attended MPS. Some students may not reside in Milwaukee, but still may wish to attend the charter school. Presumably, these provisions were enacted because the City's first charter applicants were existing private schools participating in the MPCP but seeking to convert to charter school status. *See* Milwaukee Charter Sch. Review Comm., 1998–1999 Annual Report 3 (1999). Therefore, if schools could not accept some students on a tuition basis, schools may have faced the difficult choice of turning away currently enrolled students in order to convert to charter status. Downtown Montessori, one the City's first charter schools, had three tuition students for the 2000 to 2001 school year. Telephone interview with Director, Downtown Montessori Academy (Aug. 29, 2000). In phone calls, directors of other city charter schools reported no tuition students currently enrolled.

[79] *See* Wis. Stat. § 118.40(2r)(b); Wis. Legislative Audit Bureau, Rep. 98-15, An Evaluation: Charter School Program 57 (1998).

[80] This may be the case because the agency lacks the statutory authority to challenge directly the charter school contracts created by the City or other chartering authorities. Wis. Stat. § 118.40 (2002). It is unclear what direct action DPI could take against a charter school charging tuition to some of its students under contractual provisions. Presumably, the agency could investigate a formal complaint. Another avenue might be to withhold federal grant moneys if the school in question were eligible for any. The parties could also submit the question to a court of law to construe the statute.

[81] *Id.*

[82] No Child Left Behind Act of 2001, 20 U.S.C. § 7221i (2002).

[83] 516 S.E.2d at 658.

[84] S.C. Code Ann. § 59-40-50(B)(1).

[85] Sandra Vergari, *Introduction*, *in* The Charter School Landscape 1, 2 (Sandra Vergari ed., 2002).

[86] Letter from Office of Milwaukee City Attorney to John Kalwitz, President of Milwaukee Common Council (June 25, 1998) (on file with author) (construing Wisconsin's charter school statute and concluding that the state's charter schools were not public schools). This interpretation was soundly rejected by the Wisconsin Department of Public Instruction. Julie F. Mead, *Wisconsin: Chartering Authority as Reform*, *in* The Charter School Landscape 122, 147–149, (Sandra Vergari ed., 2002). For a discussion of the controversy, see *id.*

[87] Thomas L. Good & Jennifer S. Braden, *The Great School Debate: Choice, Vouchers, and Charters* 120 (2000).

[88] 566 N.W.2d 208 (Mich. 1997).

[89] 89 Cal. Rptr. 2d 745 (Ct. App. 1999).

[90] *Id.* at 751 (internal citations omitted).

[91] *Id.* at 754 (emphasis supplied by the court).

[92] *Id.*

[93] *Id.* at 755.

[94] 727 A.2d 15 (N.J. Super. Ct. App. Div. 1999); *aff'd*, 753 A.2d 687 (N.J. 2000).

[95] On appeal, the New Jersey Supreme Court upheld the lower court's decision with little comment.

[96] *See* L.K. Beale, Note and Comment, *Charter Schools, Common Schools, and the Washington State Constitution*, 72 Wash. L. Rev. 535 (arguing that Washington's

proposed charter school statute would have violated state's constitutional duty
to provide a "general and uniform" system of public schools).

[97] *Id.*

[98] *Wilson,* 89 Cal. Rptr. 2d at 752.

[99] *Id.*

[100] William Haft, *Charter Schools and the Nineteenth Century Corporation: A Match
Made in the Public Interest,* 30 Ariz. St. L.J. 1023 (1998).

[101] Mich. Const. art. VIII, § 3.

[102] 17 P.3d 1125 (Utah 2001).

[103] Utah Const. art. X, § 3.

[104] 984 P.2d 639 (Colo. 1999).

[105] Colo. Const. art. IX, § 15.

Chapter 3

Accountability

One of the central premises upon which charter schools are based is the concept of accountability. In exchange for relief from state regulation, charter schools are held accountable in ways traditional schools are not, namely through contractual provisions. Failure to satisfactorily comply with these provisions may result in the closure of the school. In fact, the Center for Education Reform reports that as of October 2002, 194 charter schools, or 6.7 percent of the total number of schools chartered, have been closed for various reasons.[1]

This chapter explores the issue of accountability and its legal basis. Section 1 will examine how charter schools are held accountable through state systems of assessment and the accountability provisions of the No Child Left Behind Act of 2001 (NCLB). Section 2 explores issues of contractual accountability including contract contents, contract enforcement, revocation, and renewal standards. The final section considers charter school accountability enforced by parents, including charter schools' vulnerability to educational malpractice challenges.

State and Federal Accountability Standards

States have uniformly created assessment systems for tracking the achievement of their students in public schools. Charter schools are bound by the same provisions. Accordingly, charter schools in all states complete state standardized testing in the manner prescribed by state law. Although states have been willing to relieve charter schools of compliance with other provisions of state education law, they have maintained charter schools' obligation to demonstrate student learning in ways comparable to other schools.

This approach to uniform accountability was reinforced on the federal level with the enactment of the No Child Left Behind Act of 2001 (NCLB).[2] It requires that all states create accountability systems that apply to all public schools, including a state's charter schools.[3] As the U.S. Department of Education explains, this system of accountability must include several components:

- States create their own standards for what a child should know and learn for all grades. Standards must be developed in math and reading immediately. Standards must also be developed for science by the 2005–2006 school year.

- With standards in place, states must test every student's progress toward those standards by using tests that are aligned with the standards. Beginning in the 2002–2003 school year, schools must administer tests in each of three grade spans: grades 3–5, grades 6–9, and grades 10–12 in all schools. Beginning in the 2005–2006 school year, tests must be administered every year in grades 3 through 8 in math and reading. Beginning in the 2007–2008 school year, science achievement must also be tested.
- Each state, school district, and school will be expected to make adequate yearly progress toward meeting state standards. This progress will be measured for all students by sorting test results for students who are economically disadvantaged, are from racial or ethnic minority groups, have disabilities, or have limited English proficiency.
- School and district performance will be publicly reported in district and state report cards. Individual school results will be on the district report cards.
- If the district or school continually fails to make adequate progress toward the standards, it will be held accountable.[4]

As such, charter schools must complete the same testing requirements and must report scores in the same manner as other public schools. Those scores will then be used to determine whether students are making adequate yearly progress (AYP) toward state-articulated goals. The federal statute does not define AYP; rather each state must define the term as part of its overall accountability plan. Charter schools may, but are not required to, include the state's definition of AYP in the charter contract.[5] Charter schools that fail to make AYP are subject to the same penalties as other public schools under NCLB. If a school fails to make AYP for two consecutive years, it will be declared a school in need of improvement. This designation requires that the school develop a plan for improvement and notify parents of the status. Parents must also be given the option to transfer their children to a higher performing public school. Failure to make AYP for three consecutive years requires that students, on a needs basis defined by income, be provided supplemental services (such as tutoring) in addition to being allowed to transfer to another school. A fourth consecutive failure to achieve AYP must result in the implementation of "corrective actions to improve the school, such as replacing certain staff or fully implementing a new curriculum, as well as continuing to offer public school choice and pay for supplemental services."[6] After a fifth year, the school must be "restructured" through "implement[ing] significant alternative governance actions, state takeover, the hiring of a private management contractor, converting to a charter school, or significant staff restructuring."[7]

Nonregulatory guidance prepared by the Department of Education notes that, in accordance with state charter school laws, charter school authorizers are responsible for ensuring compliance with NCLB unless state statutes direct the state educational agency to assume that responsibility (See Appendix C).[8] Guidance also makes clear that local school districts are not expected to be responsible for charter school compliance with NCLB unless the school district is the charter school authorizer.[9] Finally, the guidance specifies that charter contracts may hold charter schools to more stringent standards than NCLB, but may not relieve charter schools of NCLB compliance.[10]

In addition to being held to the same academic achievement standards under NCLB, charter schools may play a role in a state's accountability plan for its other public schools. First, charter schools may be a destination of choice for parents transferring from other public schools that fail to make AYP. In fact, approximately $200 million in federal funds has been allocated for charter schools and their development through NCLB for 2002.[11] Second, charter schools may elect to become providers of supplemental services. Third, states may convert low-performing schools to charter schools under their charter school statutes.

Issues of Contractual Accountability

The introduction of contracts is probably the most radical element of charter schools that affects the legal relationships a school has with its constituencies. By its very nature, a contract creates and defines a relationship between two parties. As described in Chapter 1, charter schools trade accountability through state statutes and regulations for accountability through a charter contract. Charter contracts vary with respect to who may enter into such agreements as authorizers and the maximum term of the contract allowed by the state charter law.

Variance also exists with respect to the contents of charter contracts. Each charter school law specifies requirements for the contents of a charter school contract. Table 3.1 presents the requirements of four states as examples. As shown, some states, such as Arkansas and Indiana, dictate considerable detail with respect to the contents of a charter contract. Other states, such as Oklahoma and Wisconsin, enumerate a less detailed list. But even with this variance, common features are discernible. Contracts must define who holds the charter, the program being offered by the school, how the school will be governed, how the program will be delivered, the accountability standards to which the school will be held, and the term of the contract. Facility, liability, and funding issues may also be required elements of charter school contracts.

Table 3.1. A Comparison of Statutory Requirements for Charter Contract Provisions

| Arkansas

Ark, Code Ann. § 6-23-306 | 1. Describe the educational program to be offered;
2. Specify the period for which the charter or any charter renewal is valid;
3. Provide that the continuation or renewal of the charter is contingent on acceptable student performance on assessment instruments adopted by the State Board of Education and on compliance with any accountability provision specified by the charter, by a deadline, or at intervals specified by the charter;
4. Establish the level of student performance that is considered acceptable . . .
5. Specify any basis, in addition to a basis specified by this chapter, on which the charter school may be placed on probation or its charter revoked or on which renewal of the charter may be denied;
6. . . . [P]rohibit discrimination in admission policy on the basis of sex, national origin, race, ethnicity, religion, disability, or academic or athletic eligibility. . . .
7. Specify the grade levels to be offered;
8. Describe the governing structure of the program;
9. Specify the qualifications to be met by professional employees of the program;
10. Describe the process by which the persons providing the program will adopt an annual budget;
11. Describe the manner in which the annual audit of the financial and programmatic operations of the program is to be conducted, including the manner in which the persons providing the program will provide information necessary for the public school district in which the program is located to participate;
12. Describe the facilities to be used, including the terms of the facility utilization agreement if the facility for the charter school is owned or leased from a sectarian organization;
13. Describe the geographical area, school district, or school attendance area to be served by the program;
14. (A) Specify methods for applying for admission, enrollment criteria, and student recruitment and selection processes. . . . |

cont.

	15. Include a statement that the eligible entity will not discriminate on the basis of race, sex, national origin, ethnicity, religion, age, or disability in employment decisions including hiring and retention of administrators, teachers, and other employees whose salaries or benefits are derived from any public moneys.

Indiana
 	
Ind. Code
§ 20-5.5-4-1
	A charter must do the following:
	1. Be a written instrument.
	2. Be executed by a sponsor and organizer.
	3. Confer certain rights, privileges, and obligations on a charter school.
	4. Confirm the status of a charter school as a public school.
	5. Be granted for: (a) not less than three (3) years; and (b) a fixed number of years agreed to by the sponsor and the organizer.
	6. Provide for:
	    A. a review by the sponsor of the charter school's performance, including the progress of the charter school in achieving the academic goals set forth in the charter, at least one (1) time in each five (5) year period while the charter is in effect; and
	    B. renewal, if the sponsor and the organizer agree to renew the charter.
	7. Specify the grounds for the sponsor to:
	    A. revoke the charter before the end of the term for which the charter is granted; or
	    B. not renew a charter.
	8. Set forth the methods by which the charter school is held accountable for achieving the educational mission and goals of the charter school, including the following:
	    A. Evidence of improvement in assessment measures, including ISTEP and Graduation Qualifying Exam, attendance rates, graduation rates (if appropriate), increased numbers of Core 40 diplomas (if appropriate), and increased numbers of academic honors diplomas (if appropriate).
	    B. Evidence of progress toward reaching the educational goals set by the organizer.
	9. Describe the method to be used to monitor the charter school's:
	    A. compliance with applicable law; and
	    B. performance in meeting targeted educational performance.
	10. Specify that the sponsor and the organizer may amend the charter during the term of the charter by mutual consent and describe the process for amending the charter.
	11. Describe specific operating requirements, including all of the matters set forth in the application for the charter.
	12. Specify a date when the charter school will:
	    A. begin school operations; and
	    B. have students in attendance at the charter school.
	13. Specify that records of a charter school relating to the school's operation and charter are subject to inspection and copying to the same extent that records of a public school are subject to inspection and copying under [state statutes].
	14. Specify that records provided by the charter school to the

cont.

	department or sponsor that relate to compliance by the operator with the terms of the charter or applicable state or federal laws are subject to inspection and copying in accordance with [state statutes]. 15. Specify that the charter school is subject to the requirements of [state statutes].
Oklahoma Okla. Stat. § 70-3-135(A)	1. A description of the program to be offered by the school . . . 2. Admission policies and procedures; 3. Management and administration of the charter school; 4. Requirements and procedures for program and financial audits; 5. A description of how the charter school will comply with the charter requirements set forth in the Oklahoma Charter Schools Act; 6. Assumption of liability by the charter school; and 7. The term of the contract.
Wisconsin Wis. Stat. § 118.40 (1m)(6)	1. The name of the person who is seeking to establish the charter school. 2. The name of the person who will be in charge of the charter school and the manner in which administrative services will be provided. 3. A description of the educational program of the school. 4. The methods the school will use to enable pupils to attain the educational goals under [state statutes]. 5. The method by which pupil progress in attaining the educational goals under [state statutes] will be measured. 6. The governance structure of the school, including the method to be followed by the school to ensure parental involvement. 7. Subject to sub. (7) (a) and (am) and [state statutes], the qualifications that must be met by the individuals to be employed in the school. 8. The procedures that the school will follow to ensure the health and safety of the pupils. 9. The means by which the school will achieve a racial and ethnic balance among its pupils that is reflective of the school district population. 10. The requirements for admission to the school. 11. The manner in which annual audits of the financial and programmatic operations of the school will be performed. 12. The procedures for disciplining pupils. 13. The public school alternatives for pupils who reside in the school district and do not wish to attend or are not admitted to the charter school. 14. A description of the school facilities and the types and limits of the liability insurance that the school will carry. 15. The effect of the establishment of the charter school on the liability of the school district.

It is also important to note that such statutory guidelines specify contractual minimums. That is, contracts must include provisions addressing each enumerated item as a minimum, but contracts may include other provisions agreeable to both parties. As long as a provision creates no conflict with applicable state or federal law, charter schools and their authorizers may define their relationship any way they wish. For example, a university sponsor may wish to negotiate provisions that allow for research to be conducted in a charter school. As the discussion of revocation and renewal will detail, great care should be taken in the construction of charter school contracts, because they provide the legal authority for the existence of the school and determine the standards to which the school will be held.

Standards Guiding Revocation/Renewal Decisions

Revocation is the withdrawal of a school's charter during its term. Renewal relates to the decision by a charter-granting authority to enter into a new contract once the term of an existing contract expires. Both revocation and renewal raise legal issues of due process and contract compliance.

All but three jurisdictions (Hawaii, New Mexico, and Puerto Rico) enumerate the reasons justifying revocation in their charter school statutes. Table 3.2 details those standards. The four most common standards relate to charter contract compliance, compliance with the charter school law, and other applicable laws, fiscal management, and student performance standards. In addition to these statutory grounds, charter school contracts may delineate additional standards for revocation.

Table 3.2. Standards for Revocation of a Charter School Contract

Violation of the Charter Contract/Application	Arizona, Arkansas, California, Colorado, Connecticut, Delaware, District of Columbia, Georgia, Idaho, Illinois, Indiana, Iowa, Kansas, Louisiana, Massachusetts, Michigan, Mississippi, Missouri, Nevada, New Hampshire, New Jersey, New Mexico, New York, North Carolina, Ohio, Oregon, Pennsylvania, Rhode Island, South Carolina, Tennessee, Texas, Virginia, Wisconsin, Wyoming
Violation of the State's Charter School Law or other Laws Generally	Arizona, Arkansas, California, Colorado, District of Columbia, Florida, Georgia, Idaho, Illinois, Indiana, Iowa, Kansas, Louisiana, Massachusetts, Michigan, Minnesota, Missouri, Nevada, New Hampshire, New Mexico, New York, North Carolina, Ohio, Oklahoma, Oregon, Pennsylvania, Rhode Island, South Carolina, Texas, Utah, Virginia, Wisconsin, Wyoming
Fiscal (Mis)Management	Alaska, Arkansas, California, Colorado, District of Columbia, Florida, Georgia, Idaho, Illinois, Indiana, Iowa, Kansas, Massachusetts, Louisiana,

cont.

Fiscal (Mis)Management (cont.)	Michigan, Minnesota, Missouri, Nevada, New Hampshire, New Mexico, New York, North Carolina, Ohio, Oklahoma, Pennsylvania, Rhode Island, South Carolina, Tennessee, Texas, Utah, Virginia, Wisconsin, Wyoming
Failure of Students to Meet Educational Achievement/y Performance Goals or Educational Goals Generally	Alaska, California, Colorado, District of Columbia, Florida, Georgia, Idaho, Illinois, Indiana, Iowa, Kansas, Louisiana, Michigan, Minnesota, Missouri, New Mexico, New York, North Carolina, Ohio, Oklahoma, Oregon, Pennsylvania, Rhode Island, South Carolina, Tennessee, Texas, Utah, Virginia, Wisconsin, Wyoming
Fraud	Delaware, Pennsylvania
Financial Insolvency/Instability	Nevada, New Hampshire, Oregon
2/3 of the Licensed Teaching Staff Request Revocation	Arkansas, North Carolina
Majority of Parents Request Revocation	Georgia, Mississippi[12]
Continued Operation of the School Would be Contrary to the Best Interests of Students or Community	Georgia, Virginia
Failure to Fulfill Conditions Imposed by the State Education Agency (SEA) or Chartering Authority	Massachusetts, New Jersey
Failure of School on Probationary Status to Correct Problems Identified in a Remedial Plan	New Jersey, New York
Officials Misappropriate Funds	Delaware
Failure to Submit Required Reports	Idaho
Failure to Pay for Services Provided by a Non-Authorizing School District	Minnesota
Failure to Maintain Insurance	Oregon
Endangering the Health and Safety of Students	Nevada
Intentional Violation of Civil Service Laws Related to Discrimination	New York
Failure to Begin School by the Date Specified in the Charter	Indiana
Failure to Have Students in Attendance by the Date Specified in the Charter	Indiana
Other Good Cause	Alaska, Connecticut, Florida, Minnesota, North Carolina, Ohio, Oklahoma, Utah
Not Specified	Hawaii, New Mexico, Puerto Rico

The controversy surrounding Einstein Academy Charter School in Pennsylvania raises an interesting revocation question: What are the responsibilities of the state educational agency in relation to revocation of a charter? The Pennsylvania Department of Education (PDE) posed this question in its February 2002 petition for a declaratory judgment[13] because it believed it had actual knowledge that the Einstein Academy was not in compliance with the charter school law and its charter, and the charter-granting authority had taken no action to correct the problems identified. The PDE asked the court to declare either that the PDE had no choice under state law but to forward payments to the charter school regardless of the knowledge of the improper operation or that it had the authority to withhold payments and that the charter-granting school district "shall comply with its oversight responsibilities."[14] The Pennsylvania legislature resolved the issue by enacting provisions that now grant the educational agency the authority to revoke a cyber school's charter after notice and hearing if a material component of the student's education is not being provided.[15] Should a similar issue arise with respect to a classroom-based charter school, however, the PDE may need once again to appeal to a court to compel an authorizer to act.

Some states have explicitly addressed the issue of oversight of authorizers.[16] Iowa, for example, vests independent authority in its State Board of Education to revoke a charter in the event that a local authorizer fails to do so. Many states' charter school statutes, however, contain no provisions for oversight of authorizers or the exercise of their discretion to revoke or refuse to renew.[17] As such, charter school authorizers may enjoy largely unfettered discretion.

Another interesting issue related to charter school oversight arose in Connecticut. Although he did not seek revocation of the school's charter, the Attorney General filed a complaint against a charter school official. He alleged that she had improperly arranged lease and employment agreements with the school that benefited her personally, thus breaching her fiduciary responsibility to the school. However, the Connecticut Supreme Court determined that the Attorney General lacked the authority to bring the complaint and upheld the dismissal of the case.[18]

In addition to decisions to revoke charters, charter authorizers must also determine whether to renew a school's charter at the end of its term. Table 3.3 lists causes specified in state statutes that justify the nonrenewal of a charter. Not surprisingly, the four main causes—material violation of the charter contract, failure to meet educational goals, violations of the charter contract or other laws, and fiscal mismanagement—replicate those for revocation. The most striking issue about nonrenewal standards, however, is not what is specified, but what is not. A comparison of Tables 3.2 and 3.3 reveals that nonrenewal decisions lack the statutory guidance provided for revocation. In fact, twenty states have not established statutory provisions specifying reasons for which a charter school may be denied a subsequent contract. One state, Louisiana, which does not specify grounds for denying renewal, does condition renewal on the charter school's demonstrating student improvement in academic performance, based on standardized test scores.[19] In other states, a charter renewal is treated in a manner similar to the initial awarding of the charter.[20] The charter school seeking renewal must often satisfy the same application requirements previously met.[21] Renewal requirements may also be included in the charter contract. For example, Indiana requires that contracts specify grounds for renewal.[22] On the other end of the spectrum, some jurisdictions, such as the District of Columbia and Nevada, create a statutory presumption of renewal.[23] In this situation, renewal decisions are more analogous to revocation, since the burden shifts to the authorizer to show why a school should not be renewed.[24]

Table 3.3. Standards for Nonrenewal of a Charter School Contract

Material Violation of the Charter Contract	Arizona, Arkansas, Colorado, District of Columbia, Illinois, Iowa, Kansas, Nevada, New Mexico, North Carolina, Ohio, Oklahoma, Pennsylvania, South Carolina, Tennessee, Texas, Wyoming
Failure to Show Student Progress or Meet Educational Goals	Colorado, District of Columbia, Florida, Illinois, Iowa, Kansas, Minnesota, New Mexico, North Carolina, Ohio, Pennsylvania, South Carolina, Tennessee, Texas, Wyoming
Violations of Charter Law or Other Laws	Arizona, Arkansas, Colorado, Florida, Illinois, Iowa, Kansas, Minnesota, Nevada, New Mexico, North Carolina, Ohio, Oklahoma, Pennsylvania, South Carolina, Texas, Wyoming
Fiscal (Mis)Management	Arkansas, Colorado, Florida, Illinois, Iowa, Kansas, Minnesota, Nevada, New Mexico, North Carolina, Ohio, Pennsylvania, South Carolina, Tennessee, Texas, Wyoming
Endangering the Health and Safety of Students	Nevada
Financial Insolvency/Instability	Nevada
Failure of School on Probationary Status to Correct Problems Identified in a Remedial Plan	Hawaii

cont.

2/3 of the Licensed Teaching Staff Request Revocation	North Carolina
Fraud Conviction	Pennsylvania
Not in the Interest of the Pupils Residing in the District	Colorado
Instructional Staff and Parents Fail to Vote in Favor of Renewal	Mississippi
Other Good Cause	Florida, Ohio
Not Specified	Alaska, California, Connecticut, Delaware, Georgia, Idaho, Indiana, Louisiana, Michigan, Missouri, New Hampshire, New Jersey, New York, Oregon, Puerto Rico, Rhode Island, Texas, Utah, Virginia, Wisconsin

Charter schools in states that do not specify grounds for nonrenewal would be prudent to follow Indiana's lead and negotiate those standards as a provision of the initial charter contract. Because charters are term contracts by definition, the relationship between the parties ends at the expiration of the term. Therefore, without any statutory or contractual language to define renewal standards, the charter-granting authority enjoys unfettered discretion in determining whether to grant or deny renewal of a charter. In states that also have limited appeals of the discretionary decisions of charter-granting authorities, a charter school may be left little or no recourse outside the political arena.

One Florida case examined the issue of charter renewal.[25] On the recommendation of the school district superintendent, the St. Lucie County School Board determined not to renew the charter of the Orange Avenue Charter School.[26] After the school successfully appealed that decision to the State Board of Education, the matter was remanded to the school district for reconsideration in accordance with Florida law. For such situations, Florida statutes provides:

> [T]he district board may fail to act in accordance with the recommendation of the state board only for good cause. Good cause for failing to act in accordance with the state board's recommendation arises only if the school board determines by competent substantial evidence that approving the state board's recommendation would be contrary to law or contrary to the best interest of the pupils or the community.[27]

Ultimately, the school district board determined that, because students failed to make adequate progress on student performance measures, continuing the charter school's contract would be contrary to the best interests of the pupils.[28] The court held that substantial evidence supported the board's decision and affirmed.[29]

Charter Schools' Ability to Enforce Charter Contracts

Revocation and nonrenewal decisions are the ultimate penalty a charter-granting authority may impose on a charter school that does not comply with its contract. It is unclear, however, what recourse the charter school has when it complies with the contract, but the charter-granting authority does not. A Colorado court recently offered one answer to this question.[30] The charter school complained that its sponsor, a local school district, had withheld funds and interfered with budgeting, hiring, and contracting. The school, after the State Board of Education declined to intervene, filed suit in state court to compel enforcement of the contract. The Colorado Supreme Court distinguished between the provisions of the contract that were "service provisions" and those that concern the "governing policy provisions."[31] The court held that charter schools could sue to enforce the service provisions or those provisions of the contract "entered into in order to carry out the educational program described in the charter."[32] On the other hand, any "dispute between [a charter school] and [its sponsoring school district] arising out of [the] implementation of the statutorily required portions of the charter contract" must be submitted to the State Board of Education for resolution.[33]

Accountability Enforced by Parents

In addition to these statutory and contractual forms of charter school accountability, parents play a role in charter school accountability. Informally, parents hold schools accountable through the exercise of school choice. If parents are unhappy with the education provided by a charter school, they can simply withdraw their child and enroll him or her at a different public school. More formally, parents may file a legal challenge to a perceived failure by a charter school to educate their child. Typically, courts have declined to recognize parents' claims for educational malpractice or liability, however, charter school statutes and contracts redefine parents' relationships with the school and raise the question of whether the new relationships created make charter schools vulnerable to claims of educational liability.

Educational malpractice has not been a recognized cause of action since the decision in *Peter W. v. San Francisco Unified School District*.[34] There, a California appellate court determined that an illiterate high school graduate could not recover for the school's failure to teach him to read. The court reasoned that "classroom methodology affords no readily acceptable standards of care,"[35] an essential element in any finding of liability for negligent action. In addition, the court found it difficult to determine the cause of the problem because a child's learning is affected by a number of factors, both inside and outside the classroom environment. Public policy concerns also convinced the court that such an award would be problematic because judges would be forced to evaluate the daily happenings in schools, damages awards would impose financial burdens on schools that would implicate their ability to serve other students, and courts would become clogged with a deluge of similar claims when an administrative avenue for dispute resolution already exists in many state educational agencies.

Arguably, however, the special characteristics of charter schools, including their emphasis on accountability, may make them vulnerable to educational liability claims because the rationales used by courts to reject liability in the cases of conventional public elementary and secondary institutions do not apply to them with the same force.[36] For instance, charter schools may be vulnerable to causes of action based on contract law because the relationship between charter school and parents is more contractual in nature than the relationship between conventional schools and parents.[37] In addition, the charter contract, in combination with the state statutes, may define a "duty" difficult to identify in a more traditional public school context. In the same way that courts have recognized this contractual obligation in some cases involving private schools,[38] charter schools may be held to the promises made in order to entice parents to enroll their children. Furthermore, charter schools may be vulnerable to statutory liability because the charter school legislation makes it clear that the charter schools have a mandatory duty to meet the goals established in the statutes or face revocation or nonrenewal. Courts may conclude that a child who fails to make progress at a charter school should recover the per-pupil funds his/her parents "spent" at the charter school or be awarded compensatory education in the form of tutoring or additional years of schooling to remedy an educational injury endured at a charter school. In either case, a child would first have to show that the programming received was in some way substandard.

It might even be argued that the recent filing of a petition for declaratory judgment by the Pennsylvania Department of Education (PDE) with respect to the Einstein Academy Charter school was motivated in part by a recognition of the potential for educational liability in the charter school context. After detailing numerous complaints by parents of the school's failure to provide promised computers, texts, and services, and raising concerns that the charter-granting authority had taken no action to revoke the school's charter, the petition justifies its request for a declaratory judgment by stating, "[f]or these reasons the Secretary [of Education] and PDE are concerned that they may be exposed to potential liability in the event a court of competent jurisdiction should finally determine that Einstein has been in violation of the CSL [charter school law], its charter or other laws."[39]

Conclusion

As this chapter demonstrates, charter school accountability has three sources, statutes (both federal and state), the charter school contract, and parents. As charter schools move into their second decade of operation, it will be important to follow how these three sources interact in charter schools. Given the newness of NCLB, it will be particularly interesting to see how this federal accountability system impacts the charter school movement. Finally, the role of contracts is essential to a full understanding of charter school accountability. Little research to date explores these contracts, their variance, and their effect. Such research is needed in order to fully understand the legal relationships created by charter schools.

Endnotes

[1] Charter School Closures: The Opportunity for Accountability, Center for Educ. Reform, October 2002, (no 4), available at http://www. uscharterschools.org/cs/uscsp/view/uscs_rs/1564 (last visited Apr. 11, 2003).

[2] Public Law No. 107-110.

[3] *See* U. S. Department of Education Nonregulatory Guidance: The Impact of the New Title I Requirements on Charter Schools, Draft Guidance, March 24, 2003 (printed in its entirety in Appendix C).

[4] U. S. Department of Education, Introduction: No Child Left Behind, available at http://www.nclb.gov/next/overview/index. html (last visited April 11, 2003).

[5] *See* question A-3 of Nonregulatory Guidance: The Impact of the New Title I Requirements on Charter Schools, Draft Guidance, March 24, 2003 (printed in its entirety in Appendix C).

[6] U. S. Dep't of Educ., Frequently Asked Questions and Answers for Families and Communities, available at http://www.nclb.gov/next/faqs/accountability. html#8 (last visited Apr. 11, 2003).

[7] *Id.*

[8] Question A-2 of Nonregulatory Guidance: The Impact of the New Title I Requirements on Charter Schools, Draft Guidance, March 24, 2003.

[9] *Id.*

[10] *Id.*, Questions A-8 and A-9.

11 U. S. Dept. of Educ., *supra* note 4.

12 Mississippi allows staff and parents to request revocation by majority vote. *See* Miss. Code Ann. § 37-28-9(a).

13 *See* Petition for Review in the Nature of an Action for Declaratory Judgment, Pennsylvania Dep't of Educ. v. Einstein Acad. Charter Sch. (Pa. Commw. Ct., filed Feb. 8, 2002) (No. 51 M.D. 2002).

14 *Id*. at 10.

15 *See* 24 Pa. Cons. Stat. § 17-1741-A.

16 *See, e.g.,* Iowa Code § 256F.8(4).

17 *See, e.g.,* Tenn. Code Ann. § 49-13-122.

18 Blumenthal v. Barnes, 804 A.2d 152 (Conn. 2002).

19 *See* La. Rev. Stat. Ann. § 3992(A)(2).

20 *See, e.g.,* Mich. Comp. Laws § 380.

21 *See, e.g., id*.

22 See Ind. Code § 20-5.5-4-1(7)(B).

23 *See* D.C. Code Ann. § 38-1802.12(c) (2002); Nev. Rev. Stat. 386.530(2).

24 *Id*.

25 Orange Ave. Charter Sch. v. St. Lucie County Sch. Bd., 763 So.2d 531 (Fla. Dist. Ct. App. 2000).

26 *Id*. at 532.

27 Fla. Stat. Ann. § 228.056(4)(c) (repealed 2003).

28 *Orange Ave. Charter Sch.,* 763 So. 2d at 534–535.

29 *Id*. at 532–534. The court also noted that, when such hearings produce conflicting evidence, as occurred in this case, the board has the discretion to determine which testimony it will accept. *Id*. at 534.

30 Academy of Charter Sch. v. Adams County Sch. Dist. No. 12, 32 P.3d 456 (Colo. 2001).

31 *Id*. at 459–462.

32 *Id*. at 459. A service provision of a charter contract may involve the agreement of the sponsor school district to provide some educational service (for example, special education evaluation) or other service (for example, custodial) for the charter school.

33 *Id*.

34 131 Cal. Rptr. 854 (Ct. App. 1976).

35 *Peter W.*, 131 Cal.Rptr. at 860.

36 For a detailed discussion of charter schools and educational liability, see Julie F. Mead & Preston C. Green, *Keeping Promises: An Examination of Charter Schools' Vulnerability to Claims for Educational Liability,* 2001 BYU Educ. & L. J. 35 (2001).

37 Jennifer T. Wall, *The Establishment of Charter Schools: A Guide to Legal Issues for Legislatures,* 1998 BYU Educ. & L. J. 69 (1998).

38 Squires v. Sierra Nevada Educational Foundation, Inc., 107 Nev. 902, 823 P.2d 256 (Nev. 1991); Ross v. Creighton University, 957 F.2d 410 (7th Cir. 1992); Gupta v. New Britain General Hospital, 687 A.2d 111 (Conn. 1996).

39 Paragraph 52 of Petition for Review in the Nature of An Action for Declaratory Judgment, Commonwealth of Pennsylvania, *Department of Education v. Einstein Academy Charter School,* Case No. 51 M.D. 2002 (Pa. Cmwl., filed February 8, 2002). In its defense, the charter school contended that its trouble meeting its obligations stemmed from funds being withheld by the state. See Defendant's Proposed Findings of Fact, *Fairfield Area Sch. Dist. v. National Org. for Children, Inc.,* (Ct. Com. Pl. of Adams County, Pa., Dec. 11, 2001) (Case No. 01-S-1008); Alan Richard, *Short of Funds, Cyber School Awaits Ruling,* Educ. Week, Mar. 20, 2002, at 18.

Chapter 4

Charter Schools and Finance

Some of the most contentious issues surrounding charter schools involve how they are financed. A federally funded study of charter school finance systems, *Venturesome Capital: State Charter School Finance Systems*, observed, "[t]he survival and health of the charter school movement . . . may be determined more by questions about financing than by issues of autonomy or student achievement."[1] This chapter addresses the legal issues surrounding the funding of charter schools. First, an overview of charter school finance systems is provided. Second, this chapter examines statutory provisions designed to prevent fiscal mismanagement on the part of charter schools. Third, litigation regarding the economic impact of charter schools on school districts is analyzed. Fourth, this chapter examines statutory provisions and litigation to prevent school districts from withholding charter school funds. Fifth, this chapter discusses (1) whether charter school statutes can provide less funding to charter schools than non-charter schools; and (2) whether chartering authorities can subject charter schools to more stringent accountability measures than non–charter schools. The sixth and seventh sections discuss the vulnerability of school finance systems to challenges from charter schools that serve large populations of students with disabilities and at-risk students. The final section examines the legal issues surrounding the distribution of assets upon the closing of a charter school.

Overview of Charter School Funding Systems

Although charter school finance systems vary greatly, they generally fall under three categories.[2] Under the first category, the school district transfers its per-pupil allotment to the charter school for every student who lives in the district but goes to the charter school. The district usually maintains an overhead fee, which covers the costs it incurs for providing support services to the charter school. Alaska's charter school finance system is typical of this approach. Alaska charter schools are entitled to 100 percent of state and school district operations. However, school districts can charge for administrative costs, which are calculated by applying an indirect cost rate approved by the state department of education.[3]

Under the second category, charter schools receive all of their funding from the state. In states that rely on local property taxation for school funding, this approach has the effect of increasing the state's financial burden.[4] An example of this approach is Indiana, where charter schools receive 100 percent of the per-pupil allotment received by traditional public schools.[5] Under the third category, charter schools receive a portion of their funding from the state and a portion of their funding from school districts. Delaware is illustrative of this approach. Delaware charter schools receive 100 percent of state funding as well as 100 percent of local funding based on the per pupil expenditure from the previous year. However, the charter school pays 5 percent of the state share to the school district for administrative costs. Furthermore, the charter school and the district may negotiate for the services to be provided by the school district.[6]

In a number of states, the funding mechanism for charter schools varies depending on the chartering authority. For example, in Connecticut, local charter schools are funded according to the arrangements specified in the charter. State-authorized charter schools, on the other hand, receive 110 percent of state and school district operations funding, which is based on average school district per-pupil revenue.[7]

Charter schools have asserted that they receive insufficient funding for their educational programming. Several states (such as Colorado, Florida, and New Jersey), do not provide charter schools with 100 percent general operating funds. A recent review of the charter school finance systems by the Education Commission of the States found that only eight states and the District of Columbia provide start-up and planning grants for charter schools. This study also found that twenty-three states and the District of Columbia provide funding for facilities.[8] Charter schools have responded to this shortfall through private fundraising or by creating nonprofit corporations to raise funds for educational programming and facilities.[9]

Financial Mismanagement on the Part of Charter Schools

Charter school critics have asserted that the autonomy provided to charter schools might lead to financial mismanagement. The American Federation of Teachers (AFT) has observed: "Financial accountability is . . . a problem for charter schools. Most charter schools that have been closed were targeted because of fiscal mis-management or fraud."[10] Charter school statutes employ a variety of strategies to guard against this possibility. One approach is to have charter applicants explain their financial plans. For example, Arizona charter applications must contain a detailed business plan and a financial plan for the first three years of the schools' opera-tions. Failure to provide financial information in the application as required by statute may be grounds for denial of the charter. In *Shenango Valley Regional Charter School v. Hermitage School District*,[11] the Commonwealth Court of Pennsylvania upheld a denial of an application, in part, for failure to contain a financial plan demon-strating the proposed charter's ability to operate.

Another approach is to authorize chartering authorities to deny or revoke charters because of fiscal mismanagement. Arkansas's charter school statute is typical of this type of provision. It autho-rizes the state board of education to modify, revoke, or deny re-newal of a charter school if the board determines that the school's operators "[f]ailed to satisfy generally accepted accounting stan-dards of fiscal management."[12] A third strategy is to subject charter schools to independent audits of their finances. Independent au-dits serve to portray the school's financial position at the end of the fiscal year to ascertain the school's adherence to applicable laws and regulations governing the school.[13]

Charter authorizers should also consider including language in the charter stipulating that charter schools are liable for overpay-ments resulting from fiscal mismanagement or fraud. A recent pre-dicament faced by California's Apple Valley School District dem-onstrates the importance of such a provision.[14] In this case, the Apple Valley Unified School District granted a charter to the Education Foundation for Ethics and Principles (EPEP) for the creation of the Cato School of Reason II (Cato II). Cato II then entered into illegal agreements with private schools to convert into satellites of the char-ter school. An audit performed by the state controller revealed that the district had received $4.4 million more in funding than it was entitled to receive because of improper average daily attendance (ADA) claims for the charter school sites that were converted from private schools.

The district appealed the controller's findings to an Adminis-trative Law Judge (ALJ). The district asserted that it was not liable for the overpayments because it had exercised due diligence in its relationship with Cato II. The ALJ found that the district was not liable for the overpayment. It found that no provision in the applicable statutes held school districts liable for acts of their charter schools. The ALJ also held that tort law did not support district liability because there was no evidence that the district knew or should have known that the charter school was acting illegally. Furthermore, contract law did not support a finding of district liability because neither the charter nor the agreement supplementing the charter provided for such liability. However, the California Education Audits Appeal Panel (EAAP) remanded the case for additional evidence on the authority by which the district withheld funds from the charter school and how the district performed its oversight duties and statutory obligations.

The Apple Valley School District also brought action in a court of law against the accounting firm and the accountant who performed the audit on the charter school for accounting malpractice in misrepresenting the accuracy of the charter school's average daily records. The California Court of Appeal sustained the defendants' demurrer because (1) the two-year statute of limitations for accounting malpractice had already expired; and (2) the statute of limitations was not equitably tolled by the state controller's audit. [15]

Economic Effect of Charter Schools on School Districts

School districts have worried about the negative economic impact that charter schools might have upon them. Because per-pupil allotments generally follow the student, a public school loses money whenever a student leaves that school to attend a charter school. Districts fear that if enough students depart to attend charter schools, they might not be to meet the educational needs of those students remaining in non-charter schools. The New Jersey School Boards Association summarized this concern in the following manner:

> As much as 30 percent of district operations are in non-personnel fixed and residual costs. By way of example, in a district with 3500 pupils and five buildings, the loss of 300 students to a charter school could cost the district as much as $3 million in State and local funds.
>
> Yet if they lost the $3 million in State and local funds, they would still have five buildings to run, debt service to be paid, maintenance to be performed, space to be heated and insured.[16]

Districts have tried to prevent this negative impact by mounting state constitutional and statutory claims. An analysis of these claims follows below.

State Constitutional Challenges

School districts have claimed that funding to charter schools violates state constitutions by preventing them from providing an adequate level of education to other schools within their jurisdiction. This argument builds upon school finance litigation, in which courts have struck down funding systems for failing to provide an adequate education in poor school districts.[17]

In the *Englewood on the Palisades Charter School*[18] case, a New Jersey school district challenged a decision to grant a charter within its boundaries on constitutional adequacy grounds. New Jersey required the school district to pay the charter school for each student enrolled in the school a presumptive amount of 90 percent of the local levy budget per pupil for the specific grade level in the district. The state's commissioner of education had the discretion to require the school district to pay an amount less than 90 percent, or an amount not to exceed 100 percent of the local levy budget per pupil for the specific grade level in the district of residence. The district alleged that the state's charter school funding system prevented it from providing a thorough and efficient education to other schools located in the district by diverting funds from the school district to pay for a charter school. A state appellate court refused to rule on the district's constitutional adequacy claim because the school had not yet opened.

In *Board of Education of Roosevelt Union Free School District v. Board of Trustees of State University of New York*,[19] a New York appellate court also refused to consider a school board's constitutional adequacy challenge to a decision to fund a charter school. The board opposed the opening of the school within its boundaries because the charter school could take $1.2 million to $1.7 million dollars from the district's coffers. The board asserted that this loss of revenue would adversely affect the board's ability to provide a quality education by forcing the district to eliminate or reduce certain programs, services, and staff. The court dismissed the board's claim because the district had no proprietary interest in a specific sum of money.

Neither *Englewood* nor *Roosevelt* rules out the possibility that other courts might rule on the merits of a constitutional adequacy challenge. In order for plaintiffs to prevail in such cases, they would probably have to establish a causal link between the school districts' alleged inability to provide an adequate education and the loss of funding. Proving causation might be difficult because plaintiffs would have to rule out other possible reasons for the alleged inadequate education, such as inefficient allocation of resources within the districts' other public schools.

Economic impact litigation might also be advanced through state constitutional provisions that prohibit unfunded mandates. An unfunded mandate directs a governmental entity to spend money to implement a law without providing sufficient resources. In the *Highland Park Board of Education* case,[20] a New Jersey school district asserted that a 1998 charter school funding regulation that changed the "local levy budget per pupil" under the 1997 regulations was an unfunded mandate in violation of the state constitution and the Local Mandates Act. Under the 1997 regulations, school districts were required to transfer the lower of either 90 percent of the maximum thorough and efficient (T&E) amount per pupil or 90 percent of the program budget per pupil to the charter school. In 1998, these regulations were amended to require the district to transfer 90 percent of the program budget per pupil to charter schools. This amendment eliminated the possibility of transferring a lower amount of funding through the maximum T&E formula to the charter school.

The New Jersey Council of Local Mandates found that the amended regulation's elimination of the option to use the maximum T&E formula created an unfunded mandate. To prove that the regulation was an unfunded mandate, the challenging school district had to show that the 1998 regulation required it to pay more to the charter school in residence than was required under the 1997 regulation. The council found that the district met its burden by showing that it had to pay an increase of $25,124 for the 1998–1999 school year and a projected increase of $13,660 for the 1999–2000 school year.

Statutory Challenges

A few charter school statutes appear to prohibit the granting of charters that would drain economic resources from a school district and prevent it from performing its educational duty to other public schools located within the district. For example, Colorado's statute requires applications to provide evidence that "the plan for the charter school is economically sound for both the charter school and the school district."[21] South Carolina permits a denial of a charter application if it "adversely affects, as defined by regulation, the other students in the district."[22]

Two courts have addressed whether a charter school statute authorizes a denial of an application because of the negative economic effect on a school district in the absence of an express provision. In *Keystone Central School District v. Sugar Valley Concerned Citizens*, the Commonwealth Court of Pennsylvania ruled that a school district may not act in this manner because "[t]he General Assembly specifically provided that the funding for charter schools shall come from school district revenues. To deny the charter school because it may deplete school district revenues is inconsistent with the purpose of the [charter school law.]"[23]

By contrast, in the *Englewood* case, the Supreme Court of New Jersey ruled that the commissioner must analyze the economic impact upon a district when determining whether to grant a charter, even though the charter school statute did not expressly mandate such a consideration. The court acknowledged that the statute placed the commissioner's focus in determining the per-pupil funding amount on the charter school's needs. However, the court explained that the commissioner could not make such a determination without considering the effect of the charter on the district's ability to meet its constitutional mandate of providing a thorough and efficient education to its remaining students. The court further explained that the commissioner must consider the economic effect on school districts under the following conditions:

> [I]f a district of residence demonstrates with some specificity that the constitutional requirements of a thorough and efficient education would be jeopardized by loss of the presumptive amount, or proposed different amount of per-pupil funds to a charter school, then the Commissioner is obligated to evaluate carefully the impact that loss of funds would have on the ability of the district of residence to deliver a thorough and efficient education.[24]

Two courts have addressed the extent to which charter school statutes authorize appeals to decisions to grant charters that might have a negative economic impact on school districts. In *Roosevelt*, a New York appellate court concluded that a school district in residence may challenge the granting of a charter within its boundaries under Article 78 of the Civil Practice Law and rules. The court reached this conclusion, in part, because of a provision in the charter school statute that required charter applications to include an evaluation of the "fiscal impact of the charter school on other public and nonpublic schools *in the area*."[25] The language of this statutory provision suggests that, in addition to district of residence, adjacent districts may challenge the granting of a charter under Article 78. By contrast, in *West Chester Area School District v. Collegium Charter School*,[26] the Commonwealth Court of Pennsylvania ruled that residents of adjacent school districts did not have standing to challenge the grant of a charter school application. The court reached this conclusion because the authorizing statute permitted appeals only for the charter school and the chartering district.

Protections from Districts' Withholding Funds from Charter Schools

The concern that school districts have about the economic impact of charter schools has caused districts to withhold funds from these schools. Pennsylvania's statute sanctions districts for failure to make payments to charter schools by deducting state funds from the districts in the amount that is owed to charter schools. Section 1725-(A)(a)(5) of Pennsylvania's charter school law is typical. It provides that:

> Payments shall be made to the charter school in twelve (12) equal monthly payments, by the fifth day of each month, within the operating school year. . . . If a school district fails to make a payment to a charter school as prescribed by this clause, the [Secretary of Education] shall deduct the estimated amount, as documented by the charter school, from any and all State payments made to the district after receipt of documentation from the charter school.[27]

In *Boyertown Area School District v. Department of Education*,[28] the Commonwealth Court of Pennsylvania held that the secretary could not deduct state educational subsidies to districts pursuant to §1725(A)(a)(5) without providing the districts with notice and a hearing. The crucial question in this case was whether the secretary's decision to withhold funds constituted an adjudication under state agency law—thus requiring notice and a hearing—or a ministerial act. The court found that the secretary's action was an adjudication because (1) the districts had a property interest in the withholding of funds; (2) the secretary had exercised discretion in withholding funds to the districts; and (3) the secretary had carefully analyzed the documentation submitted pursuant to §1725(A)(a)(5) to establish facts that affected the districts' property interest.

Districts might also be tempted to interpret funding provisions in a manner that would illegally deprive charter schools of educational aid. In *Francine Delany New School for Children, Inc. v. Asheville City Board of Education*,[29] a charter school had to go to court to stop such a practice. In this case, the Court of Appeals of North Carolina held that a city board of education should include revenues from supplemental school tax, penal fines, and forfeitures in the calculation of its per-pupil local current expense appropriation to a charter school. The board had refused to provide such revenues for charter schools, but included these revenues in the per-pupil funding to non–charter public schools.

The board contended that the charter school was not entitled to revenues from supplemental school tax, penal fines, and forfeitures because they were not "appropriations." According to the board, there was a material difference between the phrase "local current expense appropriation" in the Charter School Funding Statute and the phrase "local current expense fund" in the state's School Budget Fiscal and Control Act. The board argued that an appropriation was "the authorization by a governmental body to spend up to a certain amount of money for a specified purpose."[30] A "fund," on the other hand, was an "independent fiscal and accounting entity, consisting of cash and other resources, together with related liabilities and equities, for the purpose of carrying on specific activities or obtaining certain objectives."[31] The court rejected this argument because the legislature "clearly intended charter schools to be treated as public schools subject to the uniform budget format."[32] Interpreting the Charter School Funding Statute in conjunction with other school funding statutes led the court to conclude "that the Legislature intended that supplemental taxes as well as penal fines and forfeitures be included in the operating budget of the local expense fund."[33]

Discriminatory Treatment of Charter Schools

As mentioned earlier in the chapter, some states do not provide charter schools with the same level of funding as other public schools. Also, chartering authorities might subject charter schools to fiscal accountability requirements that are more stringent than those applied to traditional public schools. Charter schools might assert that differences in funding and fiscal accountability violate the Equal Protection Clause and state constitutional provisions. An analysis of such challenges follows below.

Equal Protection Clause

The starting point for Equal Protection Clause challenges to differences in funding and fiscal accountability measures is *San Antonio Independent School District v. Rodriguez*.[34] In *Rodriguez*, the Supreme Court ruled that funding disparities among school districts caused by local property taxation did not violate the Equal Protection Clause. The Court found that classifications created by local property taxation were subject to the rational basis test: such classifications had to be rationally related to a legitimate governmental purpose. Applying the rational basis test, the Court concluded that local property taxation was rationally related to the purpose of maintaining local control.

In two cases, the Arizona Court of Appeals applied the rational basis test to deny Equal Protection Clause challenges by charter schools to differences in funding and fiscal accountability. In *Salt River Pima-Maricopa Indian Community School v. Arizona*,[35] the court found that the state "Deduct Statute" did not violate the equal protection rights of charter schools funded by the Bureau of Indian Affairs (BIA). The Deduct Statute provides that

> The base support level for a charter school or for a school district sponsoring a charter school shall be reduced by an amount equal to the total monies received by a charter school from a federal or state agency if the federal or state monies are intended for the basic maintenance and operation of the school . . . If the reduction results in a negative amount, the negative amount shall be used in computing all budget limits and equalization limits except that:
> . . . [e]qualization assistance shall not be less than zero.[36]

Applying the Deduct Statute, the state provided no equalization assistance to ten charter schools that had received funding from the BIA 's Indian School Equalization program, because the funding from the BIA exceeded the equalization assistance that would have been provided by the state.

The BIA-funded charter schools and the students attending those schools asserted that the deduct statute violated the Equal Protection Clause. The state court of appeals rejected this claim because the Equal Protection Clause required "only that the state classify reasonably and afford equal treatment to persons similarly situated."[37] The BIA-funded charter schools and the non–BIA funded charter schools were not similarly situated because the former schools received funding from government sources exceeding the state's equalization aid, while the latter charter schools did not. Thus, the court found that no violation of equal protection had occurred.

In *Shelby School v. Arizona State Board of Education*,[38] a private school that was denied a charter application alleged that the state board of education violated the Equal Protection Clause by requiring a credit check on charter applications, but not imposing such a requirement on non-charter public schools. Applying the rational basis test, the Arizona Court of Appeals rejected this assertion. The differential treatment of charter schools was reasonable because charter schools were formed and operated differently from non-charter public schools, and employees of charter schools had more access to state funds than their non-charter counterparts.

State Constitutional Provisions

Charter schools might assert that differential treatment with respect to funding and fiscal accountability requirements violates state equal protection provisions. School finance litigation suggests that charter schools might have a difficult time prevailing on these claims. After the Supreme Court held in *Rodriguez* that funding disparities created by local taxation were permissible under the federal Equal Protection Clause, plaintiffs asserted that such inequalities violated the equal protection clauses of state constitutions. These arguments were generally unsuccessful because courts applied rational basis analysis to find that local property taxation was rationally related to local control. Thus, it would appear that courts would likely apply rational basis analysis to state equal protection clause challenges to charter school funding and fiscal accountability policies. The *Salt River* and *Shelby* cases support this assertion. Applying rational basis analysis, the Arizona Court of Appeals ruled that the differential treatment was permitted by the state's Equal Protection Clause.

On the other hand, charter school finance systems that fail to provide charter schools with funding commensurate to traditional public schools might be vulnerable to constitutional adequacy challenges from charter schools. Recall that many charter schools have had to respond to funding shortfalls by raising funds for educational programming and facilities through private fundraising. This might be evidence that charter school finance systems are providing constitutionally inadequate levels of funding to charter schools.

In the *Abbott v. Burke Implementing Regulations*[39] case, a New Jersey appellate court examined whether charter schools located in school districts that were part of a court-ordered school finance reform may be foreclosed from the benefits received by those districts. The New Jersey Supreme Court directed the state department of education to adopt regulations ensuring that children in poor school districts were provided a thorough and efficient education as mandated by the state constitution.[40] The state department of education responded by promulgating regulations, which provided additional funding to special needs districts. However, these regulations excluded charter schools located within these *"Abbott* districts."

Children who attended public schools in *Abbott* districts asserted that the exclusion of charter schools was unconstitutional. The state appellate court denied this claim. First, the court observed that extending *Abbott's* fiscal benefits to charter schools "would necessarily impose upon these schools the corollary demanding regulatory framework governing *Abbott* districts."[41] This would subvert the goals of the charter school law by "erod[ing] the schools' autonomy and flexibility to offer innovative learning methods and educational choices and their ability to establish a new form of accountability for schools."[42]

Second, the court noted that the *Abbott* remedies were necessary because of the chronic failure of local school districts to achieve acceptable student outcomes. The charter school movement had not yet demonstrated such pervasive failure. Third, unlike *Abbott* school districts, a charter school would cease to exist if it failed to meet the testing and academic requirements imposed on public schools. Finally, the charter school construct did not fit into the *Abbott* concept because "it is an *optional* program available to parents and students who opt not to accept the advantages and remedial measures placed upon the *Abbott* school districts."[43]

Students with Disabilities

Charter school funding systems might be vulnerable to legal challenges from charter schools that serve a high percentage of students with disabilities. *Venturesome Capital* identified three approaches to special education funding. Charter schools in the first category match their funding to the educational needs of students actually enrolled in charter schools. These school finance systems match funding to the specific disabilities of students enrolled through (1) actual costs of services; (2) pupil weighting systems; or (3) categorical systems. School finance systems in the second category provide funding for special education through negotiations between charter schools and school districts. School finance systems in the third category base their funding of special needs students on the characteristics of the school district in which the charter school is located instead of the special education students actually enrolled in the charter school.

Charter school finance systems that are based on school district characteristics might be vulnerable to state constitutional adequacy challenges from charter schools. If the actual cost of providing for the needs of special education students in a charter school exceeds that of the school district average, that charter school might be unable to provide an adequate education to its students. Furthermore, the small size of charter schools might make it difficult for these schools to fulfill their duty to provide an adequate education. Small schools may lack the resources to deal with the high costs of a severely disabled student without weakening the educational offerings for other students. *Venturesome Capital* observes that charter school finance systems employ a variety of approaches that might protect charter schools from the financial burden of providing for students with disabilities. For example, this study reports that Pennsylvania has a contingency fund for ultra-high-cost special needs students to which all public schools have recourse, and that Massachusetts excludes charter schools from paying for expensive private and residential placements.

At-Risk Students

Some charter school financing systems might be subject to adequacy challenges from charter schools that serve at-risk or low-income students. *Venturesome Capital* observes that extra funding for at-risk students is provided primarily through (1) negotiations between charter schools and the school district; (2) the normal school district budget allocation process; or (3) pupil weighting systems that provide extra funding for these students. However, some states do not provide funding for at-risk or low-income students. Failure to provide additional funds for at-risk and low-income students might expose these states to allegations that they have failed to provide a constitutionally adequate level of funding for charter schools that serve these students.

Furthermore, the method that states use to count their students for funding purposes might expose them to adequacy challenges from charter schools serving low-income and at-risk charter students. Most states use average daily membership or the number of pupils enrolled in a charter school to count the number of students. California and Texas use average daily attendance figures (ADA) to count the number of students. ADA funding might expose these states to adequacy challenges from charter schools that serve at-risk and low-income students because such students generally have higher rates of absenteeism than other students. As a result, charter schools that serve disadvantaged children might not receive enough funding to provide for their students' educational needs. *Venturesome Capital* observes that California and Texas offset the ADA problem to some extent by providing extra funding for at-risk students. These provisions might still be vulnerable to adequacy challenges from children attending charter schools that serve at-risk students if they could establish that these extra resources are insufficient to provide for their extra educational needs.

Distribution of Assets upon Closure of Charter School

As of October 2002, 194 out of the 2,874 schools that have ever received a charter have closed.[44] These closures raise the question of how to dispose of assets purchased with public funds once a charter school has gone out of business. Some charter school laws stipulate that assets purchased with public funds revert to the school district or state once the charter school has closed. For example, Arkansas stipulates that "[u]pon dissolution of the open-enrollment charter school or upon nonrenewal of the charter, all net assets of the open-enrollment charter school purchased with public funds shall be deemed the property of the state, unless otherwise specified in the charter of the open-enrollment charter school."[45]

However, *Venturesome Capital* found that many systems in its study were silent on the issue of the distribution of assets upon the closure of the charter school. This study posited that legislators might have been so involved with the establishment of charter schools that they failed to address this important matter. *Venturesome Capital* does observe that in the absence of legislation, disposition of assets is governed by nonprofit corporation laws. Under these laws, the nonprofit's governing board has the power to dispose of assets once a charter school has closed.

If the charter school is *not* a nonprofit entity and is located in a state whose charter school statute is silent on the issue of dissolution of assets, the authorizing entity and the charter school should establish guidelines in the charter. The charter should provide for the liquidation of assets to pay off outstanding liabilities. The charter should also provide guidelines for the distribution of remaining assets after creditors have been provided for.

Conclusion

Some of the most controversial issues around charter schools involve school finance. One major concern raised by critics is that their autonomy might lead to fiscal mismanagement. Charter school statutes include a number of provisions designed to prevent the fiscal mismanagement of charter schools. Charter authorizers should also consider including a provision in the charter that hold schools liable for overpayments caused by their fiscal mismanagement or fraud.

School districts have alleged that charter schools have a negative economic impact on them in violation of state constitutional and statutory provisions. Courts have yet to rule on whether charter school funding prevents districts from providing non–charter-school students with a constitutionally adequate education. Charter school funding systems may also be vulnerable to state constitutional provisions prohibiting unfunded mandates. Several states contain statutory provisions that guard against the chartering of schools that would have a negative impact on school districts. Courts have disagreed as to whether a charter school statute authorizes the denial of an application in the absence of such provisions. They have also seemed to disagree as to whether adjacent districts may appeal decisions to grant charters on economic grounds.

Charter schools have asserted that statutory provisions and district practices that result in charter schools' receiving less funding or undergoing greater fiscal accountability violate federal and state Equal Protection Clause provisions. These challenges have been unsuccessful because courts have applied the rational basis test. However, finance systems that provide charter schools with less funding than traditional public schools might be vulnerable to adequacy challenges under state constitutions. Moreover, systems that provide funding on the basis of state or district per-pupil averages may be susceptible to state constitutional adequacy challenges from charter schools that serve high percentages of students with disabilities and at-risk students.

The districts' concern about the economic impact of charter schools might cause them to withhold educational funding illegally from charter schools. Pennsylvania has addressed this problem by authorizing the deduction of educational subsidies to districts that are equal to the amount withheld from the charter schools. Furthermore, as the *Francine Delany* case illustrates, charter schools may have to go to court to force districts to provide them with all of the funding that is guaranteed by statute.

Finally, some charter school statutes are silent on the issue of disposition of assets upon the closure of the charter school. If the charter school is operated by a nonprofit organization in such instances, then nonprofit chartering laws apply. If the charter school is *not* a nonprofit entity and is located in a state whose charter school statute fails to stipulate how assets should be distributed, then such guidelines should be established in the charter.

Endnotes

[1] D. Howard Nelson et al., *Venturesome Capital: State Charter School Finance Systems* 7 (2000).

[2] Craig E. Richards et al., *Financing Educations Systems* (2004, forthcoming).

[3] Education Commission of the States, States Notes: Charter Schools, available at http://www.esc.org/clearinghouse/24/13/2413.htm. (last updated Apr. 2003)

[4] Richards et al., *supra* note 2.

[5] Education Commission of the States, *supra* note 3.

[6] *Id.*

[7] *Id.*

[8] *Id.*

[9] *Venturesome Capital, supra* note 1.

[10] American Federation of Teachers, *Resolution on Charter Schools*, available at http://www.aft.org/about/resolutions/2000/charter.html. (last visited Feb. 21, 2003)

[11] 756 A.2d 1191 (Pa. Cmwlth. 2000).

[12] Ark. Code Ann. § 6-23-105(a)(2).

[13] *Venturesome Capital, supra* note 1.

[14] Reported in Apple Valley Unified Sch. Dist. v. Vavrinek, Trine, Day & Co., 120 Cal.Rptr.2d 629 (Cal. Ct. App. 2002).

[15] *Id.*

[16] *In re* Grant of the Charter School Application of Englewood on the Palisades Charter Sch., 753 A.2d 687, 697 (N.J. 2000).

[17] *E.g.*, McDuffy v. Secretary of Executive Off. of Educ., 615 N.E.2d 516, 554 (Mass. 1993); Rose v. Council for Better Education, 790 S.W.2d 186 (Ky. 1989).

[18] 727 A.2d 15 (N.J. Super. 1999); *aff'd* 753 A.2d 687 (N.J. 2000).

[19] 723 N.Y.S.2d 262 (N.Y. App. Div. 2001).

[20] *In re* Complaints Filed by the Highland Park Bd. of Educ. and the Borough of Highland Park, Nos. 10-98 & 12-98 (May 11, 2000), available at http://www.state.nj.us/localmandates/hpbe.pdf.

[21] Colo. Rev. Stat. § 22-30.5-106.

[22] S.C. Code Ann. § 59-40-70(C).

[23] 799 A.2d 209, 218 n.14 (Pa. Cmwlth. 2002).

[24] *In re* Grant of Charter School Application of Englewood on the Palisades Charter Sch., 753 A.2d 687, 697 (N.J. 2000).

[25] N.Y. Educ. Law § 2851(2)(q) (emphasis added).

[26] 760 A.2d 452 (Pa. Commw. 2000).

[27] 24 Pa. Cons. Stat. § 17-125-A(a)(5).

[28] 797 A.2d 421 (Pa. Commw. Ct. 2002).

[29] 563 S.E.2d 92 (N.C. Ct. App. 2002).

[30] *Id.* at 95.

[31] *Id.* (internal citations omitted).

[32] *Id.* at 97.

[33] *Id.*

[34] 411 U.S. 1 (1973).

[35] 23 P.3d 103 (Ariz. Ct. App. 2001).

[36] Ariz. Rev. Stat. § 15-185(D) (2002).

[37] *Salt River*, 23 P.3d at 106.

[38] 962 P.2d 230 (Ariz. Ct. App. 1998).

[39] *In re* 1999-2000 *Abbott v. Burke* Implementing Regs., N.J.A.C. 6:19A-1.1 *et seq.*, 792 A.2d 412 (N.J. Sup. Ct. App. Div. 2002).

[40] Abbott v. Burke, 710 A.2d 450 (N.J. 1998); Abbott v. Burke, 748 A.2d 82 (N.J. 2000).

[41] *Abbott v. Burke Implementing Regs.*, 792 A.2d. at 440.

[42] *Id.*

[43] *Id.* at 441 (emphasis supplied by the court).

[44] Center for Ed. Reform, *Charter School Closures: The Opportunity for Accountability* (last updated Oct. 2002), available at http://edreform.com/charter_schools/closures.pdf. (last updated Oct. 2002)

[45] Ark. Code Ann. § 6-23-506.

Chapter 5

Charter Schools and Employment

Given the relief that charter schools receive from various school laws and regulations, and the methods by which they come into existence, new relationships exist in charter schools between the school and its employees. As with the other areas of law reviewed in earlier chapters, these new relationships introduce unique legal issues. In particular, the new relationships and their attendant legal issues fall into three broad categories: (1) teachers' role in charter school development and approval; (2) issues related to hiring employees, including state teacher certification; and (3) issues related to working in charter schools, including unionization. Each of these categories will be reviewed in turn.

Teachers' Role in Charter School Development and Approval

Charter school statutes in several states grant teachers a decision-making role not enjoyed in more usual school district decisions to open or close schools. This statutorily defined role may be as simple as requiring charter school applicants to demonstrate support by teachers in the proposed school.[1] In other states, charter statute provisions have more "teeth" and require teacher approval of charter petitions at a given percentage before a charter can be granted by the school district serving as the charter school authority. For example, a recently enacted charter school statute requires that any existing Iowa public school applying to convert to charter school status "demonstrate the support of at least fifty percent of the teachers employed at the school on the date of the submission of the application."[2] Eighteen states and the District of Columbia have similar requirements, often in relation to the conversion of traditional schools to charter schools.[3] The District of Columbia, Rhode Island, South Carolina, and Utah have the strictest requirements, mandating that two-thirds of teachers approve of any conversion. Mississippi requires that teachers be polled by secret ballot in order to show a majority support any charter school. California requires that 50 percent of the "permanent" or tenured teachers approve of the action. Finally, Wisconsin requires any petition considered by a school district to have signatures of at least 10 percent of the district's teaching force, even when a conversion is not involved.

One challenge to New Jersey's charter school statute, *In re Grant of Charter School Application of Englewood on Palisades Charter School,*[4] considered the definition of "teacher" for the purposes of putting forth a charter school application. The Englewood School District challenged the application of the Palisades Charter School on the ground that the applicant had failed to satisfy the required involvement of teachers in the application. The relevant portion of the statute states that: "A charter school may be established by teaching staff members, parents with children attending schools of the district, or a combination of teaching staff members and parents."[5] Five founders of the school were named as teachers, three from Englewood and listed as "consultants" and two from the state of New York. The district alleged that since two teachers were from out of state and three merely served as "consultants," and not "teaching staff members," the application lacked the proper teacher involvement. The school district argued that "teaching staff members" should be read to mean local teachers who would be teaching at the charter school if approved.

A New Jersey appellate court upheld the decision of the state board of education rejecting this assertion. Since neither the act nor the regulations defined "teaching staff members," the court gave deference to the state board's reading of the statute, which found that the charter school's application had satisfied the requirement to involve teachers in the establishment of the school by using out-of-state teachers and in-state teachers in a consultative capacity.[6]

Some states have also extended teachers' decision-making role into issues of charter governance, renewal, and revocation. For example, Hawaii requires that at least one instructional staff member selected by the staff sit on each charter school's governing board. Mississippi requires that a majority of instructional staff and parents vote in favor of renewal as a prerequisite for the school's continuance. Teachers in Arkansas, Mississippi and North Carolina can also initiate just cause for revocation. The charter of any charter school in Arkansas and North Carolina may be revoked if two-thirds of the teaching staff request such action. Likewise, a Mississippi charter school could have its charter revoked if a majority of teachers and parents demand such action.

Issues Related to Hiring Employees

Traditional school law contexts raise a number of legal issues related to hiring of teachers, including teacher certification, employee contracts, and hiring practices. Not surprisingly, in the charter school context, these issues remain but with an application particular to the charter school setting. Charter schools must, of course, continue to honor the dictates of federal law with respect to antidiscrimination standards. Accordingly, Title VI of the Civil Rights Act of 1964 (barring discrimination on the basis of race or ethnicity), Title VII of the Civil Rights Act of 1964 (barring discrimination on the basis of race, religion, sex, and national origin), the Age Discrimination in Employment Act, Section 504 of the Rehabilitation Act of 1973, and the Americans with Disabilities Act (barring discrimination on the basis of disability) must all be observed in much the same way as they are observed in all public schools. However, other issues are not as clear. In fact, before any other hiring issues can be considered, charter schools must address an even more fundamental question: Who employs charter school staff?

Who Is the Employer?

The first issue that must be addressed when considering legal issues related to hiring teachers and other staff is whether the charter school serves as the employer or merely the place of employment. As illustrated by Table 5.1, charter schools act as the employer in a majority (22) of the states. For those seven states where the charter school is not the employer, the school district is. Likewise, for those states in which some charter schools employ their staff and others do not, those that do not are often either sponsored by a school district or are public school conversions. Interestingly, three states make this important determination a function of the charter contract. Even when the charter school's status as employer is unclear or granted to the school district, charter statutes often grant the charter school the control of all employment decisions (hiring, firing, supervision, and so forth).

Table 5.1. Is the Charter School the Employer?

Yes	Arizona, Connecticut, Delaware, District of Columbia, Florida, Idaho, Indiana, Illinois, Michigan, Minnesota, Missouri, Nevada, New Hampshire, New Mexico, New York, North Carolina, Oklahoma, Oregon, Pennsylvania, Rhode Island, South Carolina, Utah
No	Alaska, Arkansas, Iowa, Kansas, Mississippi, Tennessee, Virginia
Some charter schools serve as the employer; some do not.	California, Louisiana, Massachusetts, New Jersey, Ohio, Texas, Wisconsin
Determined by charter contract	Colorado, Georgia, Wyoming
Unclear	Hawaii, Puerto Rico

Identifying the employer served to ground one early complaint under the Michigan charter school statute. The issue arose with the Academy for Plastics Manufacturing Technology chartered by the St. Clair Intermediate School District. The charter school hired teachers as "at-will" non-union employees and made all decisions regarding their performance and direction. The school district served as the charter school authorizer. In 1997, the district proposed to the charter school that it expand its offerings to include a metal machine tool program by transferring the district's existing program to the charter school. The charter school accepted. Thereafter, the school district laid off the teacher in the program who was then subsequently hired by the charter school.

The teachers' union challenged this move and the school district's refusal to bargain over charter school positions and employees as an unfair labor practice. The union argued that the school district and charter school "jointly employed" all charter school staff. A Michigan Employment Relations Commission (MERC) hearing officer determined that the two entities were separate employers because the district did not exercise sufficient control over the employees to be considered a "joint employer." A Michigan appellate court agreed and upheld the reasoning of the MERC.[7]

An Oregon case also hinged on the identification of the proper employer of a putative charter school official. At issue was whether a dismissed administrator was an employee of the school district or the employee of a charter school. The administrator maintained that as a charter school employee, only the charter school's governing board could dismiss her. However, the court concluded that since the school had failed to establish as a nonprofit organization, it had never properly converted to charter school status nor operated as a charter school under the statute. Therefore, the court found proper the district's dismissal of the administrator. Interestingly, the court declined to rule on whether her reading of the charter school law was accurate had the school been operating as a charter school.[8]

In addition to statutory variations designating the employer, issues also arise when a for-profit management group subcontracts with a charter holder. For example, one recent Pennsylvania case demonstrates the complexities that may be involved when determining the "employer" of charter school staff in such circumstances. In *School District of the City of York v. Lincoln-Edison Charter School*,[9] one allegation made to challenge the decision of Pennsylvania's Charter School Appeal Board to reverse the school district's denial of a charter school application turned on whether the charter school or the Edison Corporation employed the teachers. Recall that Pennsylvania's charter school law prohibits for-profit companies from holding charters. The school district maintained that provisions of the management agreement that authorized Edison to "determine staffing levels," and "to select, evaluate, assign, and discipline personnel" and to pay the employees on behalf of the charter school demonstrated that the staff were actually employed by the for-profit company, not the school itself. The court disagreed. It held that since the same provisions of the management agreement made clear that the charter school governance board had final decision-making authority and had to approve any employment or dismissal, "there was sufficient evidence to support the [Pennsylvania's Charter School Appeal] Board's finding that the employees at the charter school are Lincoln-Edison [charter school] employees, not Edison [Inc.] employees."[10]

Must Charter Schools Contract with Employees?

An issue related to identifying the employer is determining whether pre-existing employee contracts bind charter schools, whether new employee contracts must be created, or whether charter schools are free to hire employees without contracts on an "at-will" basis. As the above discussion indicates, much of the answer to that question depends on whether the charter school employs the teachers or the school district does. When school districts serve as the charter school's employer, any collective bargaining agreements (CBAs) already negotiated must often be honored unless the parties to the CBA agree otherwise. Such agreements are then often summarized in memoranda of understanding between the parties involved.

Other times, the statutes themselves allow exemptions or partial exemptions from local CBAs. For example, Massachusetts' Horace Mann charter schools, those chartered by a school committee or school district, are "exempt from local collective bargaining units to the extent provided by the terms of its charter; provided, however, that employees of the Horace Mann charter school shall continue to be members of the local collective bargaining unit and shall accrue seniority and shall receive, at a minimum, the salary and benefits established in the contract of the local collective bargaining unit where said Horace Mann charter school is located."[11] Nevada's statute, however, creates an interesting hybrid relationship between the school district as the charter authorizer, the charter school as the employer, and charter school employees. Even though the charter school is the employer, the "terms and conditions of the employment" of the local CBA must be applied to the employment of charter school staff[12] except for provisions related to teacher preparation time, time of the work day, hours of a work day, and hours and days a teacher may work in a year.[13] Charter schools may vary those expectations of teachers as long as charter school teachers are given comparable preparation time and are compensated for any additional hours worked according to the established compensation schedule.[14]

For those charter schools not bound by specific statutory provisions stating otherwise, employees, including teachers, may be hired on an "at-will" basis. "Employment at will" is defined as "[e]mployment that is usually undertaken without a contract and that may be terminated at any time, by either the employer or employee, without cause."[15] From the employer perspective, such a relationship provides the most discretion as the employees literally serve at the will of the employer. Such discretion can be viewed as another example of the autonomy charter schools may enjoy. Of course, for teachers used to working in contexts where the terms and conditions of their employment are well-defined by a contract and their due process rights at termination or nonrenewal have been statutorily or contractually defined, at-will employment does not provide the level of employee protection they have become accustomed to in more traditional public school settings. Teachers must recognize that in an at-will relationship with an employer, the charter school may terminate their employment at any time and for any or no reason. The "due process" rights teachers in public schools may take for granted are based on the relationships defined by the contract and by statute that create an expectation of continued employment. An expectation of continued employment creates a property right in the terms of the Fourteenth Amendment to the U.S. Constitution and is therefore subject to all its protections.[16] In the absence of such definition or evidence showing the action was motivated by unlawful discrimination, teachers (or other employees) dismissed from at-will employment have little recourse.

May Teachers Receive Leaves of Absence to Work in Charter Schools?

In order to provide protection for teachers who may wish to work in charter schools but are reluctant to relinquish their rights under existing contracts with school districts, twenty-one states and the

District of Columbia have created specific language to allow teachers to receive leaves of absence from their current positions in order to work in charter schools. In addition, two other states require charter school petitions or charter contracts to describe any transfer rights for teachers currently employed in the local school district. As Table 5.2 indicates, some statutes make granting such leaves discretionary on the part of school boards, while others require any leave request to be honored. Even when statutes preserve school board discretion with respect to teachers' leaves of absence, the statute may direct that leaves may not be "unreasonably withheld"[17] or teachers required to resign in order to work at a charter school.[18]

**Table 5.2. States with Statutory Language
Regarding Teacher Leaves of Absence**

Leaves of Absence Mandatorily Available	Colorado, Connecticut, Delaware, Illinois, Indiana, Louisiana, Massachusetts, Minnesota, Nevada, New Jersey, New Mexico, North Carolina, Ohio, Oregon, Rhode Island, South Carolina.
Leaves of Absence Available at Discretion of School Board	District of Columbia, Florida, New York, Pennsylvania, Tennessee, Utah
Charter Petition/Contract Must Describe Teacher Transfer Rights	California, Idaho

In those states where leaves are granted, the length of such leaves of absence range from one year[19] to any reasonable number of years requested by the teacher.[20] Leaves may also sometimes be extended.[21] While some states appear to have granted extremely generous leave statutes with the right to return to district employment throughout the leave regardless of length,[22] others require teachers to either return to the school district or resign their positions at the end of a specified period. For example, Illinois statutes entitle teachers to a five-year leave of absence in order to work in a charter school, but then require the teacher to commit to one job or the other at the end of that period.[23]

Can Teachers Be Assigned to Work in a Charter School?

Charter schools are premised on the notion that students elect to attend, but what about teachers and other staff? May a school district, particularly when it is the charter school's authorizer and the staff's employer, assign teachers to work in a charter school? As Table 5.3 indicates, the majority of states answer this question in the negative and require that teaching in a charter school be voluntary.

**Table 5.3. May a Teacher/Employee Be Assigned
to Work at a Charter School?**

NO (specific statutory language indicates voluntary assignments of teachers/employees only)	Alaska, Arkansas, California, District of Columbia, Idaho, Indiana, Illinois, Louisiana (Types I-III), Massachusetts, Missouri, New Hampshire, New Mexico, North Carolina, Oregon, Rhode Island, Texas (open enrollment), Utah, Wyoming
NO (no specific statutory language, but other statutory language suggests assignments must be voluntary)	Kansas, New Jersey, Ohio, South Carolina, Tennessee
YES (specific statutory language retaining discretion of school district authorities to assign teachers to charter schools)	Louisiana (Type IV), Virginia
UNCLEAR *(the statute is silent on the issue)*	Colorado, Georgia, Hawaii, Iowa, Mississippi, Puerto Rico, Texas (campus), Wisconsin
NOT APPLICABLE (no specific language, but presumed not applicable as the charter school is the employer)	Arizona, Connecticut, Delaware, Florida, Michigan, Minnesota, Nevada, Oklahoma, Pennsylvania

For those states for which the statute contains no language to mandate or suggest that no employee can be assigned to a charter school, it is assumed that school authorities continue to enjoy the same discretion with respect to teacher assignments they enjoy with respect to employees in other district schools. Only two states, Virginia and Louisiana, make this discretion explicit. In the latter case, only in Louisiana's "Type IV" charter schools or district charters may charter school teachers be assigned. Of course, in all instances where assignment of staff is not precluded by statute, the charter school contract may limit that authority if both parties agree. Charter schools may wish to include specific language in their charters to ensure that all staff is hired consistent with the mission of the school.

Must Charter School Teachers Be Certified?

The certification requirements of instructional and administrative staff in charter schools may also differ from those required for professional staff in traditional public schools. Table 5.4 delineates state variation on this issue. Four states and Puerto Rico have established no certification requirements for teachers working in charter schools. That is not to suggest that those teachers are held to no standard. Rather, charter school aspirants must describe the standards to which teachers will be held in the charter application and, if approved, the charter contract. In addition, Arizona requires that each charter school maintain a book for public inspection that contains a copy of each charter school teacher's resume. Likewise, Utah requires charter schools to disclose teacher qualifications to parents.[24]

Table 5.4. Must Charter School Hire Certified Teachers?

YES	Alaska, California, Florida, Illinois, Indiana, Iowa, Michigan,[25] Minnesota, New Jersey, New Mexico, Ohio, Rhode Island, Tennessee, Utah, Virginia, Wisconsin, Wyoming
YES, unless granted a waiver	Arkansas, Colorado, Idaho
YES, for a specified percentage	Connecticut, Delaware, Louisiana, Missouri, Nevada, New Hampshire, New York, North Carolina, Oregon, Pennsylvania, South Carolina
NO	Arizona, District of Columbia, Georgia, Massachusetts, Texas
Unclear or not specified	Hawaii, Kansas, Mississippi, Oklahoma, Puerto Rico

Notwithstanding the four states and the District of Columbia that exempt charter school teachers from state certification requirements, most states require a majority of, if not all, charter school teachers to hold some type of state credential. For those states that require a percentage of teachers to be certified, requirements range from 50 percent[26] to 90 percent[27] of instructional staff. In those states, the remainder of staff may be uncertified but sometimes must still meet established criteria. New York's statute provides an example. It allows 30 percent of a charter school's teaching force or five teachers, whichever is less, to be uncertified as long as each teacher meets one of four criteria. The person must (1) have 3 years teaching experience; (2) be a tenured or tenure-track professor; (3) have two years teaching experience with Teach for America; or (4) "possess exceptional business, professional, artistic, athletic, or military experience."[28]

Similarly, even some states that require certification for all teachers have created special certificates or permits for charter school teachers. In such instances, the teacher is either certified through an alternative route[29] or is issued a provisional certification if enrolled in a program leading to traditional certification.[30] In addition to those states controlling the proportion of teachers who may be uncertified,

Ohio allows charter schools to use uncertified teachers for up to twelve hours of work per week. Likewise, both Wyoming and Oregon qualify their certification requirements by noting that full-time employees must hold licensure.

Most states that require certification for all or part of a charter school's teaching force similarly require school administrators to hold state licensure. However, this is not always the case. Neither Minnesota nor New York requires a charter school administrator to be licensed. Alaska's charter schools may operate without an administrator, but in such a circumstance, the school district must assign one of its administrators to the school for the purpose of teacher evaluation.

The certification requirements for a charter school "leader" were disputed in a New Jersey lawsuit.[31] At issue was whether a charter school leader needed to hold a New Jersey administrative license. In the school's original application, the school titled its "lead person" as a "director" and provided a detailed job description for that leadership position. The department of education informed the applicant that based on the job description, the "director" would need to hold licensure as a principal. The charter school countered that if the person selected did not have the licensure to be a principal, the title would change to "supervisor." The challenging school district complained. The charter school then listed the position as "head" of the charter school. The state board determined that the state statute did not require "headmasters" or head teachers to be certified. The district again appealed.

The appellate court disagreed with the state board.[32] It noted that although the title was systematically "downgraded" in an apparent attempt to avoid certification requirements, nothing in the job description changed. The court concluded that "the school's head, by whatever name, must have a certificate of some kind"[33] and ordered the state commissioner to direct the school to ensure that the lead administrator was so certified by the 1999 school year.

Another issue related to teacher certification involves the intersection between state charter school laws and federal education laws. Two federal laws have provisions relating to teacher qualifications. The first is the Individuals with Disabilities Education Act (IDEA), which requires that:

> The State educational agency has established and maintains standards to ensure that personnel necessary to carry out this part are appropriately and adequately prepared and trained. . . . Such standards shall be consistent with any State-approved or State-

recognized certification, licensing, registration, or other comparable requirements that apply to the professional discipline in
which those personnel are providing special education or related
services; . . . [and] where there is a shortage of such personnel, the
most qualified individuals available who are making satisfactory
progress toward completing applicable course work necessary to
meet the [State's] standards . . . within three years.[34]

As this passage demonstrates, states must ensure that all students
with disabilities, including those enrolled in charter schools, are
taught by personnel who are "appropriately and adequately"
trained. For those states that do not require charter school teachers
to be certified, IDEA dictates that the state still ensure that *qualified*
staff are working with children with disabilities. In other words,
charter schools may be asked to assure the state that the personnel
working with children with disabilities have the requisite knowledge and skills if certification is lacking. Hiring special education
staff that hold certification may be the simplest route to accomplish-
ing the requirement that staff have adequate knowledge and training, whether or not the charter school statute requires it. In fact, a
conservative interpretation of IDEA suggests that staff delivering
special education should be certified and that any uncertified charter school staff who are working with students with disabilities
should take course work to become certified within three years.

The recently enacted No Child Left Behind Act of 2001[35] (NCLB)
also contains provisions related to teacher qualifications. The NCLB
is the most recent iteration of the Elementary and Secondary Education Act, which provides federal funds for a number of projects.
A new provision of the NCLB requires that states ensure that all
public school students are taught by "highly qualified instructional
staff."[36] However, the law also contains a provision that "[t]he accountability provisions under this Act shall be overseen for charter
schools in accordance with State charter school law."[37] Further, the
provision directing states to submit plans to the federal Department
of Education (DOE) requires that the state provide a copy of any
"charter school law that exempts teachers from State certification
and licensing requirements."[38] It would appear that the language
of these two provisions directs the DOE to find a way to harmo-
nize a state's charter statute with the NCLB when monitoring its
implementation.

Recent nonregulatory guidance provided by the DOE explains
the agency's interpretation of these provisions as applied to charter
schools that receive Title I funds. It explains that although charter

school teachers do not need to hold certification if the state does not require it, they still must hold a four-year college degree and demonstrate competence in the subject area they teach.[39] This requirement applies to any teacher who teaches a "core academic subject," which includes English, mathematics, reading or language arts, science, foreign languages, civics, government, economics, arts, history, and geography.[40] Charter schools must also comply with NCLB's requirements with regard to paraprofessionals, who must have completed two years of college, possess an associate's degree or demonstrate subject-matter competence to the satisfaction of the state education agency through a formal assessment.[41] Title I charter schools must ensure compliance with these provisions by the end of the 2005–2006 school year.

These requirements could have considerable impact on existing charter schools that employ instructional staff that do not meet these requirements. In fact, the National School Boards Association notes that this interpretation may require "modifications to existing contracts with charter schools and has significant implications for professional development funding."[42] These requirements also seem to limit Title I charter school flexibility in those states with charter school laws that do not require teacher certification. Nonetheless, the NCLB is just beginning to be implemented, and it is difficult to ascertain what effect its requirements will have on charter schools' employment practices. It is, therefore, an issue that bears watching.

Issues Related to Working in a Charter School

Of course, once a charter school has hired its staff, other legal issues arise in the relationship. These include the collective-bargaining rights, retirement fund participation and availability of other benefits, transfer rights, tenure rights, and issues related to evaluation and termination. Because collective-bargaining rights often implicate other rights enjoyed by employees, they will be discussed first.

May Charter School Employees Bargain Collectively?

Of the 34 charter school jurisdictions that allow public employees to collectively bargain, 27 have some statutory language explicitly relating to collective bargaining and charter schools. When conversion schools are involved or when the school district serves as the employer, charter school employees are often presumed to be members of the existing local bargaining unit. In some cases, that relationship may be further defined or qualified by the specific charter contract itself. Six states require that if charter school employees wish to bargain collectively, they must form a separate bargaining unit from any existing bargaining unit of the local school district. Interestingly, two states, Indiana and Oregon, prohibit school districts from negotiating any language with an employee union that would waive or limit a district's authority to charter schools.[43]

Table 5.4. Charter School States and Language Regarding Collective Bargaining

Charter School Employees Are Part of Existing Local Bargaining Unit	Alaska, Hawaii
Charter School Employees May Form Separate Bargaining Unit	Connecticut, Delaware, Idaho, Illinois, New Hampshire, Pennsylvania
Charter School Employees May Be Part of Existing Unit or Form a Separate Unit	California, Florida, Indiana, Louisiana, Massachusetts, Michigan, Minnesota, Nevada, New Jersey, New York, Ohio, Oregon, Rhode Island, Tennessee, Wisconsin
Collective Bargaining Waived	Oklahoma
Collective Bargaining May Be Waived	Colorado
Charter Contract Must Describe Relationship with Employees and Existing Representative	New Mexico, Wyoming
No Specific Language	Arizona, Arkansas, District of Columbia, Iowa, Kansas, Puerto Rico, Utah
Collective Bargaining Not Allowed for Public Employees	Georgia, Mississippi, Missouri, North Carolina, South Carolina, Texas, Virginia

Not surprisingly, some courts have been asked to consider collective bargaining in relation to charter schools. In one early challenge, the Milwaukee Teachers' Education Association filed suit in 1995 with a variety of complaints concerning Wisconsin's charter school statute. One dispute centered on portions of the statute that required any school chartered by the Milwaukee Public Schools (MPS) to be a non-instrumentality, meaning that MPS could not employ any staff at the charters, even if the charter schools converted from existing public schools. No other Wisconsin school district faced the same restriction. The union also objected to sections added to the statute controlling collective bargaining that prohibited negotiations with MPS on subjects related to the charter statute. The circuit court granted the union's request for an injunction, thereby blocking the MPS from chartering any additional schools until a decision on the merits of the case could be rendered. The union eventually dropped its lawsuit in 1999 in exchange for a memorandum of understanding with the district, but only after the statute was revised to grant MPS the same authority enjoyed by other Wisconsin districts to authorize either instrumentality or non-instrumentality charter schools and to eliminate the complained-of sections in relation to collective bargaining.[44]

As mentioned earlier, a Michigan case also considered the inter-section of collective bargaining and charter schools. In that case, the union challenged the school district's relationship with a char-ter school and the implications it had for bargaining over staff posi-tions. Recall that the situation involved a school district's transfer of a program to the charter school, the subsequent termination of the affected teaching position, and then the charter school's hiring of the same teacher as an at-will employee of the charter school.[45] The teachers union complained that the situation created an unfair labor practice that if allowed would permit the school district to avoid its contractual obligations with the union by transferring as-sets and programs to the charter school while still maintaining con-trol of the program as the charter school authorizer. Accordingly, the union argued that the school district and charter school should be considered joint employers in order that the employee's rights to engage in union activities be protected.

The court rejected this argument, noting that the union's argu-ment failed to recognize that the school district had to relinquish considerable control over the program in order to transfer it to the charter school. Further, the court concluded that "while the [school district] may have been pleased with the effect that forming the acad-emy had on its dealings with the union, the [school district] did not take advantage of this situation in order to avoid its obligation to negotiate with unions under the [Public Employees Relations Act] PERA."[46]

This ruling raises an interesting hypothetical question. Had there been evidence that the school district had used its chartering au-thority consistent with the charter school act, but deliberately to avoid negotiating with its employee union, would the ruling have been the same? Although it is unknown how a court would rule in such a case, a school district so tempted should expect challenge to any deliberate act of this kind.

In fact, at least one court has noted that charter school legisla-tion may lead to litigation in order to sort out new relationships between schools, employees, and unions. The United States Court of Appeals for the Sixth Circuit made the following observation of Michigan's passage of charter school legislation in rendering a decision related to nonmembers of the union and a complaint about the propriety of certain fees charged by the Michigan Education Association:

> An act passed by the Michigan legislature in December 1993 allows nonprofit entities to establish a new breed of independent public school called charter schools. We note with more than a little trepidation that this development will in all likelihood only add fuel to the litigation fire that the nonmembers here have so carefully stoked for the past sixteen years.[47]

Does Charter School Employment Implicate Participation in State Teacher/Employee Retirement Funds?

Public employees, especially public school teachers often participate in public retirement systems. Charter school teachers may or may not have access to this system, depending on the charter school statute and its interplay with statutes creating retirement systems. As shown in Table 5.6, the majority of states extend this benefit to all charter school teachers. Eight states restrict participation in some way. For example, in Illinois only certified teachers may participate. Wisconsin limits participation to those teachers who work in instrumentality charters in which the school district employs the staff. Utah and South Carolina limit participation to those on leave from a school system or those who work for a charter school that has been converted from a traditional public school. Both Michigan and North Carolina have determined that teachers employed by a "private employer" or a management company are not eligible to participate, while those who work directly for the nonprofit charter holder may take part.

Table 5.6. Charter School Participation in State Retirement Programs

Yes (for all teachers)	Alaska, Arizona, Arkansas, Colorado, Connecticut, Georgia, Hawaii, Idaho, Iowa, Kansas, Massachusetts, Minnesota, Nevada, New Jersey, New Mexico, New York, Ohio, Oklahoma, Oregon, Pennsylvania, Rhode Island, Tennessee, Texas, Virginia, Wyoming
Yes (for some teachers)	Florida, Illinois, Louisiana, Michigan, North Carolina, South Carolina, Utah, Wisconsin
Charter School May Choose	California, Delaware, District of Columbia, Indiana, New Hampshire

In four states and the District of Columbia, the charter school may make retirement benefits available to their teachers through the state system or through some other system. In the District of Columbia, if a charter school elects to offer retirement benefits through a system other than the publicly operated one, an employee already vested in the public system may elect which program in which to participate.[48] Further, no District of Columbia charter may make switching participation from the public system to its separate retirement system a condition of charter school employment.[49]

Do Tenure Laws Apply to Charter School Teachers?

Although not all states grant teachers the right to tenure, for those that do, teacher tenure is an interesting concept in charter schools. Given the fact that schools operate on limited term contracts that must be renewed, it could be argued that the school itself does not have "tenure." Because the school's continued existence is dependent on satisfying the accountability provisions of the charter, the school has no guarantee that it will continue to need employees. Hence, the guarantee of employment usually associated with teacher tenure seems a contradiction in terms.

Yet, some charter laws preserve the right to teacher tenure in charter schools. For example, in Alaska, the charter school teacher earns tenure in the school district. In New Jersey, any charter school teacher on leave retains tenure in the parent school district, and newly hired charter school teachers may acquire tenure through a process know as "streamline tenure."[50] Nevertheless, the applicability of tenure laws varies considerably. Although tenure laws still apply in Rhode Island,[51] they do not in Massachusetts.[52] In most cases, charter statutes do not explicitly address teacher tenure. For states in which blanket waivers of school laws describe the charter school context, teacher tenure would likely not apply. However, in states in which specific waivers must be requested, an application to waive tenure laws would be necessary. Consequently, teachers who already enjoy tenure status or wish to obtain it need to be certain of the applicability of tenure to any charter school for which they wish to work.

Do Charter School Teachers Have Any Rights to Return to a Previous Position in a School District?

In addition to the statutory provisions related to leaves of absence discussed above, a teacher's right to return to a previously held position in a school district may also be addressed in charter legislation. As might be expected, the right to return from a leave of absence is often qualified by whether a position is available.[53] Even when no specific leave has been granted, teachers sometimes enjoy some rights to return. For example, both Arizona and Oklahoma grant a teacher previously employed by a school district the right to a hiring "preference" for any available position as long as the teacher re-applies within three years of leaving the district for a charter school.[54] In a similar manner, Arkansas teachers who worked for a charter school that has had its charter revoked must be given a preference for being rehired by the school district.[55] Louisiana and New Jersey even provide a right to return for teachers dismissed by charter schools.[56] However, a charter school teacher discharged from a New Mexico charter school for just cause is considered similarly discharged from the school district.[57] Remember, too, that specific charter contract language may describe any right to return to previously held positions whenever the school district is the chartering authority.

Do Any Provisions Relate to Termination of Charter School Teachers?

Few states specifically address the termination of charter school teachers. Often, there is a generic requirement that charter school applications and/or contracts describe all personnel policies, which would presumably include issues related to dismissal.[58] For charter schools bound by collective-bargaining agreements, that contractual language would likely define the procedures required for dismissal. Only eight states explicitly address teacher termination in one form or another. Delaware requires that termination of any employee be conducted consistent with the school's personnel policies or the collective-bargaining agreement reached with the employee representative.[59] Iowa requires charter schools to abide by existing statutes relative to the issue, while Massachusetts charter schools are exempt from them.[60] California requires that if the charter school will not follow existing laws on teacher dismissal, the charter must describe how the issue will be handled.[61] Oklahoma requires that "suspension, dismissal, [and] nonreemployment" be addressed in the application, and New Mexico requires an "employee discipline" policy,[62] while Nevada requires that personnel policies provide the "same level of protection" as enjoyed by teachers in traditional schools.[63]

Finally, Pennsylvania statutes provide language relative to procedure. Although the statute does not direct charter schools to apply any particular procedure, it allows a school district to likewise dismiss any teacher terminated by a charter school. It then provides that the school district may use information from the charter school, including (1) reasons for dismissal; (2) list of witnesses; (3) descriptions of any physical evidence; (4) a copy of the record at the dismissal hearing.[64] By inference then, the provision seems to suggest that charter schools must use some sort of process characterized by these four components.

The notion of procedures, of course, evokes issues of due process under the Fourteenth Amendment to the Constitution. What process is due to teachers who work in charter schools and face adverse disciplinary action? As mentioned earlier in the chapter, the answer to that question lies, as it does for all teachers, in the type of contract held and the timing of the action being taken. For at-will employees, no process would be due unless school policies dictate it. For those on term contracts, the process due would depend on whether the action was taken during the term of the contract or at its expiration. In the first instance, at least some process would be due because the remainder of the term contract would create a protected property interest for the employee. If taken at the contract's expiration, no process would be due because the legal relationship between the parties would have expired with the contract— no relationship, no expectation of employment, no process due.

If the employee holds a tenure contract, the relationship has no defined end point. Therefore, the employee has an expectation of continued employment that requires proper process to sever. Although the Supreme Court has never specified the exact contours of that process, at a minimum it must include proper justification of the action, notification of that justification, an opportunity for the individual to counter that evidence, and a decision based on the facts. As with many other issues, charter school operators should be careful to determine what statutes and existing arrangements apply to them. In addition, charter school authorizers should consider whether such policies need incorporation into the charter.

In addition to issues of procedural due process, employee termination raises the subject of substantive due process. That is, whether the termination of an employee is fundamentally fair. An Ohio case illustrates this point. The case raised a question regarding the application of constitutional protections in relation to the termination of a charter school teacher by a principal employed by a for-profit management company. The teacher alleged that her termination was an improper retaliation for her outspokenness regarding failures of the school to appropriately deliver special education services. As such, she claimed the principal had violated her rights to freedom of speech under the First Amendment. The school, principal, and management company argued that her case should be dismissed because the principal, as the employee of the private management company, was a private, not a state, actor. Therefore, they maintained that First Amendment considerations with regard to employees did not apply and the teacher had no claim. The court discarded this theory, ruling that the school's status as a public charter school rendered the principal a state actor regardless of the fact that he was an employee of the for-profit management company.[65]

What Other Provisions of Charter School Statutes Relate to Employees?

Finally, some statutes have created provisions in addition to those reviewed above that implicate charter school employees, especially teachers. Three states, Iowa, Massachusetts, and Pennsylvania require charter schools to describe staff development plans in their petitions, charters, or policies. Arizona, North Carolina and Tennessee allow charter school participation in state insurance plans, while New Jersey requires that teachers on leave be allowed to receive continued coverage by the health plans used by their school districts. Both Missouri and Oklahoma specify that no district may make any reprisals against any employee involved in a charter school application or petition. Finally, Hawaii's statute contains an interesting provision that compels charter schools to write a "detailed implementation plan" that "provides for the basic protections of employees and their reasonable academic freedom."[66]

Is It Fair to Treat Charter School Teachers Differently from Other Public School Teachers?

This chapter has reviewed the legal relationships between charter schools and their employees. As might be expected, states, to varying degrees, have granted charter schools the flexibility to experiment with employee relationships and what effect they might have on children's learning. In many of the issues raised above, some may wonder whether it is fair to treat public school teachers differently based on whether they work in a traditional or charter school or even whether they work in one type of charter school versus another within the same state. Such issues of fairness are generally examined under the Fourteenth Amendment's Equal Protection

Clause. In this instance charter school states have often created two or more classes of teachers and make benefits, rights, and protections available to them based on those classifications. Unlike classifications of race or gender, however, such classifications would not cause any court to apply anything but the lowest level of judicial scrutiny. As such, any state so challenged would only need to demonstrate to the satisfaction of the court that the classifications rationally relate to a legitimate interest of state policy making. Such a rationale would not be difficult to construct in the context of charter schools. In fact, simply noting that charter schools exist to examine new ways of doing things in public education would probably be sufficient to satisfy the demands of this so-called rational basis test. Controlling costs could be another rationale. Accordingly, although the laws create differences, these differences would not likely rise to the level of unfairness necessary for them to be declared unconstitutional. Rather, as the provisions were at least ostensibly designed to do, the focus will be on the public policy question of whether the created differences produce the desired results or create problems of teacher recruitment, quality, or retention.

Conclusion

The new relationships between employees and schools created by charter school legislation range from substantially the same as those that occur in traditional public schools to those that differ considerably. The state variance described here suggests that charter schools need to clearly understand all requirements in state and federal law regarding employee issues before negotiating the charter contract with their authorizers. This prudent step is needed both to develop knowledge about the boundaries of charter schools' discretion in this area and to determine what, if any, contract provisions should be developed to clearly establish charter schools' employment policies.

Endnotes

1   *See, e.g.,* Colo. Rev. Stat. § 22-30.5-106(c).
2   Iowa Code § 256F.3 (3).
3   Arkansas, California, Delaware, District of Columbia, Florida, Idaho, Indiana, Minnesota, Mississippi, New Jersey, New Mexico, North Carolina, Pennsylvania, Rhode Island, South Carolina, Texas, Utah, Wisconsin, Wyoming.
4   727 A.2d 15 (N.J. Super. A.D. 1999).
5   N.J. Stat. Ann. § 18A:36A-4a as cited in *Englewood,* 727 A.2d 15, at 25.
6   *Englewood,* 727 A.2d at 27.

[7] St. Clair County Intermediate Sch. Dist. v. St. Clair County Educ. Ass'n., 630 N.W.2d 909 (Mich. App. 2001).

[8] Nuffer v. Molalla River Sch. Dist,, 65 P.3d 1111 (Or. App. 2003).

[9] 798 A.2d 295, (Pa. Cmwl. 2002).

[10] *Id.*, at 303.

[11] Mass. Gen. Laws ch. 71, § 89(u).

[12] Nev. Rev. Stat. § 336.595(1).

[13] Nev. Rev. Stat. § 336.595(2).

[14] *Id.*

[15] Black's Law Dictionary 545 (7th ed. 1999).

[16] *See* Board of Regents v. Roth, 408 U.S. 564, (1972); Perry v. Sindermann, 408 U.S. 593 (1972).

[17] N.Y. Educ. Law § 2854(3)(d); Pa. Stat. 1723-A(E); D.C. Code Ann. § 38-1802.07(a).

[18] Fla. Stat. § 228.056(12)(e).

[19] *See, e.g.*, Colo. Rev. Stat. § 22-30.5-111(1).

[20] *See, e.g.*, Minn. Stat. § 124D.10(20); N.C. Gen. Stat. § 115C-238.29F(e)(3).

[21] *See, e.g.*, Colo. Rev. Stat. § 22-30.5-111(1); R.I. Gen. Laws § 16-77-3(e).

[22] Minnesota and North Carolina for example.

[23] Ill. Comp. Stat. § 5/27A-10(b).

[24] Utah Code Ann. § 53A-1a-512(3)(b).

[25] Michigan statutes exempt university and college faculty members teaching in charter schools from certification requirements. Mich. Comp. Laws Ann. § 380.505(2).

[26] *See e.g.*, Conn. Gen. Stat. § 10-66dd(b), or Or. Rev. Stat. § 338.135(6)(c).

[27] S.C. Code Ann. § 59-40-50(B)(5); 75 percent of teachers in new charter schools must be certified and 90% of teachers in public school conversion charters must be certified.

[28] N.Y. Educ. Law § 2854(3)(a-1).

[29] *See, e.g.*, Del. Code Ann. tit. 14, § 507(c).

[30] *See, e.g.*, Wis. Stat. § 118.40(1m)(b)(7) & § 118.19(1).

[31] *In re* Charter School Appeal of Greater Brunswick Charter School, 753 A.2d 1155 (N.J. Super. A.D. 1999).

[32] *Id.*, at 1161.

[33] *Id.*

[34] 20 U.S.C. 1412(a)(15).

[35] Public Law No. 107-110

[36] Id, § 1111(b)(8)(C).

[37] Id, § 1111 (b)(2)(K).

[38] Id, § 2112(b)(11).

[39] U.S. Dep't. of Educ., Nonregulatory Guidance: The Impact of the New Title I Requirements on Charter Schools, Draft Guidance (March 24, 2003). See Appendix C.

[40] *Id.*, Section E.

[41] *Id.*

[42] Charter School Guidance: NSBA Sees Issues for Local School Boards, available at http://www.nsba.org/site/doc.asp?TRACKID=&VID=2&CID=89&DID=11337 (last visited Apr. 17, 2003).

[43] Ind. Code § 20-5.5-6-8; Or. Rev. Stat. § 338.135(9).

[44] For a history of the case and discussion of the issues, see Milwaukee Teacher's Educ. Ass'n v. Milwaukee Bd. of Sch. Directors, Case No. 97-2110, (Wis. Ct. App. 1998).

[45] St. Clair County Intermediate Sch. Dist. v. St. Clair County Educ. Ass'n., 630 N.W.3d 909 (Mich. App. 2001).

[46] *Id.*, at 921.

[47] Jibson v. Michigan Educ. Ass'n., 30 F.3d 723, 725 n.1 (6th Cir. 1994) (internal citations omitted).

[48] D.C. Code Ann. § 38-1802.07(b).

[49] D.C. Code Ann. § 38-1802.07(b)(4).

[50] N.J. Stat. Ann. § 18A:36A-14(e).

[51] R.I. Gen. Laws § 16-77-11(7).

[52] Mass. Gen. Laws ch. 71, § 89(t).

[53] *See, e.g.*, N.C. Gen. Stat. § 115C-238.29F(e)(3); N.M. Stat. Ann. § 22-8B-10(F).

[54] Ariz. Rev. Stat. § 15-187(B); Okla. Stat. § 70-3-139(B).

[55] Ark. Code Ann. § 6-23-205.

[56] La. Rev. Stat. Ann. § 3397(B)(2)(c); N.J. Stat. Ann. § 18A:36A-14(f).

[57] N.M. Stat. Ann. § 22-8B-10(G).

[58] *See, e.g.* Ga. Code. Ann. §20-2-2063(8).

[59] Del. Code Ann. tit. 14, § 504A(7).

[60] Iowa Code § 256F.4 (2)(h); Mass. Gen. Laws ch. 71, § 89(t).

[61] Cal. Educ. Code § 47611.5(d).

[62] Okla. Stat. § 70-3-134(A)(4); N.M. Stat. Ann. § 22-8B-8(k).

[63] Nev. Rev. Stat. § 386.520D(2)(m).

[64] Pa. Stat. § 1723A(H).

[65] Riester v. Riverside Community Sch., 257 F.Supp.2d 968 (S.D.Ohio 2002).

[66] Haw. Rev. Stat. § 302A-1182(c)(1).

Instructional Delivery
in
Charter Schools

Chapter 6

Charter Schools and Race

Critics of charter schools have expressed the concern that whites and minorities would use these schools to segregate themselves from each other. This concern has a historical basis: After the Supreme Court ruled in *Brown v. Board of Education*[1] that separate-but-equal schools were unconstitutional, white parents used freedom-of-choice plans as a means of circumventing desegregation. This chapter examines the variety of legal questions regarding race that arise in the charter school context. First, this chapter provides an overview of the Equal Protection Clause. This summary is provided because many of the discrimination challenges examined in this chapter are brought under the Equal Protection Clause. Second, the constitutionality of charter school racial balancing provisions, which require charter schools to reflect the racial composition of the surrounding school districts, is examined. Third, this chapter explores the legal issues surrounding race-neutral, charter school admission policies that might have the effect of creating one-race charter schools. Fourth, an examination of the legal issues pertaining to school desegregation decrees is provided. Finally, this chapter analyzes the constitutionality of charter schools that have curricula that appeal to particular ethnic and racial groups.

Overview of the Equal Protection Clause

As explained above, many of the legal challenges involving discrimination implicate the Equal Protection Clause of the Fourteenth Amendment. The Equal Protection Clause provides that no state may "deny to any person within its jurisdiction equal protection of the laws." Courts have applied three levels of scrutiny to determine whether a governmental classification violates the Equal Protection Clause. These classifications are set out in Table 6.1.

Courts apply strict scrutiny, which is the most difficult level for the state to overcome, in two situations: (1) when the government classification affects "suspect classes" such as race; or (2) the classification involves a fundamental right protected by the Constitution (e.g., the right to vote). Classifications subject to strict scrutiny must

101

be narrowly tailored to satisfy a compelling governmental interest. Heightened scrutiny is usually applied to gender classifications. Such classifications must be substantially related to important state interests. All other classifications are subject to the rational basis test, which is the lowest level of scrutiny. Such classifications must be rationally related to a legitimate governmental interest. This level of scrutiny provides a great deal of latitude to the government. If a court can find a conceivable basis for the classification, it will uphold the differential treatment under the Equal Protection Clause.

Table 6.1. Equal Protection Clause Framework

Classification	Test Employed
1. Suspect class (race) 2. Fundamental rights recognized under the Constitution	Strict scrutiny: Narrowly tailored to satisfy a compelling government interest
Gender	Heightened scrutiny: Substantially related to important state interest
All other classes (e.g., age, economic status, sexual orientation)	Rational basis: Rationally related to a legitimate state interest

Racial Balancing Provisions

Racial balancing provisions are one strategy employed by enabling statutes to prevent charter schools from becoming racially segregated. Table 6.2 depicts the variety of racial balancing provisions. Seven states require charter schools to adopt policies to ensure that they reflect the racial composition of the surrounding school districts. For example, California's statute authorizes school districts to deny an application if it "does not contain reasonably comprehensive descriptions [of] . . . [t]he means by which the school will achieve a racial and ethnic balance among its pupils that is reflective of the general population residing within the territorial jurisdiction of the school district to which the charter petition is submitted."[2]

Three states require the racial composition of charter schools to reflect that of the surrounding school districts. For example, North Carolina's statute requires that:

> [w]ithin one year after the charter school begins operation, the population of the school shall reasonably reflect the racial and ethnic composition of the general population residing within the local school administrative unit in which the school is located or

the racial and ethnic composition of the special population that the school seeks to serve residing within the local school administrative unit in which the school is located.[3]

Finally, Nevada goes further still by compelling the charter school's racial and ethnic population to differ by not more than 10 percent from the racial composition of the surrounding school district.

Table 6.2. Charter School Racial Balancing Provisions

Must Adopt Policies That Ensure Student Body Reflects Racial Composition of Surrounding School District	California, Florida, New Jersey,[4] Ohio, South Carolina, Wisconsin, Wyoming
Student Body Must Reflect Racial Composition of Surrounding School District	Kansas, Minnesota, North Carolina
Student Body Must Fall within 10 Percent of Racial Composition of Surrounding School District	Nevada

If a racial balancing provision were challenged under the Equal Protection Clause, a court would have to determine the applicable level of scrutiny. If the provision required charter schools to use race in their admissions decisions, then a court would likely apply strict scrutiny analysis. Provisions requiring charter schools to adopt policies ensuring that they reflect the racial composition of the surrounding school districts might not be subject to strict scrutiny. This is because such provisions appear merely to require charter schools to use approaches designed to increase the pool of under-represented races available for selection, such as outreach and advertising. They do not seem to require charter schools to use race as a criterion in their selection of students. This distinction is significant: "Efforts geared toward outreach or inclusion in the selection pool are generally not deemed a racial classification worthy of strict scrutiny so long as the selection is itself race-neutral. The results of the efforts may alter the selection pool (in fact, this is the clear intent of the efforts), but no race-conscious selection methods are employed. In other words, methods designed to avoid disparate impact are permissible when race-neutral selection occurs."[5]

By contrast, provisions that require charter schools to reflect the racial composition of the districts in residence are more likely to be subject to strict scrutiny. This is because they appear to require noncompliant charter schools to use race in their selection process in order to exist. *Beaufort County Board of Education v. Lighthouse Char-*

ter School Committee supports this assertion. In 1996, the South Carolina legislature enacted a charter school law; § 59-40-50(B)(6) of that
statute stated that "under no circumstances may a charter school
enrollment differ from the racial composition of the school district
by more than ten percent." The Beaufort County Board of Education denied an application for a charter school to be located in the
Hilton Head section of the county for failing to identify its prospective students. Thus, it was impossible for the board to determine
whether the school would be in compliance with the state's racial
balancing requirement. The Supreme Court of South Carolina found
that the board's finding of noncompliance was not clearly erroneous; however, the court remanded the case to the circuit court to
determine the constitutionality of the racial balancing provision.[6]

On remand, the circuit court found that § 59-40-50(B)(6) violated the Equal Protection Clause.[7] Strict scrutiny was applicable
because the provision was an admissions policy that classified applicants on the basis of race. The court reached this conclusion because the provision "specifically requires that a charter school may
not exist if the provision is not satisfied."[8] The court rejected the
board's argument that strict scrutiny was inapplicable because the
provision merely expressed the legislature's goal that charter schools
have a racially diverse student body. Although the court agreed that
some of the language of the statute contradicted its interpretation
of the racial balancing provision, it concluded that the legislature
"was very clear in the requirement that the charter school can operate if its enrollment satisfies § 59-40-50(B)(6)."[9]

Applying strict scrutiny, the court found that the racial balancing provision was unconstitutional. It rejected the assertion that the
provision satisfied the interest of promoting student diversity among
charter schools. Although the court took notice of Supreme Court
Justice Lewis Powell's separate opinion in *Regents of the University
of California v. Bakke*[10] that universities could use race as a factor in
their admissions decisions to benefit from the effects of student diversity, it rejected the legal import of Powell's opinion, noting that
"[n]either of the two major opinions [in *Bakke*] shared Powell's view
of the law."[11] The racial balancing provision was further constitutionally deficient because "[w]hile a charter school may not even
use race as a factor in its admissions decisions, race becomes the
only factor when a certain racial make-up is reached."[12]

The court further held that even if diversity were a compelling
governmental interest, the provision was unconstitutional because
it failed the narrow tailoring requirement. In making this determi-

nation, the court employed the five-part test applied by the Fourth Circuit in *Tuttle v. Arlington County School Board*:

> (1) the efficacy of alternative race-neutral policies, (2) the planned duration of the policy, (3) the relationship between the numerical goal and the percentage of minority members in the relevant population or work force, (4) the flexibility of the policy, including the provision of waivers if the goal cannot be met, and (5) the burden of the policy on innocent third parties.[13]

With respect to the first factor, the court was unaware of the feasibility of race-neutral alternatives, but found the provision failed the other criteria used in *Tuttle*. The provision violated the second factor because the charter school had to satisfy the enrollment percentage requirement in perpetuity. Section 59-40-50(B)(6) violated the third factor because its numerical goal was unrelated to the charter school's pool of students. Although the racial composition of the Beaufort County school district was equally divided among black and white, the charter school would have been located in an area that was 75 percent white. Thus, the court concluded that there was no relationship between the legislature's goal and the racial composition of the pool of students from which the charter school would draw.

The provision failed the fourth factor because "the policy's rigidity would result in the entire establishment of a charter school being based on race."[14] The policy would have forced the charter school to recruit students from 50 miles away, resulting in excessive transportation requirements. Additionally, the court observed that "requiring students to travel one hundred miles a day is absurd, and would in no way support the Legislature's goal of diversity."[15] With respect to the fifth factor, § 59-40-50(B)(6) was excessively burdensome on third parties because of the transportation problems discussed above and the racial classifications that the charter school would have to employ. The court further explained that students were burdened by the racial classifications because "this cutting edge tool which seeks to teach young children to view people as individuals rather than as members of certain racial and ethnic groups classifies those same children as members of certain racial and ethnic groups."[16]

The court also rejected the assertion that the racial balancing provision satisfied the compelling governmental interest of eliminating *de jure*, or official, segregation. The court also acknowledged that eliminating past discrimination may be a compelling governmental interest. However, this provision failed to satisfy that interest because it applied to all districts regardless of whether they were operating in a segregated fashion. Because the provision was not severable from the state's charter school statute, the court concluded that the entire statute was unconstitutional.

The charter school and the state attorney general appealed the trial court's ruling on severability to the Supreme Court of South Carolina. The school board cross-appealed on the constitutional question. While the appeal was pending, the charter school statute was amended by adding a severability clause and changing the racial composition requirement. The amended statute now provides that "it is required that the racial composition of the charter school enrollment reflect that of the school district or that of the targeted student population which the charter school proposes to serve, to be defined for the purposes of this chapter as differing by no more than twenty percent from that population. This requirement is also subject to the provisions of Section 59-40-70(D)."[17] Furthermore, Section 59-40-70(D) states:

> In the event that the racial composition of an applicant's or charter school's enrollment differs from the enrollment of the local school district or the targeted student population by more than twenty percent, despite its best efforts, the local school district board shall consider the applicant's or the charter school's recruitment efforts and racial composition of the applicant pool in determining whether the applicant or charter school is operating in a nondiscriminatory manner. A finding by the local school district board that the applicant or charter school is operating in a racially discriminatory manner may justify the denial of a charter school application or the revocation of a charter. . . . A finding by the local school district board that the applicant is not operating in a racially discriminatory manner shall justify approval of the charter without regard to the racial percentage requirement if the application is acceptable in all other aspects.[18]

Citing the amendments to the charter school statute, the Supreme Court of South Carolina vacated the trial court's opinion and dismissed the appeal as moot. The court found that the new provisions regarding racial composition superseded the original provision. Further, the court held that the new provisions had substantially "changed the character of the racial composition requirement by injecting a fact-based determination regarding discrimination rather than mandating a straightforward racial quota."[19]

The Supreme Court's subsequent decision in *Grutter v. Bollinger*[20] would probably not have convinced the state circuit court in *Beaufort* to conclude that South Carolina's racial balancing provision was constitutional under *Bakke*. In *Grutter*, the Court held that the University of Michigan Law School's race-conscious admissions policy did not violate the Equal Protection Clause. Admissions officials were required to assess each applicant on the basis of all available information in his or her file, including a personal statement, letters of recommendation, an essay describing how the applicant would contribute to the school's life and diversity, undergraduate grade point average, and Law School Admissions Test (LSAT) score. The policy also required officials to consider "soft variables," such as "enthusiasm of recommenders, the quality of the undergraduate institution the quality of the applicant's essay, and the areas and difficulty of undergraduate course selection."[21] Although the policy did "not restrict the types of diversity contributions eligible for 'substantial weight' in the admissions process,"[22] it did affirm the law school's commitment to African-Americans, Hispanics, and Native Americans, who would otherwise not be represented at the law school in meaningful numbers. The law school further argued that enrolling a "critical mass" of underrepresented groups would ensure their ability to make contributions to the law school and the legal profession.

The Supreme Court endorsed Justice Powell's opinion in *Bakke* that diversity was a compelling governmental interest that could justify race-conscious university admissions policies. The Court also found that "the Law School's concept of critical mass is defined by reference to the educational benefits that diversity is designed to produce," such as cross-racial understanding and the breaking down of racial stereotypes.[23] Moreover, the law school's admission policy was narrowly tailored to satisfy this compelling interest. The law school's policy was similar to the Harvard plan approved by Justice Powell because race served as a "plus" in a particular applicant's file instead of a quota, there was a serious consideration about the ways that each applicant might contribute to the diversity of the law school, and the law school meaningfully considered diversity factors other than race. The Court rejected the contention that narrow tailoring required the law school to exhaust all other conceivable race-neutral possibilities before using race-conscious policies. Rather, the Court was satisfied that the law school had adequately considered all available alternatives. Finally, the Court observed that race-conscious policies must be limited in time, and the Court took the law school at its word that it would terminate the race-conscious admissions policy as soon as possible.

It is doubtful that *Grutter* would have changed the *Beaufort* circuit court's conclusion that South Carolina's charter school racial balancing provision was impermissible under *Bakke*. The primary problem would have been that *Grutter* affirmed Justice Powell's finding in *Bakke* that race and ethnicity could not be the only diversity factors that school officials could consider.

Other courts might find that racial balancing provisions that require charter schools to use race in their admissions decisions are narrowly tailored to satisfy to satisfy two interrelated compelling interests not analyzed in *Beaufort*: to prepare students for life in a multicultural society and to eliminate the effects of *de facto* segregation.[24] One can find support for this position in *Comfort* ex. rel. *Newmeyer v. Lynn School Committee*.[25] In this case, plaintiffs challenged a district's voluntary desegregation plan, which took race into account when determining whether to permit a student from transferring out of a neighborhood school. The plan classified schools either as "racially balanced," "racially imbalanced," or "racially isolated." Elementary schools were racially balanced if their minority populations fell within 15 percent of the percentage of minority students in the district. Middle and high schools were racially balanced if their minority populations fell within 10 percent. Schools were classified as racially imbalanced when the proportion of minority students surpassed the range of racial balance. Schools were categorized as racially isolated if the proportion of white students exceeded the range of racial balance. The desegregation plan prohibited white students from transferring into schools and minority students from transferring out of schools that were considered racially isolated.

Parents of elementary children in the district challenged the desegregation plan on the ground that it violated the Equal Protection Clause. The United States District Court of Massachusetts granted the defendants' motion to dismiss because the desegregation plan was narrowly tailored to achieve the compelling interests of promoting ethnic and racial diversity and eliminating the effects of *de facto* segregation. The goal of promoting racial and ethnic diversity was "inextricably tied to the mission of a public K–12 school system."

With respect to narrow tailoring, the plan was necessary to achieve the district's curricular interests for the following reasons: (1) apportioning resources in a race-neutral fashion would not accomplish the goal of "train[ing] citizens to function in a multiracial world";[26] (2) "intergroup contact cannot be achieved with only token numbers of minorities in an overwhelmingly white school (or *vice versa*)";[27] and (3) "there is a tipping point of 20 percent white or not-white students, well-recognized by experts . . . and dubbed the 'critical mass,' that is crucial to catalizyng positive intergroup contact."[28]

The race-conscious plan was proportional to the district's curricular goals, in part, because "only the demographics of Lynn at this time (42 percent to 58 percent nonwhite) make it possible to achieve that number systemwide."[29] As the demographics of the district changed, so would the parameters of the plan: "it foists no more or less 'diversity' on the schools of the city than the demographics of a system and a neighborhood system allow."[30]

The court also concluded that the plan placed a minimal burden on third parties. Students had no entitlement to attend a particular school and there were no special qualifications for admission into a school. Also, students were not stigmatized by the government's recognition of their race. Rather, the plan informed students that "notwithstanding racial segregation, students of different races can and should coexist in integrated, cooperative learning environments."[31]

The court rejected a number of narrow tailoring challenges advanced by the plaintiffs. Plaintiffs' first argument was that the plan was not narrowly tailored to achieve the curricular goal of advancing diversity because it sought to ensure contact only between whites and nonwhites. The plaintiffs asserted that such notions of racial balance were antithetical to the "genuine diversity" that was called for in *Bakke* and *Wessman v. Gittens*.[32] In *Wessman*, the First Circuit held that a district's racial preference to African Americans and Hispanic applicants for admission into a competitive high school violated *Bakke* because it merely sought racial diversity. The district court distinguished the "diversity" sought by the desegregation plan from the diversity sought in *Bakke*. *Bakke*-like diversity was concerned with fostering a diversity of viewpoints that was "predicated on the notion that people of different backgrounds will make unique contributions to academic discourse." School officials could not achieve viewpoint diversity by limiting diversity consideration to racial and ethnic factors. The diversity sought by the desegregation plan could be distinguished from viewpoint diversity because "it reflects a concern that elementary school children simply get used to being in classrooms with people different from themselves."[33] The best way to "block the formulation of stereotypes and racist attitudes . . . is to promote multiracial interaction."[34]

Second, the court rejected the claim that additional resources would have achieved the curricular goal of intergroup contact. Students would fail to learn racial tolerance from abstract instruction without meaningful contact with students from other races. Social psychology literature indicated that the most significant benefits derived from intergroup contact occurred when a school's minority students exceeded 20 percent. The court found that the direct observation of the defendants' experts and the testimony of the district's teachers, students, and administrators supported this view. The court rejected the claim that the critical mass concept was inessential because some schools with minority student populations below 20 percent achieved positive race relations. Defense experts convinced the court that there existed "a continuum of effects leading to the point where intergroup contact is finally significant."[35] Thus "[i]t would be absurd to suggest that when a school dips marginally below a 20 percent critical mass, a climate of racial tolerance evaporates."[36] The court rejected the claim that the plan was not narrowly tailored because it failed to ensure a 20 percent critical mass of minority students in every school. If the "plan were calibrated to yield, without fail, a 20 [percent] critical mass in every school, it would risk the characterization as a quota, be needlessly rigid and neglectful of the changing conditions in Lynn."[37]

The court found that the desegregation plan was narrowly tailored to the goal of remedying the effects of *de facto* segregation. The court observed that the "increasing polarization of Lynn schools, created in part through official misconduct, led to documented inequalities within the system: minority schools had inferior materials and facilities and the more experienced teachers transferred to the better funded, managed, and maintained white schools."[38] Quoting precedent from the Second Circuit, the court concluded that "[p]lainly the 'reduction of racial isolation resulting from *de facto* segregation can be a compelling governmental interest justifying the racial classifications.'"[39] The court further noted that although *Brown* and its progeny did not mandate schools to redress *de facto* segregation, nothing in the case law prohibited school districts from acting in good faith to remedy the negative effects of *de facto* segregation. The desegregation plan was narrowly tailored to this interest because the plan was tied to the demographics of the school district, the demographics of the district ensured that even the most racially isolated schools had a critical mass of minority students, and the plan minimized racial isolation while maintaining neighborhood schools and avoiding busing.

Lynn suggests that it is possible for a mandatory charter school racial balancing provision to be narrowly tailored to the interests of preparing students to live in a racially diverse society and eliminating the effects of *de facto* segregation. The critical question would be whether such racial balancing provisions could satisfy the narrow tailoring requirement. The *Lynn* court identified three questions for making this determination: (1) Are the means necessary? (2) Is the policy proportional to the interest? (3) What is the impact on third parties? With respect to the necessity question, race-neutral options such as random selection from a voluntary pool might be less likely to produce racially balanced charter schools. In fact, research on magnet schools indicates "that reliance on a random selection process will likely not produce a pool reflective of the larger population because minority parents, particularly those who are poor, are less likely to choose."[40]

With respect to the proportionality question, *Lynn* suggests that an important factor for any *de facto* desegregation plan is whether it takes into account the demographics of the district. This is the case with charter school mandatory racial balancing provisions. Only charter schools that are located in desegregated school districts would have to be desegregated. Additionally, the racial demographic requirements of charter schools would change with those of the district. Finally, a court might be convinced that the burden to students who are denied enrollment in the charter school is minimal. As was the case in *Lynn*, no student has a right to attend a charter school. Also, in the case of most charter schools, there are no prerequisites for enrollment.

Non–Racial Preferential Admissions Policies

Charter schools generally use lotteries if more students apply for admission than can be admitted. However, as Table 6.2 illustrates, several states and the District of Columbia permit charter schools to enroll automatically certain categories of students. Such categories include siblings of students admitted into a charter school, children of the charter schools' board of trustees, children of a charter school's board of directors, children of a charter school's employees, and students living within the attendance zone of the charter school.

Table 6.2. Examples of Charter School Admissions Preferences

Siblings of Charter School Students	Arizona, Connecticut, Delaware, District of Columbia, Florida, Georgia, Illinois, Indiana, Iowa, Louisiana, Massachusetts, Minnesota, Missouri, New Jersey, New Mexico, New York, North Carolina, Ohio, Oregon, Pennsylvania, South Carolina, Tennessee,[41] Utah, Wisconsin
Children of Charter School's Founders	Delaware, Pennsylvania, Utah

cont.

Children of Charter School's Board of Directors	Florida, North Carolina,[42] Tennessee
Children of Charter School Employees	Delaware, Missouri, North Carolina,[43] South Carolina, Tennessee, Utah
Students within a Charter School's Attendance Zone	California, Delaware, District of Columbia, Florida,[44] Georgia, Massachusetts, Minnesota, New Hampshire Ohio, Oklahoma, Oregon, Pennsylvania, Tennessee, Texas, Utah, Wisconsin

Such preferences might lessen the possibility that charter schools would reflect the racial composition of the surrounding school district. It is possible that students within the school's attendance zone, the charter school's founders, board of directors, and employees might consist of predominantly one race. Thus, granting preferences to these categories might reduce the number of slots in the charter school that are available to students from other racial groups.

The experience of Wisconsin's Core Knowledge Charter School is illustrative. As the Wisconsin Legislative Audit Bureau (WLAB) observed: "Some individuals are concerned that the admissions practices of Core Knowledge Charter School . . . were designed to minimize the number of minority students attending the school."[45] Administrators adamantly denied that they engineered the racial composition of the school. They increased advertising efforts in minority communities, resulting in increased minority applications. However, the racial composition of the school remained substantially the same because of the limited number of seats and the continuing eligibility of returning students. As the WLAB concluded, "the school's racial demographics are unlikely to change significantly in the future unless the board expands the school's enrollment, because no existing students will be compelled to leave."[46]

Non–racial preferential admissions provisions might be challenged on equal protection grounds. Plaintiffs might try to have these provisions analyzed under strict scrutiny analysis. In *Washington v. Davis*,[47] the Supreme Court ruled that the Equal Protection Clause is not violated merely because a governmental action has a disproportionate effect on members of one racial or ethnic group. Plaintiffs would instead have to show that these nonpreferential provisions were enacted with the intent to discriminate.

In *Village of Arlington Heights v. Metropolitan Housing Development Corporation*, the Court explained that several factors should be examined, in addition to disparate impact, to determine whether the government acted with the intent to discriminate: (1) historical background of the challenged decision; (2) specific events leading up to the challenged decision; (3) departures from normal procedures; and (4) legislative or administrative history.[48] Also, in *Personnel Administrator of Massachusetts v. Feeney*,[49] the Court explained that discriminatory intent implied more than mere awareness of the consequences. Plaintiffs would have to demonstrate that the government chose a course of action "because of," rather than "in spite of," its disproportionate impact.

Supreme Court case law suggests that charter school enrollment preferences would not be analyzed under strict scrutiny. Plaintiffs would have to demonstrate that the enrollment preferences were used because of the likelihood that they would create one-race charter schools. The experience of Wisconsin's Core Knowledge Charter School shows that enrollment preferences might create a one-race school despite the best efforts of charter schools to obtain a racially diverse student body.

Courts would probably instead employ the rational basis test to charter school admissions preferences. Recall that courts would generally uphold a governmental classification under this test if there is a conceivable rationale for it. Courts might find that enrollment preferences advance several legitimate concerns. For example, preferences for students within a charter school's attendance zone might be rationally related to the goals of simplifying planning and transportation concerns, and maintaining predictable enrollment patterns. Defendants might also assert that attendance zone preferences are a reasonable means of ensuring that a school district's residents enjoy the benefits of their residency.[50] Moreover, preferences for the children of the charter school's founders, governing board, and employees might be rationally related to the goal of encouraging the development of educationally innovative ideas.

Charter school admissions preferences might also be subject to a substantive due process challenge under the Fourteenth Amendment. Admissions preferences would violate substantive due process if they are not rationally related to a legitimate governmental interest. As the equal protection discussion makes clear, non-racial preferential admissions policies probably satisfy legitimate governmental concerns. Finally, charter school admissions preferences might run afoul of the uniformity provisions of state constitutions. Chapter 2 points out that the constitutions of a number of charter school states contain provisions that might limit the variability of charter schools. Plaintiffs might assert that charter school admissions preferences violate such provisions, insofar as they differ from the admissions policies of other public schools. In *Wilson v. State*

Board of Education,[51] the California Court of Appeal found that California charter schools were sufficiently similar to other public schools so as not to constitute a separate system of public schools.

Court-Ordered School Desegregation Decrees

Several charter school states have school districts that are still under court-ordered desegregation decrees. These decrees require school districts to eliminate the vestiges of their segregative practices to the extent practicable with respect to student assignments, faculty assignments, transportation, facilities, student activities, and the quality of education. School districts that are under a desegregation decree are under a heavy burden to show that policies that would continue the effects of segregation serve important and legitimate ends. They are also generally prohibited from adopting policies that would have the effect of maintaining school segregation. The charter school statutes of 13 states—Arizona, Colorado, Delaware, Illinois, Iowa, Louisiana, Nevada, North Carolina, Ohio, Oklahoma, Pennsylvania, Tennessee, and Virginia—require charter schools to comply with court-ordered school desegregation decrees.

Charter schools might violate court-ordered desegregation decrees by being more segregated than other public schools within the school district. Charter schools might also make it difficult for school districts to satisfy school desegregation decrees by attracting a disproportionately high percentage of students and faculty of one race away from other public schools within the districts.[52] Charter school proposals should explain how they minimize the impact on desegregation decrees. Failure to do so could result in the rejection of the proposals.

In *Berry v. School District of the City of Benton Harbor,*[53] for example, a federal district court permitted the funding of the Benton Harbor Charter School because the charter school's faculty and staff recruitment policies, curricular requirements, and diversity training of faculty, staff, and board of directors were consistent with a desegregation decree. However, the court prohibited the funding of the Benton Harbor Community Academy because the school failed to provide sufficient information regarding the racial composition of the student body. Therefore, the court could not determine whether the charter school would have impeded the state and school district's ability to satisfy their obligations under the decree.

Courts may have to address the question of whether desegregation decrees extend to applications for charter schools that are located in segregated school districts and serve the same attendance zones of these districts, but are sponsored by entities that are not under federal court supervision. *Wright v. Council of the City of Emporia*[54] suggests that desegregation decrees apply to such charter schools. In *Wright*, a town that was part of a county school system that was under a desegregation decree attempted to establish a separate school system. This action would have increased the proportion of white students attending town schools, while decreasing the percentage of white students in the county schools. The Supreme Court prohibited the town from forming its own school district because this action would have had the effect of impeding the process of dismantling the existing unconstitutional system. In reaching this decision, the Supreme Court expressed its agreement with other federal courts "that have held that splinter school districts may not be created 'where the effect—to say nothing of the purpose—of the secession has a substantial adverse effect on desegregation of the county school district.'"[55]

Courts might conclude that charter applications for schools that reside in *de jure* segregated school districts and serve the same attendance zones, but are sponsored by entities that fall outside the decrees, are analogous to splinter school districts. Both situations involve the removal of a portion of *de jure* segregated school districts. Also, the proposed charter schools and the splinter school districts serve the same student populations as the *de jure* segregated school districts. Thus, a court might examine whether such proposed charter schools would have a substantially negative impact on the enforcement on the desegregation decree before permitting the schools to open. *Milliken v. Bradley*[56] would not appear to mandate a different conclusion. In *Milliken*, the Supreme Court held that a court-ordered desegregation decree that was designed to dismantle a *de jure* segregated city district could include predominantly white suburbs only if their intentionally discriminatory acts contributed to the racial segregation within the city district. *Milliken* can be distinguished from *Wright* because (1) *Milliken* involves districts that were already in existence at the time of the decree, and (2) the districts in *Milliken* did not serve the same attendance zones.

In *Rufo v. Inmates of Suffolk County Jail*,[57] the Supreme Court suggested that under certain circumstances a federal district court may modify a desegregation decree to permit the operation of a charter school that would be out of compliance. *Rufo* involved a consent decree between county officials and prison inmates, which called for construction of a new jail that would provide single occupancy cells for pretrial detainees. Construction on the jail was delayed and the inmate population outpaced projections. To raise the capacity of the jail, the sheriff moved for a modification of a decree permitting double bunking of certain cells. Both the federal district court and the First Circuit denied the sheriff's motion.

The Supreme Court vacated and remanded the case to the district court and in doing so, articulated the following standard for the modification of consent decrees. The party seeking modification bears the burden of establishing that a significant change in circumstances warrants revision of the decree. A modification may be warranted when (1) changed factual conditions make compliance with the decree substantially more onerous; (2) the decree proves to be unworkable because of unforeseen obstacles; or (3) enforcement of the decree without modification would be detrimental to the public interest.

If the moving party meets this standard, the district court would then determine whether the proposed modification was suitably tailored to address the changed circumstance. In making this determination, the district court would have to take three matters into account: (1) the modification should not perpetuate or create a constitutional violation; (2) the modification should resolve the problems created by the change in circumstances; and (3) the district court should defer to local government administrators, who have the "primary responsibility for elucidating, assessing, and solving the problems of institutional reform, to resolve the intricacies of implementing a decree modification." [58]

A charter applicant who was seeking the modification of a desegregation decree under *Rufo* would most likely try to demonstrate that denial of the proposed school would be against the public interest. The applicant might advance arguments concerning the benefits of choice and experimentation in public education. If the school's student body were predominantly minority, the applicant might be able to satisfy its burden by citing statistics, such as suspension rates and standardized test scores, demonstrating that minority students have not benefited from desegregated schools in the district.[59] Of course, if a court were to conclude that preparation for a multicultural society is in the public interest, it might refuse to allow the charter school to operate.

If the applicant were to satisfy its burden, the court would then have to determine whether the proposed charter school was suitably tailored to address this change in circumstances. If the proposed charter school were sufficiently small, the applicant might be able to show that the school would not perpetuate discrimination.

Charter schools tend to be much smaller than traditional public schools. In the 1998–1999 school year, the median size of a charter school was 137 students. The median size of all public schools for this period was 475 students.[60] Thus, a typically sized charter school might not have a large impact on a desegregation decree.

The court would probably examine the educational program of the proposed charter school to determine whether the proposal addressed the change in circumstances. For instance, if an applicant asserted that minority students were not performing well on standardized tests in desegregated schools within the district, the court might examine how the charter school's educational program would attempt to raise test scores for its minority students.

Finally, *Rufo* indicates that a court would defer to the educational opinion of school district administrators who are primarily responsible for the implementation of the decree. Such deference would be helpful in situations where the proposed noncompliant school would be chartered by an entity other than the *de jure* segregated school district. These chartering entities might not have the goals of the desegregation decree in mind when granting a charter. However, because such charter schools might be considered "splinter districts" that would still have to comply with school desegregation decrees, it would certainly be prudent for a court to listen to the concerns of officials in the *de jure* segregated district when deciding whether to permit the proposed school to operate.

Charter Schools with Curricula That Appeal to Particular Racial and Ethnic Groups

A number of charter schools have curricula and educational programming that might appeal to a particular racial or ethnic group. For example, the El-Hajj Malik El-Shabazz Academy, a Detroit charter school, uses a holistic, Afrocentric curriculum.[61] The purpose for California's All Tribes American Indian Charter School is to address the needs of Native American students from the five reservations in the Valley Center region and to reduce middle school and high school dropout rates. In 2001, all but one of the school's students were of Native American descent.[62]

These schools might be vulnerable to Equal Protection Clause challenges on the ground that they violate *Brown v. Board of Education*'s mandate against *de jure* segregated public schools. If the chartering entity were a *de jure* segregated school district, or considered a splinter school district under *Wright*, then a federal district court could deny the operation of the school if it would have the effect of substantially impeding the operation of the decree. The analysis would be more complex for charter schools that were not located in school districts that were under a desegregation decree. A court might find no constitutional violation if the racial composition of the school reflected that of the surrounding school district. This is because the school's segregation might have been caused by factors unrelated to its educational theme, such as housing patterns.[63]

A court might reach a different conclusion in the case of a culturally specific charter school that is located in a desegregated school district. Plaintiffs would have an easier time showing that the educational theme was the cause of the school's segregation.[64] Furthermore, a court might find that the charter school's founders violated *Feeney* because "there is more than knowledge of the potential for segregation; indeed the very purpose of the school is segregative."[65] Using this analysis, a court might conclude that the charter school has employed a racial classification, even though the school permits other races to enroll. This finding would subject the race-centric charter school to strict scrutiny. The school would have to demonstrate that its educational programming satisfied a compelling governmental interest and was narrowly tailored to serve that interest. The charter school might be unconstitutional under such a scenario.[66]

On the other hand, a court might conclude that such culturally specific charter schools do not employ racial classifications and thus would not be subject to strict scrutiny. Children of all races are permitted to attend these schools and might be attracted to their educational programming. For example, the mission statement of All Tribes Indian Charter School is: "To meet the academic, social, cultural and developmental needs of the Native American students, *and all* students, in an environment that respects the integrity of the individual student and diverse cultures and knowledge."[67] Because students of all races are permitted to attend these charter schools, courts might conclude that culturally specific charter schools are race-neutral, even if their student populations are racially segregated.[68]

Conclusion

As this chapter indicates, charter schools raise a number of legal questions regarding race. The enabling statutes of a number of states hold racial balancing provisions, which might violate the Equal Protection Clause. Several statutes contain non–racial admissions preferences, which might create one-race schools, that might be less susceptible to legal challenges. Charter schools located in *de jure* segregated school districts may have to comply with court-ordered desegregation decrees. However, federal courts may modify a decree to permit the existence of charter schools that are not in compliance. Finally, the constitutionality of culturally specific charter schools may turn on a variety of factors, such as the racial composition of the school district, and whether courts view these schools as racial or cultural classifications.

Endnotes

1. 347 U.S. 483 (1954).
2. Cal. Educ. Code § 47605(b)(5)(G).
3. N.C. Gen. Stat. § 115C-238.29F(g)(5)(ii).
4. New Jersey's charter school statute states: "The admission policy of the charter school shall, to the maximum extent practicable, seek the enrollment of a cross section of the community's school age population, including racial and academic factors." N.J. Stat. § 18A: 36A-8e. This provision would suggest that factors other than race and ethnicity would be considered. However, the legislative history of the state's charter school act suggests that the primary purpose of this provision was to ensure that the charter schools had a racial and ethnic composition that was similar to that of the surrounding district. *In re* Grant of Charter School Application of Englewood on Palisades Charter Sch., 753 A.2d 687, 692 (N.J. 2000).
5. Wendy Parker, *The Color of Choice: Race and Charter Schools*, 75 Tul. L. Rev. 563, 592 (2002).
6. Beaufort County Bd. of Educ. v. Lighthouse Charter Sch. Committee, 516 S.E.2d 655 (S.C. 1999).
7. Beaufort County Bd. of Educ. v. Lighthouse Charter Sch. Committee, No. 97-CP-7-794 (S.C. Ct. Com. Pleas May 8, 2000).
8. *Id.*, slip op. at 2.
9. *Id.*, slip op. at 3.
10. 438 U.S. at 265 (opinion of Powell, J.).
11. *Beaufort*, No. 97-CP-&-794, slip op. at 3 n.7. The court also observed that the Fifth Circuit had subsequently rejected the use of race as a factor to achieve diversity in Hopwood v. Texas, 78 F.3d 932 (5th Cir. 1996). *Id.*
12. *Id* (emphasis supplied by court).
13. *Id.*, slip op. at 4 (*quoting* Tuttle v. Arlington County Sch. Bd., 195 F.3d 698, 706 (4th Cir. 1999)).
14. *Id.*, slip op. at 5.
15. *Id.*
16. *Id.*
17. S.C. Code Ann. § 59-40-50(B)(7).
18. *Id.* § 59-40-70(D).
19. Beaufort v. Lighthouse Charter Sch. Committee, 576 S.E.2d 180, at 182 (S.C. 2003).
20. 123 S.Ct. 2325 (2003).
21. *Id.* at 2332.
22. *Id.*
23. *Id.* at 2339-2340.

[24] For a discussion about the constitutionality of the voluntary use of race in K–12 education, *see* Julie F. Mead, *Conscious Use of Race as a Voluntary Means to Educational Ends in Elementary and Secondary Education: A Legal Argument Derived from Recent Judicial Opinions*, 8 Mich. J. of Race & L. 63 (2002).

[25] 263F. Supp. 2d 209 (D.Mass. 2003).

[26] *Id*. at 257.

[27] *Id*.

[28] *Id*.

[29] *Id*.

[30] *Id*.

[31] *Id*. at 258.

[32] 160 F.3d 790.

[33] *Comfort*.

[34] *Id*. 263 F. Supp. 2d. at 259.

[35] *Id*. at 263.

[36] *Id*. at 263-64

[37] *Id*. at 264.

[38] *Id*.

[39] *Id*. at 265 (*quoting* Brewer v. West Irondequoit Cent. Sch. Dist., 212 F.3d 738, 753 (2d Cir. 2000)) (vacating district court's injunction suspending race-conscious elements of interdistrict transfer plan).

[40] Amy Stuart Wells, *The Sociology of School Choice: Why Some Win and Others Lose in the Educational Marketplace*, *in* Examining the Evidence (Edith Rassell & Richard Rothstein Eds., 1993).

[41] Tennessee permits preferences for the siblings of charter school students, and to the children of a teacher, sponsor, or member of the governing board as long as attendance does not exceed 10 percent or 25 students, whichever is less.

[42] North Carolina's enabling statute provides: "[O]nly for its first year of operation, the charter school may give enrollment priority to children of the initial members of the charter school's board of directors, so long as (i) these children are limited to no more than ten percent (10%) of the school's total enrollment or to 20 students, whichever is less, and (ii) the charter school is not a former public or private school." N.C. Gen. Stat. § 115C-238.29F.

[43] North Carolina gives preferences to the children of the school's principal, teachers, and teacher assistants.

[44] Florida gives preference to students residing within a reasonable distance to the charter school, but this provision is subject to the state's race balancing requirement.

[45] Wisconsin Legislative Audit Bureau, *An Evaluation: Charter School Program*, Report 98-15, at 35 (1998).

[46] *Id*. at 36.

[47] 426 U.S. 229 (1976).

[48] 429 U.S. 252, 266–268 (1977).

[49] 442 U.S. 256 (1979).

[50] *See* Martinez v. Bynum, 461 U.S. 321, 328 (1982) (finding that a bona fide residence requirement furthers the substantial state interest in assuring that services provided for its residents are enjoyed only by residents).

[51] 89 Cal. Rptr. 2d 745 (Ct. App. 1999).

[52] Parker, *supra* note 5, at 617–618.

[53] 56 F. Supp. 2d 866 (W.D. Mich. 1999).

[54] 407 U.S. 451 (1972).

[55] *Id.* at 462 (citing Lee v. Macon County Bd. of Educ., 448 F.2d 746, 752 (5th Cir. 1971); Stout v. Jefferson County Bd. of Educ., 448 F.2d 403, 404 (5th Cir. 1971); Haney v. County Bd. of Educ., 410 F.2d 920, 924 (8th Cir. 1969); Burleson v. County Bd. of Election Commissioners of Jefferson County, 308 F.Supp. 352, 356 (D.C.Ark. 1970), *aff'd*, 432 F.2d 1356 (8th Cir. 1970); Aytch v. Mitchell, 320 F.Supp. 1372, 1377 (D.C.Ark. 1971)).

[56] 418 U.S. 717 (1974).

[57] 502 U.S. 367 (1992).

[58] *Id.* at 392.

[59] *See* Robin D. Barnes, *Group Conflict and the Constitution: Race, Sexuality, and Religion: Black America and School Choice: Charting a New Course*, 106 Yale L.J. 2375 (1997) (arguing that charter schools might be more likely to meet the needs of African-American students than desegregated schools).

[60] Office of Educ. Research & Improvement, U.S. Dep't of Educ., *The State of Charter Schools 2000: National Study of Charter Schools* 10 (2000).

[61] www.uscharterschools.org, *El-Hajj Malik El-Shabazz Academy*, available at http://www. uscharterschools.org/lpt/s/1874 (viewed on January 16, 2003).

[62] Eleanor Wang, *Charter Members of Change*, San Diego Union Tribune, Dec. 16, 2001.

[63] Parker, *supra* note 5.

[64] *Id.* at 611.

[65] *Id.*

[66] *Id.*

[67] Canku Ota (Many Paths): An Online Newsletter Celebrating Native America, December 29, 2001, Issue 52, *Charter Members of Change*, available at http://www.turtletrack.org/Issues01/Co12292001/CO_12292001_Charter_School.htm (viewed Jan. 16, 2003) (emphasis added).

[68] Parker, *supra* note 5, at 612.

Chapter 7

Charter Schools and Gender

In addition to taking measures to make charter schools free from racial discrimination as discussed in the previous chapter, legislators have been careful to remind charter school operators and sponsors that gender or sex discrimination is likewise prohibited. This prohibition can be found in both federal and state laws. In fact, although states vary in terms of what state statutory and regulatory exemptions charter schools enjoy, they uniformly hold charter schools bound by the antidiscrimination provisions of their state laws. This fact alone sends the clear message that charter schools are expected, as are all public schools, to serve the entire public without regard to various status characteristics—among them, gender.

Interestingly, however, the federal government has not yet reported the gender proportions of students served by charter schools. Data are available to describe the racial and ethnic composition and distribution of charter school students, the proportion of students who receive free and reduced lunches, the proportion of students with disabilities, and the proportion of students who have limited English proficiency.[1]

This chapter will first briefly review the legal foundation for this commitment to avoid gender discrimination in schools. The requirements these sources of legal authority place on charter schools with respect to hiring and employee relations, programming and curricula, athletic and extracurricular opportunities, and sexual harassment will be outlined. Secondly, this chapter will explore the question of whether a charter school could be targeted to serve only one gender consistent with these nondiscriminatory requirements. This examination culminates with guidelines for those who may be interested in exploring further the creation of single-gender charter schools.

Charter Schools and Requirements for Gender Equity

Like all notions of equity, the foundation for gender equity has its home in the Equal Protection Clause of the Fourteenth Amendment to the United States Constitution. However, unlike alleged racial discrimination, courts reviewing allegations that policies create gender discrimination do not employ strict scrutiny, the most exacting of all legal reviews. Neither are policies alleged to be gender-biased reviewed under a traditional, but easy to satisfy, rational basis test. Rather, gender classifications require the court to use a heightened mid-level scrutiny in order to ascertain whether the state has a proper justification for the use of gender classifications.[2] Heightened scrutiny will be explained in more detail in the second section of this chapter. Suffice it to say here that whenever a state actor, including a charter school, uses sex as a determinative factor in some decision-making, there must be a substantial and defensible reason for it to be constitutional. Two federal laws codify our conceptions of gender equity. The first is Title VII of the Civil Rights Act of 1964.[3] Title VII applies to charter schools as employers. As such, charter schools are required to be certain that all hiring, promotion, and other personnel decisions occur without gender discrimination. Title VII requires that each employer adopt and publish a statement of nondiscrimination. In addition, the charter school must designate someone to handle complaints and must adopt a grievance procedure for the investigation and resolution of any complaint of gender discrimination, including sexual harassment.[4]

The second federal law proscribing gender discrimination is Title IX of the Education Amendments of 1972.[5] Title IX prohibits sex discrimination by any educational program that is a recipient of federal financial assistance. The law's regulations define a "recipient" as:

> [A]ny State or political subdivision thereof, or any instrumentality of a State or political subdivision thereof, any public or private agency, institution, or organization, or other entity, or any person, to whom Federal financial assistance is extended directly or through another recipient and which operates an education program or activity which receives or benefits from such assistance, including any subunit, successor, assignee, or transferee thereof.[6]

Thus, most charter schools would be "recipients" by definition. Either the charter school directly receives federal funds itself, or its chartering authority likely does. Even if by an unusual circumstance, neither of these entities met the definition of "recipient" under the law, the state itself unquestionably does. The state, therefore, is bound to ensure that each of its programs, in this case the charter school program established by the state legislature, operates free from discrimination on the basis of sex.[7] Accordingly, each charter school, owing its existence to this legislative scheme, falls under the state's assurance that all programs operate without sex discrimination.

Like Title VII, Title IX requires that the charter school adopt a policy of nondiscrimination and that a person be designated to investigate allegations of sex discrimination, including sexual harassment.[8] In general, Title IX requires that all curricular and extracurricular offerings be freely available to students of either sex. It also requires that extracurricular athletic activities provide balanced opportunities for competition. In the classroom, Title IX generally prohibits assigning students to classes based on sex, including courses such as health, physical education, vocational education, home economics, and music. However, the regulations allow classes to be segregated by sex in certain circumstances. For example, lessons dealing with human sexuality may be delivered to single-gender classes. Music classes or choral groups that separate students according to vocal range are allowable even though they result in groups of all or nearly all the same sex. Likewise, physical education classes derived by objective standards of ability that result in classes of one gender are permitted, as are classes dealing with sports that involve bodily contact (wrestling, football, boxing, and so forth). However, care must be taken that the standard is objective and related to the activity. As an example of an inappropriate standard, the Office for Civil Rights (OCR) notes that using the ability to lift a certain weight as a predicate for entry into a swimming class would fail this requirement, as the likely result would unnecessarily exclude some girls.[9] The OCR also cautions that whenever such classes exist, schools must be certain that the separate courses, services, and facilities are comparable.

In a related manner, Title IX requires that care be taken with course counseling to ensure that students of one gender are not encouraged to pursue a course of study while students of another gender are discouraged from the same discipline. Accordingly, Title IX requires that "where a recipient finds that a particular class contains a substantially disproportionate number of individuals of one sex, the recipient shall take such action as is necessary to assure itself that such disproportion is not the result of discrimination on the basis of sex."[10] This passage should also carry particular import for charter school operators. If applicatants to the school are predominantly one gender, it will be necessary to carefully review recruiting materials to be certain no sex discrimination stands as the cause of the situation.

Finally, gender equity is protected by state constitutional provisions for equal protection of the laws and specific state legislation to prohibit sex discrimination. Although a review of these provisions is outside the scope of this chapter, charter school authorizers and operators should be cognizant of the independent requirements these sources of legal authority may add to the federal foundation reviewed here.

Could a Charter School Be Targeted to Serve Only One Gender?

The short answer to this question at this time is, at best, "perhaps."[11] The first step to getting a more definitive answer would be to check with state authorities to be certain state antidiscrimination laws do not preclude single-gender schools. If they do not, then the answer lies in an examination of the issue with both the Equal Protection Clause and Title IX in mind.

On January 8, 2002, President George W. Bush signed the No Child Left Behind Act of 2001.[12] The law broadly describes its purpose as "[a]n Act to close the achievement gap with accountability, flexibility, and choice, so that no child is left behind." This funding statute reauthorizes the Elementary and Secondary Education Act and permits the expenditure of federal funds for a number of educational initiatives. The act itself fills over 500 pages of text and has garnered considerable attention from policymakers at all levels as they try to determine how this act changes the legislative landscape upon which they strive to develop educational programs that improve learning for all students. However, one sentence included in this voluminous record has application here. Section 5131 announces that "[f]unds made available to local educational agencies . . . shall be used for innovative assistance programs, which may include . . . [p]rograms to provide same-gender schools and classrooms (consistent with applicable law)."[13]

Does single-gender education have a place in public school reform efforts? Can our definition of public education allow such gender concentration and the exclusion that defines it? These are more than hypothetical questions. In addition to this recent invitation from Congress to consider single-gender schools and classrooms in schools' innovative efforts, public funds are currently flowing to single-gender schools in a number of contexts, including both magnet and charter schools.[14] Of course, it is the parenthetical, "consistent with applicable law" that provides a caveat to any single-gender bandwagon and raises the question: Under what circumstances is single-gender education "consistent with applicable law"? Or stated another way, is it within the bounds of school officials' discretion to "innovate" by separating children on the basis of sex?

The National Association for the Advancement of Single Sex Public Education[15] lists eleven public single-gender schools currently in operation in the United States.[16] Table 5.1 provides basic information about each of those schools.

Table 7.1. Public Single-Sex Schools and Programs Currently in Operation

School	Type of Program	Type of Choice Program	Year Begun
Western High School Baltimore, MD	All girl high school	Intradistrict choice	1844
Philadelphia High School for Girls Philadelphia, PA	All girl high school	Intradistrict choice	1848
Robert Coleman Elementary School Baltimore, MD	Single-sex classrooms for both sexes	Intradistrict choice	1993
The Young Women's Leadership School New York, NY	All girl middle/high school, grades 7–12	Magnet school	1996
The San Francisco 49ers Academies East Palo Alto, CA	Paired single-sex academies for each sex on the same campus	Magnet school	1996
Lewis Fox Middle School (Mary McLeod Bethune Institute for Girls & Benjamin Mays Institute for Boys) Hartford, CT	Paired single-sex programs for each sex within a larger host school	Intraschool choice	1996
Maria Mitchell Elementary School Denver, CO	Single-sex classrooms for 4th & 5th grades	Intradistrict choice	1998
Jefferson Leadership Academies Long Beach, CA	Paired single-sex academies for each sex on the same campus (grades 6–8)	Magnet school	1999
Thurgood Marshall Elementary School Seattle, WA	Single-sex classrooms in grades 1–5	Intradistrict choice	2000
Young Women's Leadership Charter School Chicago, IL	All-girl middle/high	Charter school	2000
Brighter Choice Charter School Albany, NY	Paired single-sex academies for each sex on the same campus (Grades K–1 for fall 2002, growing to K–5)	Charter school	2002

As shown, two of the schools are charter schools that employ single-sex approaches to education. Modeled after the Young Women's Leadership Academy, the Young Women's Leadership Charter School began serving students in grades 6–9 in the fall of 2000, employing an academic focus on mathematics, science, technology, and leadership. The school was specifically designed to address concerns that coeducational environments did not adequately encourage the development of girls in these subjects. Chartered by the Chicago Public School District, the school intends to add a grade each year until it reaches a capacity of approximately 500 students in grades 6–12.[17]

The newest single-gender school provides paired single-gender education on the same campus. The newly approved pair of charter schools, Brighter Choice Charter School for Boys and Brighter Choice Charter School for Girls, began operation in fall of 2002. Located in Albany, New York, the school received its charter from the Board of Regents of the State University of New York. The school began by serving a total of 90 students in kindergarten and first grade, particularly "at-risk children from economically disadvantaged families."[18] The school eventually intends to grow to 290 students in grades K–5. The school considers itself a "third generation" single-sex school. As its web site explains:

> "First generation" single-sex schools, like VMI's [Virginia Military Institute's] all-male school, were established at a time in the nation's history when the educational rights of African-Americans and women were not yet realized. "Second generation" single-sex schools, like the new Harlem and Chicago all-girls schools, were devised as an affirmative remedy to discrimination and educational neglect but offer single-sex instruction to just one sex. "Third generation" single-sex schools, such as the Brighter Choice Charter School, offer the opportunity for single-sex instruction to boys and girls—on an equal basis.[19]

After reviewing research on single-gender education, the school declares that academic research provides "sound support for the school's particular approach to single-sex education."[20]

Legal Authority Guiding Single-Sex Education

Determining whether the single-sex educational options operate "consistent with applicable law" requires attention to both federal constitutional and statutory provisions.[21] In this case, the "applicable law" is formed by the Equal Protection Clause of the

Fourteenth Amendment to United States Constitution and Title IX of the Educational Amendments of 1972. Any understanding of the principles of gender equity must begin with these sources.

The constitutional principle of equal protection of the laws is grounded in the constitution's Fourteenth Amendment. In short, that principle requires that governmental authorities at all levels articulate adequate justification for any classification that determines recipients of its benefits. That is, if the government creates groups of people who are then treated differentially, that it does so within the bounds of its legitimate authority and can justify the groupings in relation to the policy goal the groupings serve. The tightness of fit required between governmental ends and means depends on the criterion used for sorting. For example, as explained in the previous chapter, the Supreme Court has determined that governmental classifications based on race are highly suspect and must only be used in rarest of circumstances when the state furthers a compelling state interest and the use of a racial criterion is necessary and narrowly tailored to that goal.[22] Determining whether this exacting relationship between governmental ends and means exists is termed "strict scrutiny."[23] In contrast, more common classifications (e.g., those based on age to determine when someone is eligible for a drivers license) need not satisfy this level of scrutiny. Instead, non-suspect classifications need only satisfy the so-called rational basis test or be rationally related to a legitimate state interest. Accordingly, the dispositive question with regard to gender equity and single-sex education must begin with a determination of the level of scrutiny to which courts will subject separation on the basis of sex.

In *Frontiero v. Richardson*,[24] four members of the Court, Justices Brennan, Douglas, White, and Marshall, determined that strict scrutiny should be applied to gender classifications. Justice Brennan explained that because of the nation's "long and unfortunate history of sex discrimination,"[25] "we can only conclude that classifications based on sex, like classifications based on race, alienage, or national origin, are inherently suspect and must therefore be subjected to strict judicial scrutiny."[26] In subsequent cases, however, the Court backed away from this level of scrutiny, crafting, instead a mid-level or heightened scrutiny standard for consideration of gender classifications.[27]

The Supreme Court has considered gender-specific education three times. However, the Court has never definitively answered the question of single-gender education at the K–12 level. One K–12 case reached that level of review in the late 1970s. The case,

Vorchheimer v. School District of Philadelphia,[28] involved a challenge by female students to the existence of the Central High School, which admitted only boys. The district also operated (and, as noted on Table 7.1, continues to operate) the Philadelphia High School for Girls. The Third Circuit Court of Appeals determined that since attendance at either school was voluntary and that equal educational opportunities had been provided at both schools, no violation of the Fourteenth Amendment had occurred. An equally divided Supreme Court affirmed the decision without opinion, thereby limiting the precedent's application to those states under the jurisdiction of the Third Circuit.

The issue was later retried in state court.[29] That court found that substantial facts had been misrepresented in the original case (the boys' school was larger, had a larger library and computer lab, and commanded double the funds in college scholarships than did the girls' school) and therefore concluded that the admissions policy of Central High School violated both the federal and Pennsylvania constitutions. Thereafter, Central High became coeducational while the Philadelphia High School for Girls continued operation unaffected by the controversy. The girls' school was reportedly the subject of an investigation by the Office for Civil Rights (OCR) in 1992, but the agency found no violation of Title IX because males could apply for admittance if they desired (although none did at that time) and "officials had no policy of excluding males from the school."[30]

The Supreme Court first substantively considered the issue of single-gender education in 1982 when it heard *Mississippi University for Women v. Hogan.* This case involved the exclusion of men from a state-operated program for nursing. The Supreme Court's decision established a heightened scrutiny standard that single-sex education must be founded on an "exceedingly persuasive justification" and must show that "the classification serves important governmental objectives and that the discriminatory means employed are substantially related to the achievement of those objectives."[31] This "mid-level" standard of review, although not as rigorous as strict scrutiny, which is the yardstick applied to all racial classifications, is intended to hold state officials to a tighter relationship between goals sought and means employed than the rational basis test to which most state policies are subjected. In this instance, the state of Mississippi could not justify why the nursing program was only available to women and the Court held that the school's admission policies violated the Equal Protection Clause of the Fourteenth Amendment.

Although not decided by the Supreme Court, a 1991 Michigan case is instructive concerning the constitutionality of single-gender schools. In the 1990s, the Detroit School District attempted to create an all-boys school. The school was designed to address the issue of high dropout rates and to provide positive male role models for boys in this urban setting. The court in *Garrett v. Board of Education of the School District of the City of Detroit*[32] rejected the plans as unconstitutional. Applying the heightened scrutiny test from *Mississippi v. Hogan*, the court accepted that the district had an "important governmental interest" in improving the education of boys, but was unwilling to accept that segregating boys from girls is substantially related to that goal. The court stated that "there is no evidence that the co-educational system is failing urban males because females attend schools with males."[33]

Fourteen years after deciding *Mississippi v. Hogan*, the Supreme Court again considered the issue of single-gender education in relation to the all-male Virginia Military Institute (VMI). The case, *United States v. Virginia*,[34] articulated the Court's most recent analysis on the issue of single-gender education, finding that the state-funded and state-operated VMI violated the Equal Protection Clause of the Fourteenth Amendment by excluding women. Seven justices formed the majority. Justice Ginsburg wrote for the Court with Justices Stevens, O'Connor, Kennedy, Souter, and Breyer joining the opinion. Chief Justice Rehnquist concurred with the Court's judgment, but not its reasoning and filed a separate opinion explaining his rationale for the same conclusion. Justice Scalia dissented, and Justice Thomas took no part in the case. *United States v. Virginia*, then, presents the best window into how the Court might settle any dispute over single-gender education at the public elementary or secondary level. A strong majority of seven members concurred in the holding, and all the justices continue to sit on the Supreme Court today. As such, it is important to examine precisely what the Court held and the reasoning supporting that holding.

The Court first discussed the boundaries of mid-level or heightened scrutiny in controversies regarding gender classification. Ginsburg termed the analysis "skeptical scrutiny"[35] and explained that there exists a "strong presumption that gender classifications are invalid."[36] The Court further held that the presumption of invalidity can only be rebutted if the "proffered justification is 'exceedingly persuasive.'"[37] Moreover, the Court determined that "[t]he burden of justification is demanding and rests entirely on the State."[38] In addition, the Court instructed that "[t]he justification must be genuine, not hypothesized or invented post hoc in response to litigation. And it must not rely on overbroad generalizations about the different talents, capacities, or preferences of males and females."[39] Then applying this standard to the VMI facts, the Court determined that the state of Virginia had failed to adequately justify VMI's exclusion of "women who have the will and capacity" to pursue "the training and attendant opportunities that VMI uniquely affords."[40] As Justice Ginsburg summarized the state's error: "Virginia, in sum, has fallen far short of establishing the exceedingly persuasive justification that must be the solid base for any gender-defined classification."[41]

The Court further found that the state's remedy for the violation of the Equal Protection Clause, the creation of the Virginia Women's Institute for Leadership (VWIL), was insufficient and did not place women in the position they would have occupied absent the discrimination. Specifically, the Court found that the all-female academy did not offer a sufficiently comparable program to satisfy constitutional principles of equity. In fact, the Court described the VWIL "as a 'pale shadow' of VMI in terms of the range of curricular choices and faculty stature, funding, prestige, alumni support and influence."[42]

As demonstrated above, litigation on the issue of single-gender education exists to guide the issue of single-gender education, but most controversies have arisen in higher education contexts, and therefore a question remains as to whether similar conclusions would be applied to public elementary and secondary contexts.[43] These cases exemplify the difficulty that may be present in meeting the constitutional standard set for single-gender education: that policymakers must have an "exceedingly persuasive justification" that demonstrates that separating children by virtue of sex is substantially related to an important governmental interest. What the Supreme Court might accept as "exceedingly persuasive" in elementary and secondary context remains an open question. The considerations applied in the VMI case suggest that the Justices will look for more than simple assurances from educators that sex-segregated education constitutes sound educational policy. These cases also demonstrate that although the court has not declared single-sex education unconstitutional in all situations, it has yet to find that a challenged single-sex institution met the constitutional standard for continuance. Accordingly, although states may be able to justify single-sex education in theory, the Court has not provided assistance in constructing such a justification in practice.

In addition to satisfying the broad principles associated with the Fourteenth Amendment's Equal Protection Clause, single-sex education must also meet the requirements established by Title IX of the Education Amendments of 1972 and its implementing regulations. As explained earlier, Title IX prohibits sex discrimination. In general, Title IX prohibits single-sex educational programs, but there currently exists a regulatory exception for single-gender schools. That exception allows a local educational agency (LEA) *with proper justification* to operate a single-gender school that is not a vocational school as long as the LEA "makes available . . . pursuant to the same policies and criteria for admission, courses, services, and facilities comparable to each course, service, and facility offered in or through such schools."[44]

This exception, read in conjunction with the language quoted earlier, has led to considerable confusion concerning under what circumstances single-gender education is allowable under Title IX. For example, Datnow, Hubbard, and Woody report that fear of litigation under Title IX motivated some school officials participating in California's Single Gender Academy Pilot Program to abandon the single-gender academies once state funding ended in 1999.[45] Reportedly, the same confusion motivated the recently enacted provision of the No Child Left Behind Act explicitly authorizing single-gender "innovations" by LEAs.[46] Accordingly, the provision was intended by its sponsors to clarify congressional intent under Title IX that public single-gender education be allowed when appropriately justified. Signed into law in January 2002, congressional intent now appears unambiguous on the issue.

However, it must be emphasized that single-sex education, even with congressional approval, must comport with, not conflict with, the Constitution's guarantee of equal protection. Not surprisingly then, in addition to the clarifying language of § 5131 quoted earlier, Congress directed the Department of Education to provide guidelines to guide LEA efforts within 120 days of the signing of the bill into law.[47] The department provided published guidance in the form of a four-page summary of existing law, but did not provide guidance as to how or under what circumstances single-sex programs need to be justified. In addition, on May 3, 2002, the agency published a "notice of intent to regulate" in the Federal Register.[48] The notice invited public comment on "whether, and under what circumstances, schools should be permitted to offer single-sex classes under the Title IX regulations" and specifically sought input on the following questions:

(1) Should a school district have to explain the benefits of single-sex classes for its students? If so, what kinds of explanations would be adequate? To what extent should these explanations be supported by scientifically based research, assessments of the needs of local students, or other reliable evidence?

(2) Assuming that a school district provides a single-sex class to students of one sex, would it be possible for a coeducational class to provide equal opportunity for students of the other sex? If so, under what circumstances?

(3) If it is not possible for a coeducational class to provide equal opportunity for students of the other sex, and a single sex class would be required, what happens if there is little interest in a single-sex class among students of one sex?

(4) Must student assignments to single-sex classes always be voluntary? If not, when are mandatory assignments permissible?

(5) Are there any classes that should not be permitted to be single-sex? For example, at the time that Title IX was enacted, Congress was particularly concerned about discrimination in single-sex vocational education classes and sex-segregated physical education classes (although students could be separated by sex in physical education classes involving contact sports).[49]

Regarding the issue of single-sex schools, the department sought input on three additional questions:

(1) If a school district provides a single-sex school to students of one sex, would it be possible for a coeducational school to provide equal opportunity for students of the other sex? If so, under what circumstances?

(2) Are there special considerations with regard to single-sex charter schools or magnet schools? Should a school district, state, or chartering agency be required to offer a school for students of the other sex? If so, under what circumstances?

(3) Given the Supreme Court's decision in *United States v. Virginia*, 518 U.S. 515 (1996), should a school district that establishes single-sex schools or classes for one sex be required to establish schools or classes for the other sex that are "comparable" or that meet some other standard?[50]

It is interesting to note that while the department sought input on the issue of comparable benefits, no question asked respondents to identify what justifications would rise to the level of "exceedingly persuasive." In fact, only the first of the eight total questions queries interested parties about possible rationales for single-gender classes, and then the department asks not *what* rationale would be sufficiently substantial, but *whether* any justification should be required at all.

The comments collected during the period from May to July are currently being analyzed. The next step will be for the Department of Education to publish proposed regulations on the issue, followed by another period of time for public comment. Once comments are analyzed, the department will issue final regulations. It therefore remains to be seen what definition the Department of Education will bring to "consistent with applicable laws." It is also likely that any definition they provide will require further judicial interpretation of the issue before any truly clear image emerges.

Nonetheless, given the sources of legal authority reviewed above and the current scrutiny applied to single-gender schools, three primary guidelines can be distilled regarding single-gender educational programs and their constitutionality:

1. The state or any of its political subdivisions (e.g., a public school district, a public university serving as a charter school authority, a municipality, a public charter school) must justify any single-gender decision made at the outset of that decision, not as an afterthought to maintain the status quo, and that justification must be based on exceedingly persuasive rationales unrelated to stereotypic notions of sex-roles and abilities.

2. The state or any of its political subdivisions must be able to show how separating children by virtue of sex is substantially related to an important governmental interest.

3. If justifiable single-gender options are used, the State or any of its political subdivisions must be able to demonstrate that comparable benefits are available to each sex, comparable both in terms of quality and in terms of scope.

These three principles suggest that single-gender schools could survive judicial scrutiny at least in theory. As described above, the primary hurdle is crafting a rationale sufficient to satisfy the first criterion. It is only with such an "exceedingly persuasive justification" that a single-gender school or program would survive any challenge to its existence.

Applying the three principles discerned from a review of case law and statutory authority and applying them to the existing public single-gender educational programs reveals a number of interesting issues for policymakers regarding the constitutionality of such approaches.

Principle 1: Exceedingly Persuasive Justification

As mentioned earlier, the first and dominant challenge to demonstrating the constitutionality of single-gender education is the
crafting an "exceedingly persuasive" justification. Interestingly,
the taxonomy described by the Brighter Choice Charter Schools'
web site concerning "generations" of single-sex schools and programs also provides a helpful way to organize the complex issues
associated with justifying the programs. Recall that "first-genera-
tion" schools commenced single-sex education early in our
country's history at a time before the concept of equal educational
opportunity had materialized. "Second-generation" single-sex
schools were ostensibly established to remedy discrimination or
at least the alleged disparate educational effects available to girls
in the coeducational setting. "Third-generation" single-sex schools
seek to provide the benefits of single-gender education to both
sexes. Accordingly, the Young Women's Leadership Charter School
would be considered a second-generation single-sex school and
the Brighter Choice Charter School would fall under the third generation of such schools.

As a "second-generation" single-sex school, the Young Women's
Leadership Charter School may be able to withstand challenge.
Some commentators[51] have suggested that meeting the level of justification articulated by *United States v. Virginia* may be more readily
made for all-girls' education than for all-boys' education because
there is research that suggests that girls are "shortchanged" in coeducational environments and achieve better in single-sex environments.[52] As one writer noted, all-girls' schools may better
withstand constitutional scrutiny because they are "designed to
provide girls with educational opportunities equivalent to those
enjoyed by boys in coeducational schools, and because [they are]
based upon scientific research rather than sex-role stereotypes."[53]
This notion, however, is not universally accepted, and other writ-
ers have taken pains to suggest that such conclusions are based on
flawed research and invalidated by a substantial number of contrary research studies.[54]

This argument illustrates one of the problems this school might
face if challenged. A reviewing court would be forced to referee a
battle of competing experts. In the face of such competition, the
court may conclude that since research does not reach a definitive
result, the justification cannot meet the "exceedingly persuasive"
standard. In addition, it has been suggested that such arguments
to support all-girls' education may actually undermine a legal ar-

gument because the separation may actually "serve to enforce debilitating stereotypes" about girls' abilities in math and science, rather than counter them.[55]

Given these problems, it would appear that second-generation single-sex programs must be justified on more than academic research that makes generalizations concerning the state of girls' education nationwide. Rather, a district (or charter school authorizer) might reasonably be asked to show that girls are disadvantaged in that local system. In other words, does evidence show that the problems that some identify truly exist in that particular educational context? If districtwide data support such a conclusion, a court may be swayed that the explanation that the single-sex school serves a compensatory purpose has a foundation in fact, rather than theory. If district data are inconclusive or contrary, that fact would support any challenger's argument that the program is not adequately justified.

"Third-generation" single-sex schools, those that offer programs to both sexes, have an advantage in that they may be able avoid problems associated with the first two types of single-sex schools. The programs are all relatively new, so that they cannot be accused of using pretextual rationales in order to preserve a tradition. In addition, both sexes are served, so there is no issue of compensation for or remedying discriminatory effects for one sex and not the other. And yet such schools must show that they began their programs with a proper justification or at least that there is an articulated reason for continuing the separation now that it has begun. For example, it seems unlikely, that the reason given by the Maria Mitchell Elementary School of "assist[ing] our children with transitioning into their teen years" without more explanation would be sufficient to conclude that the school has an adequate basis for gender separation.[56]

It would also seem that the charter school application process provides an opportunity for those proposing single-gender charter schools to make such a justification. That process creates a mechanism by which a charter school authority can require a charter applicant to forcefully substantiate why such an approach is being sought. The fact that charter schools are, by definition in many states, intended to examine and spur educational innovation may work to a single-gender charter school's advantage. It might be argued that a charter school conceived to explore the viability of single-gender education, given current research, justifies the approval of a single-gender charter school.

Principle 2: Substantial Relationship

As demonstrated by *Garret*, the Michigan case reviewed earlier, it is not sufficient for single-sex educational programs to articulate a reason for being; they must also demonstrate that separating the sexes substantially relates to meeting the educational objectives targeted.[57] In other words, it is not enough to say that single-gender education has benefits; the school must also be able to show that those benefits substantially relate to an identifiable problem. *Garret* also demonstrates that a court may require a showing that the problems being attacked by adopting a single-sex approach stem from coeducational failures.

Regardless of the "generation" of single-sex schools, these linkages may be difficult to make, given the rift on the issue within the educational community. Several authors note that no clear consensus demonstrates the benefits of single-gender education to either sex.[58] Indeed, even the Brighter Choice Charter Schools briefly outline the "counterarguments" related to single-sex education after reviewing its purported benefits. Their materials then conclude, "The academic research suggests positive educational benefits of single-sex schooling for girls (if not affluent), at-risk students, and African American and Hispanic students (regardless of sex). Further, white males either benefit slightly or at worst realize a neutral outcome."[59] Whether such conclusions are sufficient to rebut the presumption of invalidity of gender classifications identified by the Supreme Court in the VMI case remains to be seen.

It would also be interesting to observe what role comparative achievement data would play in the schools that converted to single-gender approaches for all or part of their school population. Reportedly, achievement test scores rose after instituting single-gender class groupings in the Robert Coleman Elementary School, Maria Mitchell Elementary School, Lewis Fox Middle School, and Thurgood Marshall Elementary School.[60] These successes may provide the persuasion necessary. They may not. Nonetheless, a question remains. Would such increases be sufficient to demonstrate the veracity of the claims made, or would a court require that schools prove that the improvements could be attributed to the single-gender approach and not to other factors that may explain the changes noted? What needs to be emphasized is that single-gender schools and programs need to be equally persuasive when articulating the reason for adopting that approach and in connecting that approach to the desired outcomes.

Principle 3: Comparable Benefits

Assuming for the sake of argument that a single-sex charter school could successfully navigate the challenges associated with the first two principles, the program would still have to demonstrate that comparable benefits are available to the opposite sex. This raises the question of to what group single-sex educational programs must be compared. Need the school show that students of the non-targeted gender in coeducational schools enjoy comparable opportunities? Or must the school demonstrate that each sex enjoys an equal opportunity for single-gender education? The first argument seems applicable only if the school is designed to remedy or compensate for problems experienced by one gender in comparison to the other a coeducational environment. However, such a comparison would need to be avoided by any paired single-sex program serving both genders in sexually homogeneous settings. For, if programs like the Brighter Choice Charter Schools use those in traditional settings to gauge comparable benefits, it risks undermining the justification for the separation in the first place. If comparable benefits exist in the traditional coeducational schools, how can separating the sexes be justified? The DOE instructs that "[i]t has been our longstanding interpretation, policy, and practice to require that the 'comparable school' must also be single-sex."[61]

Consistent with this stance, "third-generation" schools would be best able to argue that comparability is achieved by having both sexes educated in homogeneous settings. That is, in order to balance single-sex opportunities for both boys and girls, combinations of boys-only schools and girls-only schools offer comparable programming, and a reasonably similar (if not equivalent) number of seats to eligible students in the same community or recruitment area. In that way, the benefits of the single-gender programs would arguably be available without regard to sex.

In fact some commentators have concluded that such paired single-sex programs are in the best position to withstand legal challenge after VMI.[62] Boland concludes:

> An ideal [single-sex] program would most likely consist of peer schools started at the exact same time, to avoid the prestige and alumni problems inherent in *Vorchheimer* and *Virginia*. Physical facilities should be identical. They would have to have faculty of an equal caliber, although the male school could have all male teachers and the female school all women instructors. Curriculum could include classes focusing on issues relevant to each sex, including past accomplishments of individuals sharing the stu-

dents' gender and race. Finally, as the *Virginia* Court revealed its willingness to consider the legitimacy of each sex's "general tendencies" in designing pedagogically advantageous single-sex programs, the methods of teaching could be adjusted to the dictates of research on the preferable methods for each sex.[63]

As stated earlier, this analysis was designed to explore the question: Under what circumstances is single-gender education "consistent with applicable law"? As the analysis above reveals, the most honest answer is that the question cannot be unmistakably answered until the Supreme Court addresses the issue of single-gender public education at the elementary and secondary level.[64] Some have argued that single-sex programs can withstand scrutiny,[65] while others are just as convinced that single-sex public education cannot be constitutionally justified.[66]

Only three conclusions appear beyond question. First, school leaders who support single-sex education need to clearly articulate their rationales for that decision, else the judicial system will give their policy decisions little deference. Second, social science research will play a pivotal role in persuading jurists as to the constitutionality or lack thereof associated with single-gender approaches. Finally, litigation will be required to ultimately settle the issue.

Conclusion

As this chapter has demonstrated, charter schools are bound by the same prohibitions against gender discrimination as are other public schools. Accordingly, charter school authorizers and charter school operators must familiarize themselves with the broad principles of equal protection guaranteed by the Fourteenth Amendment and the specific requirements of Title VII, Title IX, and their state's nondiscrimination statutes. These laws also have implications for charter school authorizers. First, authorizers must be certain that gender equity is considered when determining whether a charter school applicant should be granted approval. Curricular offerings and the policies guiding student assignment should be examined for consistency with gender equity. Should any applicant seek to develop single-gender charter schools, particular care will be required to be certain that proper justification exists for such institutions and that comparable benefits are available to each sex. Whether coeducational or single-gender, once a charter school becomes operational, charter school authorizers should require evidence that the school has met its policy requirements under both

Title VII and Title IX. Charter school authorizers need not directly provide assistance on these matters but should guide charter school officials to appropriate assistance at both state and federal levels.[68] Finally, as monitors of charter contract compliance, authorizers should be certain that assurances of nondiscrimination on the basis of gender made by charter schools are realities in operation. Therefore, gender equity should be part of any contract compliance review.

Endnotes

[1] Office of Educ. Research & Improvement, U.S. Dept. of Educ., *The State of Charter Schools 2000: National Study of Charter Schools*, Fourth-Year Report, available at http://www.ed.gov. (last visited Apr. 2002)

[2] This test merely requires the policymakers to articulate a "rational relationship" between a legitimate state interest and the means selected to address that interest.

[3] 42 U.S.C. § 2000e *et seq.* (as amended by the Civil Rights Act of 1991).

[4] For an explanation of requirements and current judicial standards for workplace harassment, *see* M. David Alexander, et al. *Sexual Harassment in the Workplace*. pp. 227–237 *in* The Principal's Legal Handbook 227 (William E. Camp, et al., eds., 2000).

[5] 20 U.S.C. §1682 et seq. "No person in the United States shall, on the basis of sex, be excluded from participation in, be denied the benefits of, or be subjected to discrimination under any program or activity receiving federal financial assistance."

[6] 34 C.F.R. § 106.2.

[7] "Every application for Federal financial assistance for any education program or activity shall as condition of its approval contain or be accompanied by an assurance from the applicant or recipient, satisfactory to the Assistant Secretary, that *each education program or activity operated by the applicant* or recipient and to which this part applies will be operated in compliance with this part" 34 C.F.R. § 106.4 (emphasis added).

[8] For a discussion of the legal standards for liability for sexual harassment, see Genevieve Frazier Bryant, et al., Sexual Harassment in the Schools: Avoiding Liability. (2000).

[9] Office for Civil Rights, Title IX and Education, available at http://www.ed.gov.offices/OCR/ocrttl9.html (last visited Mar. 2002).

[10] 34 C.F.R. § 106.36(c).

[11] General Accounting Office, *Public Education, Issues Involving Single-Gender Schools and Programs, A Report to the Chairman, Committee on the Budget, House of Representatives*. (May 1996).

[12] Pub. L. No. 107-110.

[13] *Id* § 5131(a)(23).

[14] Public funds also support single-gender education through the publicly funded private school voucher programs operating in Cleveland and Milwaukee. Analysis of the constitutionality of these programs, although similar, is outside the scope of this commentary.

[15] National Association for the Advancement of Single Sex Public Education (NAASSPE) (2002), available at http://www.singlesexschools.org. (last visited Apr. 2002)

[16] For a discussion and analysis of each of these single-sex schools, see Julie F. Mead, *Single-Gender 'Innovations': Can Publicly Funded Single-Gender School Choice Options be Constitutionally Justified?* 39 Educ. Admin. Quart. 164 (2002).

[17] Young Women's Leadership Charter School (2002), available athttp://www.ywlcs.org. (last visited Feb. 2002)

[18] Brighter Choice Charter Schools (2002), available at http://www.brighterchoice.org/single_sex.htm. (last visited Feb. 2002)

[19] *Id.*

[20] *Id.*

[21] Gender equity is also protected by state constitutional provisions for equal protection of the laws and specific state legislation to prohibit sex discrimination. Although a review of these provisions is outside the scope of this analysis, educational authorities either operating or considering the operation of single-gender educational programs should be cognizant of the independent requirements these sources of legal authority may add to the federal foundation reviewed here. Such provisions may or may not place more stringent requirements on gender separation in public educational settings.

[22] Adarand Constructors, Inc. v. Pena, 515 U.S. 200 (1995).

[23] Regents of Univ. of Cal. v. Bakke, 438 U.S. 265, 357–362 (1978).

[24] Frontiero v. Richardson, 411 U.S. 677 (1973).

[25] *Id.* at 684.

[26] *Id.* at 688.

[27] Craig v. Boren, 429 U.S. 190 (1976); Kirchberg v. Feenstra, 450 U.S. 455 (1981); Mississippi University for Women v. Hogan, 458 U.S. 718 (1982); J.E.B. v. Alabama *ex rel.* T.B., 511 U.S. 127 (1994).

[28] Vorchheimer v. School Dist. of Philadelphia, 430 U.S. 703, (1977) *aff'g*, 532 F.2d 880 (3d Cir. 1976).

[29] Newberg v. Board of Public Educ., 26 Pa. D. & C.3d 682 (1983).

[30] General Accounting Office, *supra* note 11.

[31] *Mississippi Univ. for Women*, 458 U.S. at 724 (1982) (internal quotation marks and citation omitted).

[32] 775 F. Supp. 1004 (E.D. Mich. 1991).

[33] *Id.* at 1008.

[34] 518 U.S. 515 (1996).

[35] *Id.* at 531.

[36] *Id.* at 532 (*quoting J.E.B.*, 511 U.S. at 152 (1994) (Kennedy, J., concurring)).

[37] *Id.* at 533.

[38] *Id.*

[39] *Id.*

[40] *Id.* at 542.

[41] *Id.* at 546 (internal quotations and citation omitted).

[42] *Id.* at 553 (*quoting* U.S. v. Virginia, 44 F.3d 1229, 1250 (4th Cir. 1994) (Phillips, J. dissenting)).

[43] In recognition of this distinction and the deference often shown to educators in cases involving young children in contrast to young adults, Pherabe Kolb argues for application of the more relaxed rational basis review of single-sex educational programs. *Reaching for the Silver Lining: Constructing a Nonremedial Yet "Exceedingly Persuasive" Rationale for Single-Sex Educational Programs in Public Schools*, 96 Nw. U. L. Rev. 367 (2001).However, in contrast to Kolb, the analysis provided in this chapter assumes that the more stringent "skeptical scrutiny" applies. Nonetheless, Kolb's arguments may be used to demonstrate to a reviewing court that

single-gender education is substantially related to improved public education in ways that would not be so persuasive in a higher education context.

44 34 C.F.R. 106.35(b).

45 A. Datnow, et al., *Is Single Gender Schooling Viable in the Public Sector? Lessons From California's Pilot Program.* (2001). Available at http://www.oise.utoronto.ca/depts/tps/adatnow/final.pdf (last visited Feb. 2002).

46 K. Hutchinson, *The Lesson of Single-Sex Public Education: Both Successful and Constitutional,* 50 Am. U. L. Rev. 1075; (2001); NAASSPE, *supra* note 15.

47 Pub. L. No. 107-110, § 5131(c).

48 67 Fed. Reg. 31097, 31098.

49 *Id.*

50 *Id.*

51 A. Koman, *Urban Single-Sex, Public Secondary Schools: Advancing Full Development of the Talent and Capacities of America's Young Women,* 39 Will. & Mary L. Rev. 507 (1998); C. Krupnick, *Legal and Policy Issues Raised by All-Female Public Education,* 14 N.Y. L. Sch. J. Rs. 155 (1998); A. Nemko, *Single-Sex Public Education after VMI: The Case for Women's Schools,* 21 Harv. Women's L. J. 19 (1998); C. Ramsey, *Subtracting Sexism from the Classroom: Law and Policy in the Debate over All-Female Math and Science Classes in the Public Schools,* 8 Tex. J. Women & L. 1 (1998); A. Bellman, *The Young Women's Leadership School: Single-Sex Public Education after V.M.I.,* 1997 Wis. L. Rev. 827 (1997); B. Sandler, *Publicly Supported Single Sex Schools and Policy Issues,* 14 N.Y. L. Sch. J. of Hum. Rs. 61 (1997).

52 S. Bailey, *How Schools Shortchange Girls.* (1992); M Sadker & D. Sadker. *Failing at Fairness, How America's Schools Cheat Girls* (1994).

53 A. Bellman, *Supra* note 15.

54 C. H. Sommers, *The War against Boys: How Misguided Feminism Is Harming Our Young Men.* (2000); K. Schuld, *Rethinking Educational Equity: Sometimes, Different Can Be an Acceptable Substitute for Equal,* 1999 U. Chi. Legal F. 461 (1999); R. Tovey, *Gender Equity: A Narrowly Gender-based Mode of Learning May End up Cheating All Students.* Harv. Educ. Letter (1995); H. Marsh, *Effects of Attending Single-Sex and Coeducational High Schools on Achievement, Attitudes, Behaviors, and Sex Differences,* 81 J. Educ. Psychol. 70 (1989).

55 T. Boland, *Single-Sex Public Education: Equality Versus Choice.* 1 U. Pa. J. Const. L. 154, 172 (1998).

56 Denver Public Schools, Maria Mitchell Elementary School Profile, available at http://www.denver.k12.co.us/schools/e/Elementary/255.shtml (last visited Feb. 26, 2002).

57 L. Hsiao, *'Separate But Equal' Revisited: The Detroit Male Academies Case,* 1992/1993 Ann. Surv, Am. L. 85 (1993).

58 Datnow, *supra* note 15. N. Levit, *Separating Equals: Educational Research and the Long-Term Consequences of Sex Segregation,* 67 Geo. Wash. L. Rev. 451 (1999); P. Campbell & E. Wahl, *Of Two Minds: Single-Sex Education, Coeducation and the Search for Gender Equity in K-12 Public Schooling,* 14 N. Y. L. Sch. J. of Hum. Rts. 289 (1997); General Accounting Office *supra* note 15.

59 These quotes also suggest another potential problem. If school authorities use rationales based on the race of their students to justify gender separation, they risk allegations of race as well as gender discrimination. Since race-based classifications are analyzed using the more rigorous strict scrutiny standard, such rationales would likely make the school more, not less, vulnerable to legal challenge.

60 NAASSPE, *supra* note 15.

[61] U.S. Department Of Education, Appendix A, Guidance for Title V, Part A of the Elementary and Secondary Education Act, as reauthorized by the No Child Left Behind (NCLB) Act (State Grants for Innovative Programs), August 2002.

[62] J. Reiter, *California Single-Gender Academies Pilot Program: Separate but Really Equal*, 72 S. Cal. L. Rev. 1401(1999); Boland, *supra* note 55, at 172.

[63] Boland *supra* note 55, at 171.

[64] Datnow, *supra* note 45, Boland, *supra* note 55. General Accounting Office *supra* note 11.

[65] Kolb, *supra* note 43. Nemko, *supra* note 51.

[66] The Office for Civil Rights within the U.S. Department of Education provides a number of resources on-line at: http://www.ed.gov.offices/OCR/.

Chapter 8

Charter Schools and Students with Disabilities

The principles that govern the access of children with disabilities to appropriate educational settings are grounded in the Fourteenth Amendment of the Constitution, the same provision that guarantees equal opportunity on the basis of other status characteristics such as race and gender. Determining a charter school's specific responsibilities for children with disabilities requires examination of three sources of legal authority: federal law, state law, and the charter contract. In this instance, federal law drives the process, because three federal statutes direct delivery of services to children with disabilities in addition to the general protections afforded by the Constitution. Although state legislatures through their statutes may relieve charter schools of state rules and regulations, including those related to special education, they have no authority to waive federal requirements such as federal disability law.

Federal laws clearly contemplate that charter schools are public schools that will serve students with disabilities comparably as students with disabilities are served in more traditional public schools. In fact, the Charter Schools Expansion Act (CSEA), which provides grant money to states and their charter schools, defines a charter school as a "public school" that, among other requirements, "complies with . . . section 504 of the Rehabilitation Act of 1973 [Section 504], and part B of the Individuals with Disabilities Education Act [IDEA]."[1] Accordingly, Section 504[2] and IDEA,[3] together with Title II of the Americans with Disabilities Act (ADA),[4] form a foundation that dictates special education responsibility in charter schools. However, due to variance across the country regarding the legal status of charter schools in relation to school districts, understanding *that* federal law applies is just the beginning. Precisely *how* federal law applies and what obligations a charter school has with regard to students with disabilities lie at the intersection of federal, state, and contract law.

This chapter discusses the obligations charter schools have for students with disabilities. The first section examines Section 504 and

Title II of the ADA as applied to charter schools. The second section examines the IDEA and issues related to its delivery in the charter school context. This discussion explains how both state law and individual charter contract provisions determine how the IDEA is implemented in a given charter school. The third section examines what special issues attach when a charter school seeks to serve only children with disabilities. Finally, this chapter explores the implications of special education law for charter school authorizers.

Section 504/ADA and Charter Schools

Section 504 is a civil rights statute analogous to Titles VI and IX. It provides no funding, but prohibits discrimination on the basis of disability by any recipient of federal financial assistance. The ADA extends these nondiscrimination provisions to the workplace regardless of whether the employer receives federal money.[5] Title II of the ADA addresses the schools' treatment of children with disabilities. Its requirements mirror those of Section 504 in public school contexts. Therefore, Section 504/ADA will be treated together for the purposes of this chapter.

Inherent in the Section 504/ADA prohibition of discrimination is the consideration of access. The pertinent question is whether charter school attendance is open to children with disabilities in a manner comparable to that of nondisabled children. Accordingly, the admissions policies and practices of charter schools must be carefully considered, and a charter school must ensure that any entry criterion it adopts does not discriminate against students with disabilities. For example, a charter school that required students to have IQ scores within a particular range may be vulnerable to a Section 504/ADA challenge because IQ scores may create a complete bar to some children with mental disabilities. A better strategy would be for a school to require demonstrated achievement on some standard measures coupled with grades and/or teacher recommendations, in much the way children now qualify for "gifted" programs in traditional public schools. Although achievement and measured IQ are closely related, they focus on different issues. IQ tests are designed to measure intellectual potential, while achievement scores measure accomplishment. IQ scores are also sometimes used by states to define cognitive and learning disabilities. Therefore, since achievement measures what a child can do, it is not as likely to raise the same concerns under Section 504/ADA as is an IQ score criterion.

This example, however, is extreme. The more likely application of Section 504/ADA's guarantee of access would be programmatic in nature. It is insufficient to simply admit children with disabilities into the charter school to demonstrate nondiscriminatory access. The substance of Section 504/ADA demands that access be meaningful, which means that educational needs arising from a child's disabilities are met with appropriate programming and that each child is guaranteed a free appropriate public education (FAPE). In other words, access must be both physical and programmatic.

A decision by the Office for Civil Rights (OCR) following an investigation of a complaint against the Boston Renaissance Charter School in 1997 provides an illustration.[6] A student enrolled in kindergarten began exhibiting frequent behavioral difficulties. The school responded with suspension. Eventually, the school recommended that the child be evaluated for special education eligibility pursuant to the IDEA and Massachusetts law. The school also required that the child attend school for only one half of the scheduled school day. The school did not inform the parents of Section 504 or their rights under its provisions. The parents refused special education testing at first, but after problems persisted for several months, they agreed. The child was not found eligible under the IDEA, but did qualify as a child with a disability under Section 504's functional definition,[7] given his hyperactivity and the possible Attention Deficit Hyperactivity Disorder (ADHD). Although the school made some minor changes in the child's program, the school continued frequent suspension and its restriction that the child could attend school for only half of the school day. The parents withdrew him from the charter school during first-grade and enrolled him in a traditional public school where he completed his first grade year without the need for early dismissal or suspension.

The OCR found the charter school had committed a number of Section 504 violations. First, it had failed to satisfy the regulations with regard to notice. The school had not adopted or disseminated the required notice of nondiscrimination on the basis of disability. It had also failed to designate a staff member to receive grievances and to investigate and resolve complaints. Furthermore, the school had neglected to inform the parents of their rights under Section 504, including the right to file a complaint and request an impartial hearing to resolve any dispute. The school had likewise failed to explain to the parents the safeguards provided by the law and its regulations for students facing suspension or expulsion to ensure that disciplinary procedures are equitably applied.

In addition to these procedural errors, OCR found that the charter school had violated the child's substantive rights to FAPE in two ways. First, the school failed to provide supplementary aids and services within the regular classroom in order to accommodate the child's disability. Second, the school violated Section 504 when it restricted the child's school day. Section 504 requires that children with disabilities have access to a school day of the same length as that of nondisabled peers unless school officials can demonstrate that the child, due to the nature and severity of his disability, requires the shortened day as an accommodation. The school agreed to a settlement that required it to make the necessary policy changes, train its staff appropriately, and reimburse the parents for the childcare and tutorial expenses they had incurred while the child was enrolled in the charter school.

Similarly, OCR found violations at TOVAS Charter School in Temple, Texas. While investigating a complaint for wrongful discharge, OCR discovered irregularities in the school's compliance with Section 504. Specifically, the school had failed to implement procedures to identify and serve children with disabilities, to adopt a proper notice of nondiscrimination, or to establish complaint procedures.[8]

As the experiences of the Boston Renaissance School and the TOVAS Charter School depict, Section 504/ADA dictate more than good intentions on the part of a charter school. Assurances of nondiscrimination must satisfy both procedural and substantive requirements set forth in federal regulations. Charter schools must determine how they will acquire services for children with disabilities from the onset of operations. For charter schools that are part of larger school districts, this should not be problematic. For more independent charter schools, it may be. Like any small school district, a freestanding charter school lacks the economy of scale that provides the necessary impetus and cost savings for establishing programs and hiring staff in anticipation of students. Accordingly, many charter schools must essentially stand ready to serve a child with a disability if and when that child enrolls. Understandably, such a process makes planning and budgeting difficult. Yet, charter schools must understand when developing their programs that serving children with disabilities is an obligation that cannot be avoided.

In addition, since charter schools have considerable autonomy in designing programs, care must be taken in the development of programming such that students are not excluded either by design or by default. For example, Nevada's charter school law has a provision that reads:

> If the governing body of a charter school determines that the charter school is unable to provide an appropriate special education program and related services for a particular disability of a pupil who is enrolled in the charter school, the governing body may request that the board of trustees of the school district of the county in which the pupil resides transfer that pupil to an appropriate school.[9]

If a Nevada charter school purposely limited the special education programming it offered in order to invoke this provision and limit the number of children with disabilities the school accepted, a viable § 504/ADA complaint might be made that the school discriminated on the basis of disability. This example demonstrates that in order to be responsive to the public in a nondiscriminatory manner and minimize vulnerability to legal challenge, charter schools must consider the needs of children with disabilities as the school is being designed, not as an afterthought to their enrollment.

The issue of programming also brings up a practice that some have called "counseling out."[10] Some research has suggested that charter schools often counsel parents of children with disabilities that the charter school cannot meet the child's needs and that the child should attend another school. To the extent that all parents are counseled about the fit between the child's learning style and the curricular approach adopted by the charter school, this practice is not troublesome. However, when such sessions are used to discourage the enrollment of children with disabilities with the intent of avoiding responsibility for serving children whose disabilities require accommodation (including special programming), the practice would violate Section 504/ADA, as it results in the categorical exclusion of students on the basis of disability.[11]

The lessons learned in other school choice contexts, such as magnet schools and open enrollment, provide further insight into this issue of programmatic access. First, a parental choice cannot be honored if it does not meet the requirements of federal disability law.[12] A free appropriate public education (FAPE) is a child's entitlement that must be protected and ensured as long as the child is enrolled in any form of public school. No child should have to trade FAPE in order to get "choice." Nor can school authorities either require such a trade by forcing parents to waive their child's access to services or allow such a trade by agreeing with a parental request to forgo services that the child needs in order to receive FAPE.[13]

This reasoning is not to suggest that a child's needs might not change in the charter school context. Depending on the educational environment created there, it is certainly conceivable that a child's disability could manifest itself differently in the new school environment, thereby requiring fewer or at least different interventions. The key is that the school honors the mandated commitment to equal educational opportunity by ensuring that the child's needs (not programmatic availability, administrative convenience or teacher convenience) dictate any changes and that all changes occur through the proper procedures.

It should be clear after this discussion that charter schools can take some affirmative steps to truly serve all children that desire their unique form of public education. The following six directives, while not exhaustive, form a minimum response by charter school operators to Section 504/ADA. They should:

1. Familiarize themselves with Section 504/ADA and its requirements;[14]
2. Adopt a formal policy of nondiscrimination on the basis of disability;
3. Designate a staff person to receive and investigate any complaints of discriminatory treatment;
4. Prepare materials to inform parents of their rights under Section 504/ADA;
5. Consider how the school will acquire the necessary expertise to evaluate and serve children with disabilities during the charter school design or development phase;
6. Train all staff concerning their role in making the charter school free from discrimination on the basis of disability.

Charter Schools and the IDEA

The IDEA forms a companion piece of legislation to Section 504/ADA. While Section 504 and the ADA prohibit discrimination, the IDEA provides funding to serve those children with disabilities whose impairments "adversely affect educational performance" such that they require special education. This complex federal law requires states, as a condition of the funding provided, to ensure that the educational needs of its children with disabilities are appropriately met. As such, the state through its state educational agency (SEA) is the ultimate guarantor of FAPE for each child with a disability that resides there.[15] The SEA, then, must ensure that each local educational agency (LEA)[16] meets the act's mandates.[17] In the most basic terms, an LEA must

1. Identify, locate and evaluate all eligible children;
2. Make FAPE available through special education and related services;
3. Include children with disabilities in large-scale assessments (those dictated by the state or those the charter school has determined that all children must take);
4. Establish written policies and procedures for implementing the law.

In other words, each LEA has an affirmative obligation to identify and serve appropriately all eligible children with disabilities within its jurisdiction and have written policies and procedures in place to effect that result. An LEA is the legal entity that ensures appropriate educational programming at the local level under the guidance, direction, and oversight of the state. Therefore, what specific responsibilities a charter school has under the IDEA depends initially on whether the charter school is an LEA for the purposes of the act.

In 1997, the amendments to the IDEA included specific provisions regarding charter schools.[18] The first section requires that for "charter schools that are public schools of the local educational agency [LEA]," the LEA must serve students attending those schools in the same manner it serves students in its other schools and must provide funds received through the IDEA to the charter schools in a like manner to its other schools.[19] In addition, the IDEA makes provision for charter schools that are designated as LEAs independent of any larger district.[20] The regulations further note that a third kind of charter school may exist, which is neither an LEA nor part of another LEA. In such a case, "the SEA [state educational agency] is responsible for ensuring that the requirements of this part are met."[21] A clear decree underlies these requirements—namely, that "[c]hildren with disabilities who attend public charter schools and their parents retain all rights under the [IDEA]."[22] As the OCR explained: "It has long been the Department's position that public school choice programs must maintain openness and equity, vital components of publicly supported education."[23]

Table 8.1 depicts how each state has handled the LEA issue. In 16 states, the school district in which the charter school is located always serves as the LEA. New Hampshire, New York, and Oregon designate the child's resident district as the responsible agency to ensure that a child's needs are being met. Connecticut has created a statutory scheme that contemplates cooperation between the charter school and the resident district, assigning some duties to the school district (holding Individualized Education Program (IEP) team meetings and paying for costs) and leaving others (ensuring service delivery) to the charter school. Sixteen states consider charter schools to be LEAs themselves. California charter schools may petition the state for approval to operate as their own independent LEAs. Somewhat similarly, a charter school in the District of Columbia may "elect" whether to be its own LEA or part of the DC school district's service delivery plan. Finally, three states, Illinois, Louisiana, and Wisconsin, have a mixture of types of charter schools for special education purposes. Some of the schools, generally those sponsored by local school districts, are schools within LEAs. Others, typically those sponsored by other charter school authorities, are independent LEAs. A Wisconsin school district may decide whether a charter school it sponsors will be an instrumentality or a non-instrumentality of the school district. In special education terms, since the district employs all the personnel for instrumentality charter schools, those schools fall under the district's LEA umbrella, while non-instrumentality charter schools are independent LEAs. Therefore, a Wisconsin school district may sponsor some charter schools for which it serves as the LEA and some charter schools for which each charter school is its own LEA.

Table 8.1. Charter School LEAs under State Statutes

LEA	States
School District	Alaska, California, Colorado, Florida, Georgia, Idaho, Iowa, Kansas, Mississippi, New Mexico, Nevada, Oklahoma, South Carolina, Tennessee, Virginia, Wyoming
Resident School District	New Hampshire, New York, Oregon
Shared Responsibility	Connecticut
Charter School Elects, Petitions	California, District of Columbia
Charter School	Arkansas, Arizona, Delaware, Hawaii, Indiana, Massachusetts, Michigan, Minnesota, Missouri, New Jersey, North Carolina, Ohio, Pennsylvania, Rhode Island, Texas, Utah
Mixture of LEA Types	Illinois, Louisiana, Wisconsin

As Table 8.1 illustrates, while all charter schools must serve children with disabilities consistent with the IDEA, the entity responsible for ensuring such compliance varies from state to state and even from charter school to charter school within a state. Knowing what agency serves as the LEA is the first step to understanding the obligations a given school has. An additional layer of complexity is added by each charter contract. The specific terms of the contract may define further how the IDEA is implemented in a given charter school. Each type of charter school addressed under the IDEA and its regulations will be addressed in turn. Issues related to individual charter contracts associated with each type will also be discussed.

As noted above, the first charter school type named in the IDEA is the charter school that is part of a larger LEA, usually a school district. In that instance, the school district serves as the LEA for IDEA purposes and owes the same obligation to charter school students as it does to its students in more traditional schools. Charter schools that fall into this category need to work with their parent school district to develop their special education delivery pattern. It will also be important to consider these issues at the time the charter school contract is being negotiated. For example, how will special education staff be hired? Will the charter school have this duty as it does with its other teachers, or do the parties (the charter school and the school district) agree that the LEA will assign special education staff? Who will supervise special education staff? How will funding be affected? It may also be necessary for the sponsoring school district to examine and alter its service delivery pattern to ensure that a charter school is as programmatically accessible as possible. These are just a sampling of the issues that need to be discussed and described in the contract, in order to fully allocate responsibility for the IDEA delivery in a district charter school.

The second charter school type named in the IDEA is the LEA charter school, a charter school that is independent of any larger district and serves as its own LEA. These independent charter schools have the same obligations as larger school districts that serve as LEAs. Being an independent charter school does not, however, necessarily mean that the charter school is its own LEA. Independent charter schools should first consult with state law to be certain they are LEA charter schools. This step is necessary because states may designate another entity to assume this responsibility for independent charter schools.

As Table 8.1 indicates, some states, through statutes, may require local or resident school districts to serve as LEAs, even for those charter schools that are otherwise independent of a school district. For example, Oregon law assigns the duty to serve children

with disabilities to the child's "resident district" for schools chartered by the state board of education and that are otherwise independent from local districts.[24] In addition, LEA charter schools must
consider the same questions raised above for district charters and
may wish to consider entering into agreements on those issues with
the serving LEA or LEAs. However, if state law has not designated
the LEA for independent charter schools, each individual charter
school bears those LEA responsibilities.

LEA charter schools are free to enter into cooperative agreements or contracts with other agencies or schools to provide the
needed services. The manner in which a LEA charter school meets
these obligations is at the discretion of the school with oversight
from its chartering authority. The obligations may not, however, be
abrogated. Whatever arrangements a charter school makes to satisfy the IDEA's mandates, the school retains the responsibility to
ensure that all federal obligations are indeed being met.

An interesting issue that arises in the LEA charter school context might be termed the state statute conundrum (see Figure 8.1).
Seven states (Hawaii, Illinois, Mississippi, New York, Oregon, Pennsylvania, and Wisconsin) and the District of Columbia relieve charter schools from compliance with state statutes and rules regarding
special education. Idaho relieves charter schools from state rules,
but not its statutes. This relief creates an interesting situation for
those charter schools. These sources of state authority typically define how a state will implement the IDEA. State statutes and regulations often create more detailed eligibility definitions and criteria
for determining whether a child qualifies as a child with a disability beyond that delineated in the federal statute and regulations.
Whatever is contained within those exempted state provisions, according to federal law, an LEA charter school must adopt written
policies and procedures to implement the mandates of the IDEA
that must meet with the satisfaction of the state educational agency.[25]
Accordingly, LEA charter schools find themselves faced with a
choice. They must choose between (1) creating their own independent policies and procedures based solely on federal law and (2)
following the state's rules and regulations despite being technically
relieved from them. Many charter schools may decide that the most
practical route may be the latter, given the myriad other issues involved in charter school operation. In addition, because the SEA
must be satisfied with whatever is developed and the state statutes
and regulations effectively create an existing template, voluntary
compliance may be the simplest way to assure SEA satisfaction.

Figure 8.1. State Statute Conundrum for Independent LEA Charter Schools Relieved from State Special Education Statutes and Regulations

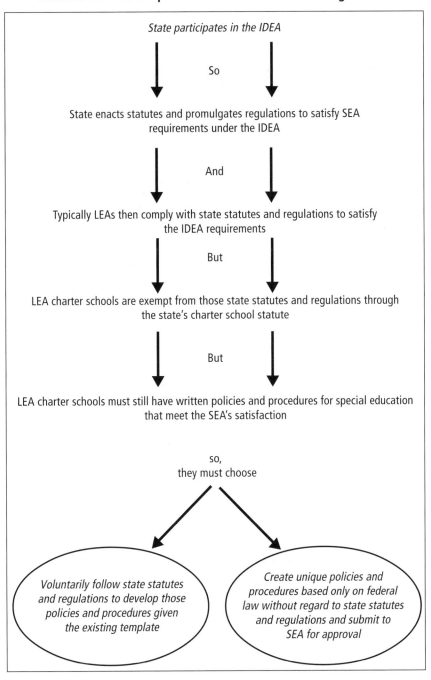

Charter schools located in states that allow schools to request waivers of state statutes and regulations (such as Kansas and Rhode Island) might also wish to consider this conundrum if they are contemplating petitioning the state for an exemption from state special education rules.

Finally, as explained in federal law, some charter schools are neither part of a larger LEA nor independent LEAs. It is for these schools that a section was added to the regulations when they were promulgated in 1999.[26] As explained by the U.S. Department of Education in the explanatory materials accompanying the release of the IDEA's final rules and regulations, the agency added this section to make clear congressional intent that all public charter schools comply with the IDEA. By creating this catch-all category, the regulations reiterate the state's ultimate obligation to ensure that the IDEA is fully implemented in all public schools. Additionally, this section makes explicit the requirement that all public charter schools must meet the IDEA mandates regardless of whether the IDEA funds are received by the school or not.[27] This section of the regulations also includes a provision that notes that SEAs may assign an entity to assume some or all of the "initial responsibility," but that the SEA bears ultimate responsibility for ensuring that compliance occurs in a consistent manner.[28] This provision would apply in Connecticut, New Hampshire, New York, and Oregon. In each of these states, legislatures have declined to name the charter school as the LEA or to make charter schools part of larger LEAs. Rather, each has created a situation in which the charter school and the resident school districts of its students must work together to be certain the needs of children with disabilities are met. As such, no single LEA is responsible for serving a particular charter school. The designation of responsibility to the resident district of each eligible charter school child means that charter schools with students from multiple districts will need to coordinate with more than one LEA for the purpose of serving their students with disabilities. In this situation, federal law serves as a reminder that the state must ensure that this process results in the proper implementation of the law where responsibility has not been assigned to a single entity.

As mentioned above, regardless of the type of charter school for special education purposes, the charter contract may contain provisions that add to or describe how obligations will be met. Therefore, charter schools must examine their contracts to determine whether there exist provisions specific to special education responsibilities. In addition, as with all contract provisions, care must be taken to ensure that charter contract provisions violate neither state nor federal law.

Two recent administrative decisions reaffirm charter schools' obligation to comply with the various provisions of the IDEA and provide illustrations of the definition of that obligation in a charter school context. A due process complaint against a Texas charter school succeeded because the parents demonstrated that their child did not receive the services necessary to achieve FAPE. The hearing officer also noted that even though the charter school was new and had limited resources it was still bound by all the IDEA requirements.[29] Lack of resources was no excuse for noncompliance. In a due process complaint against an Arizona charter school, a state hearing officer held for the parents, finding numerous procedural and substantive violations of the IDEA, involving a charter school's failure to appropriately address a child's learning disability.[30] In that case, the charter school had used a letter from personnel in the state department of education that provided erroneous advice concerning the charter school's obligations as a defense against the allegations. The hearing officer rejected this thinking, noting that following "flawed" advice provided no justification for ignoring the child's needs for special educational services. Both of these decisions and others like them reinforce the necessity of charter school personnel to fully understand the IDEA and its requirements.[31]

Given all these requirements, the following directives form a point of departure for charter school operators and their compliance with IDEA. They should:

1. Familiarize themselves with IDEA and its requirements;[32]
2. Determine whether, under state law, the school will be an LEA for the purposes of special education;
3. Consider whether any contract provisions are needed to make explicit the various responsibilities of the school and its authorizer, particularly if the authorizer is the school's LEA;
4. Adopt policies and procedures for compliance with IDEA's requirements;
5. Prepare materials to inform parents of their rights under IDEA;
6. Consider how the school will acquire the necessary expertise to evaluate and serve children with disabilities during the charter school design or development phase;
7. Train all staff concerning their role in IDEA implementation.

May a Charter School Serve Only Children with Disabilities?

Strict requirements under both the IDEA and the regulations of Section 504 mandate that children with disabilities be educated in the least restrictive environment (LRE) given their unique needs to the maximum extent appropriate. [33] That is, children with a disability are required to be educated with their nondisabled peers unless the nature and severity of the child's disability make achieving a free appropriate public education (FAPE) unfeasible in such a setting. The plain reading of these LRE requirements suggests that they may create an implementation challenge to a charter school developed to serve a special population of children with disabilities. In essence, school officials in such a charter school would have to ensure that each child enrolled could only receive a free appropriate public education in a setting essentially segregated from children without disabilities.

In fact, since the advent of various forms of public school choice, the Office of Special Education Programs (OSEP) of the United States Department of Education has long advised that parental choices must be consistent with FAPE and the LRE requirements of the IDEA and Section 504.[34] The fact that a parent chooses such a setting is irrelevant to the issue of whether it satisfies the dictates of federal disability law. As OSEP explained in response to an inquiry from Indiana officials regarding parents' selection of the Indiana School for the Blind or the Indiana School for the Deaf under statewide open enrollment, "[u]nder Part B [of the IDEA], parent preference cannot override the decision of the child's case conference [IEP] team."[35] Therefore, only those parental choices that are consistent with federal disability law can be honored. This long-held position of OSEP emphasizes the fact that FAPE is the child's entitlement, and parents may not waive their child's rights, even in the name of parental choice.

An examination of the U.S. Charter Schools web page maintained by the United States Department of Education reveals that over thirty schools[36] nationwide have been established under state charter school provisions that specifically target and/or limit their student populations to children with disabilities.[37] These charter schools have been designed to address the particular needs of children with learning disabilities, developmental and cognitive disabilities, autism, psychiatric disabilities, deafness, and hearing impairments. These schools must take particular care to ensure that, consistent with federal law, children enrolled in their schools have contact with nondisabled children to the "maximum extent appropriate." Fulfilling this obligation may even mean that some children will have to be denied admission if the child's nature and severity of disability is such that he or she should be educated in more typical classroom settings that include more contact with children without disabilities than is provided for at the special education charter school. Operationally, that would require that each prospective student's IEP be evaluated to determine whether the parent's choice could be honored. The IDEA requires that each child's IEP include "an explanation of the extent, if any, to which the child will not participate with nondisabled children in the regular class."[38] This provision creates a presumption of regular class placement[39] that cannot be ignored, regardless of school setting. A core principle of the IDEA is that programming (as defined by an IEP) must be designed to fit the child's needs. The IEP dictates placement (the special education services delivered and the environment in which delivery occurs). Placement does not dictate the IEP. Therefore, it would violate the IDEA to simply rewrite a child's IEP to comport with the characteristics of the special education charter school if the nature and severity of the child's disability did not direct that change.

Charter schools that serve students at risk for school failure may face a related problem. Although these schools do not target children with disabilities explicitly, the nature of the programming may be attractive to the parents of children with disabilities who struggle in traditional school settings. If the voluntary enrollment of students in such charter schools for at-risk populations results in significantly higher than average numbers of children with disabilities, it raises issues of whether the setting is integrated or segregated according to disability. Therefore, care will be necessary to ensure that children with disabilities have appropriate contact with children who are not disabled; otherwise the LRE provision of the IDEA may be violated.

Implications for Charter School Authorizers

Charter school authorizers (CSAs), regardless of whether they are also SEAs or LEAs, also play a role in ensuring that children with disabilities are appropriately served in charter schools. That role presents itself in four stages of the development and operation of a charter school: (1) proposal review, (2) charter contract negotiations, (3) oversight, and (4) contract renewal. First, authorizers must demand that charter school proposals clearly articulate how the school plans to meet the needs of students with disabilities. Are admissions processes nondiscriminatory with respect to disability? Has both physical and programmatic access for children with disabilities been considered and addressed in the school's design? Will the charter school hire its own personnel or contract with others for special education delivery? What other resources does the charter school expect to tap? Are there aspects of the proposed curriculum that might create an over- or under-representation of children with disabilities, either intentionally or unintentionally? If so, how will the charter school address the particular issues that arise in that instance?

The second point of consideration should be during charter school contract development. Schools at this point have cleared the proposal review and have entered into negotiations of contract provisions. It is important at this point to remember that contract provisions dictate the relationship between the school and the charter school authority. The manner and frequency of contract oversight, special educator hiring, special educator supervision, teacher training, adequate policy development, and funding are just a few of the issues that will need to be considered with regard to special education. Depending on the type of charter school, the charter school authorizer may wish to require further provisions to ensure that the charter school curriculum is provided consistent with federal disability law. For example, the authorizer may require that an LEA charter school provide copies of its special education policies and procedures to ensure that the school is satisfying its obligations.

Once the school becomes operational, the charter school authorizer's role shifts to oversight or contract supervision. The CSA periodically examines whether the charter school is in compliance with the charter school contract. This compliance review, whenever it occurs, should include an examination of whether children with disabilities are being appropriately enrolled and served in the charter school. Failure to properly serve children with disabilities could become an issue of revocation for the charter school during the term of the charter contract. Or if less severe problems occur, the CSA should at least insist that the charter school correct any inadequacies identified in this regard.

Finally, the CSA must consider renewal or nonrenewal of the charter at the end of the contract term. Again, the charter school's treatment of students with disabilities should be an issue used as part of the calculation to determine whether or not the charter contract will be renewed. In fact, in those states that do not specify cause for renewal, a charter school authorizer may determine not to renew a school's charter because it failed to attract adequate numbers of children with disabilities, even if the school adequately served those who did attend. The opposite might also cause concern; that a school over-enrolled children with disabilities, and the authorizer determined that public policy was not appropriately served by what some might describe as a school segregated on the basis of disability. If problems do not implicate outright nonrenewal, a CSA could require as a condition for renewal that a charter school create a plan to recruit more children with disabilities or more children without disabilities, as the case may be, in order to create a student body more reflective of expected local norms. Finally, CSAs should keep in mind that failure to take reasonable steps to ensure compliance with federal disability law may create legal vulnerability for the CSA if a child with a disability is not properly served. In any administrative due process hearing that ensued under either Section 504/ADA or the IDEA, the LEA would be named as the respondent. However, particularly when no single LEA is identified for a school, an attorney may believe it prudent to protect the child's interests by naming the school and the CSA as well as the "resident" school district, arguing that all played a role in the denial of FAPE for a particular child.

Conclusion

As the discussion in this chapter illustrates, a charter school must examine the interplay between federal law, state law, and its individual charter contract to fully understand its responsibilities for serving children with disabilities. Charter school personnel must develop a working knowledge of Section 504 and the IDEA, just as all of their public school colleagues must. The unique situations created by charter school statutes with respect to special education delivery can be complex. Understanding these issues and their implications for charter school design, contract development, and program delivery is necessary for all involved, so that charter schools truly stand as an educational option for all the public's children.

Endnotes

[1] 20 U.S.C. § 8066.
[2] 29 U.S.C. § 794; 34 C.F.R. 104 *et seq.*
[3] 20 U.S. C. 1400 et seq.; 34 C.F.R. 300 *et seq.*
[4] 42 U.S.C. § 12101 *et seq.* (1994).
[5] For a detailed explanation of Section 504 and the ADA, *see* D. Huefner, *Getting Comfortable with Special Education Law: A Framework for Working with Children with Disabilities* (2000).

[6] Boston (MA) Renaissance Charter School, 26 IDELR 889 (OCR 1997).

[7] The regulations define a person with a disability as someone who "(i) has a physical or mental impairment which substantially limits one or more major life activities, (ii) has a record of such an impairment, or (iii) is regarded as having such an impairment." 34 C.F.R. § 104.4(l).

[8] TOVAS Charter School, 37 IDELR 290 (OCR 2002).

[9] Nev. Rev. Stat. § 386.580(3).

[10] Jerry Horn & Gary Miron, *An Evaluation of the Michigan Charter School Initiative: Performance, Accountability, and Impact*, The Evaluation Center, Western Michigan University (2000); Thomas A. Fiore, et al., *Charter Schools and Students with Disabilities: A National Study, United States Department of Education, Office of Educational Research and Improvement* (2000).

[11] For a discussion of this issue see the transcript of a Special Education Workshop held at the 1997 Charter Schools National Conference. Tom Hehir, the Director of the Office of Special Education Programs and Anne Hoogstraten, then a Senior Staff Attorney for the Office of Civil Rights discuss this issue. Available at http://www.uscharterschools.org/lpt/uscs_docs/4.

[12] Lunar Letter, 17 EHLR 834 (OSEP 1991); Evans Letter, 17 EHLR 836 (OSEP 1991); Bina Letter, 18 IDELR 582 (OSEP 1991).

[13] *See* San Francisco Unified School District, 16 EHLR 824 (OCR 1990) (finding that parents enrolling their children in the district's alternative high schools could not be required or allowed to waive their children's right to special education services); Fallbrook Union Elementary Sch. Dist., 16 EHLR 754 (OCR 1990) (finding that a school district participating in California's statewide open enrollment program could not exclude children with disabilities even though meeting their needs increased costs to the district); Chattanooga (TN) Public Sch. Dist., 20 IDELR 999 (OCR 1993) (finding a violation of § 504 where the school district required parents to waive their children's rights to special education as a condition of participation in the district's magnet school programs).

[14] Helpful references on § 504/ADA include Perry A. Zirkel and Jeanne M. Kincaid, *Section 504, the ADA, and the Schools*. Horsham, PA: LRP Publications, 1995; Susan Gorn, What Do I Do When . . . The Answer Book on Section 504 (Horsham, PA: LRP Publications, 2000). In addition to many fine books detailing these laws, charter schools should access the resources available from their state educational agency on the topic. The U.S. Office for Civil Rights also provides assistance in understanding the dictates of § 504/ADA. Available at http://www.ed.gov/policy/rights/guid/ocr/disability.html (last visited Sept. 15, 2003).

[15] "A State is eligible for assistance…if the State demonstrates to the satisfaction of the Secretary that the State has in effect policies and procedures to ensure that….A free appropriate public education is available to all children with disabilities residing in the State between the ages of 3 and 21, inclusive, including children with disabilities who have been suspended or expelled from school." 20 U.S.C. § 1412(a).

[16] "A local educational agency is eligible for assistance…if such agency demonstrates to the satisfaction of the State educational agency that it…has in effect policies, procedures, and programs that are consistent with the State policies and procedures established under § 1412." 20 U.S.C. § 1413(a).

[17] It is beyond the scope of this chapter to provide an in-depth examination of all that IDEA entails. Numerous references are available that have accepted that

mission. *See, for example*, D. Huefner, *supra* note 5. For a short handbook on the subject developed especially for charter schools, see Elizabeth Giovannetti, et al., *Charter Schools and the Education of Children with Disabilities* (2001).

[18] For a pre-IDEA 97 discussion of charter school's responsibilities for children with disabilities, see Jay P. Heubert, *Schools without Rules? Charter Schools, Federal Disability Law, and the Paradoxes of Deregulation*, 32 Harv. C. R.-C.L. L. Rev. 303 (1997). Heubert argues that charter schools must fully implement IDEA and that doing so may be difficult given their size and focus. The amendments contained in IDEA 97 provide further foundation for Heubert's arguments.

[19] 20 U.S.C. § 1413(a)(5).

[20] *Id.*, § 1413(e)(1)(B).

[21] 34 C.F.R. § 300.312 (d)(1); The Office of Special Education Programs (OSEP) reaffirmed these requirements in a recent letter (Letter to Gloeckler, 33 IDELR 222 (OSEP 2000).

[22] 34 C.F.R. § 300.312(a).

[23] Letter to Bocketti, 32 IDELR 225 (OCR 1999). For a discussion regarding the inclusion of children with disabilities in parental choice plans, see Julie F. Mead, *Including Students with Disabilities in Parental Choice Programs: The Challenge of Meaningful Choice*, 100 Educ. L. Rep. 463 (1995).

[24] Or. Rev. Stat. § 338.165.

[25] 20 U.S.C. § 1413(a).

[26] 34 C.F.R. § 300.312(d).

[27] 64 Fed. Reg. 12546.

[28] 34 C.F.R. § 300.312(d)(2).

[29] Seashore Learning Center Charter School, 32 IDELR 224 (TX SEA 1999).

[30] The Basis School, 32 IDELR 187 (Arizona SEA 2000).

[31] *See also* Thompson v. Board of the Special Sch. Dist. No. 1, 144 F.3d 574 (8th Cir. 1998) (holding that when a child enrolled in a charter school, he could no longer file a complaint against his previous district as the charter school now was responsible for providing FAPE); Houston Independent Sch. Dist., 32 IDELR 79 (Texas SEA 1999) (finding for the parent in part in a dispute over the services provided a boy at a HISD charter school); Megan C. v. Independent Sch. Dist. No. 625, 30 IDELR 132 (D. Minn. 1999) (noting that when a mother withdrew her child from a district school and enrolled her at a charter school, the charter school became responsible for the development and implementation of an appropriate individualized educational program (IEP)); Letter to Stager, 33 IDELR 248 (OSEP 2000) (discussing requirement that charter schools accurately count children with disabilities and maintain adequate records to allow for an audit by state authorities); ABC Alternative Learning Center (OSERS 2002) (upholding the Arizona Department of Education's withholding of funds from the charter school in response to its failure to properly place a child with a disability after being ordered to do so).

[32] *See* Joseph R. McKinney. *Charter Schools' Legal Responsibilities Toward Children with Disabilities*, 126 Educ. L. Rep. 565 (1998); E. Ahearn, et al., *Project Search: Special Education as Requirements in Charter Schools, Final Report of a Research Study*, National Association of State Directors of Special Education (2001).

[33] 20 U.S. C. § 1412(a)(5)(A); 34 C.F.R. § 104.33(b).

[34] Lunar Letter, 17 EHLR 834 (OSEP 1991); Evans Letter, 17 EHLR 836 (OSEP 1991); Bina Letter, 18 IDELR 582 (OSEP 1991).

[35] Bina Letter, 18 IDELR 582 (OSEP 1991).

[36] This number is undoubtedly less than the actual number of charter schools designed for children with disabilities, as only those charter schools that have voluntarily completed profiles of their programs appear on the web site. Numerous charter schools of all types have not submitted information.

[37] The phenomenon was also noted by Fiore, *supra*, note 10.

[38] 20 U.S.C. § 1414(d)(1)(A)(iv).

[39] Senate Committee Report on Pub. L. N. 105-17, at 26. For a discussion of the statutory shift from a preference to a presumption for placement in regular classes, see Julie F. Mead, *Expressions of Congressional Intent*, 127 Educ. L. Rep. 511 (1998).

Chapter 9

Charter Schools and Religion

Religious institutions have expressed interest in operating charter schools. This interest may seem surprising because charter schools are public schools that must comply with the Establishment Clause of the Constitution.[1] Furthermore, religious institutions might soon have the opportunity to receive public funding through school voucher programs that give parents a percentage of their children's per-pupil allotment for public education to pay for the tuition at sectarian and nonsectarian private schools. In *Zelman v. Simmons-Harris*,[2] the Supreme Court held that such voucher programs are permissible under the Establishment Clause. Religious institutions might prefer to participate in voucher programs instead of charter schools because they could receive public money for their educational programs without having to comply with federal constitutional restrictions.

Despite these considerations, religious institutions have several reasons for participating in the charter school movement. First, many religious institutions already provide a variety of secular services, including housing, counseling, meals, athletics, daycare, and tutoring. Operating charter schools would be consistent with these secular activities. Second, charter schools may provide churches with a means of educating students who cannot afford to pay private tuition. Third, many religious institutions are struggling to keep their schools open because of declining enrollment. Charter schools may provide these institutions with the opportunity to stay involved in education. Fourth, charter schools may enable religious institutions to improve their educational programming. Parochial schools generally pay their teachers less than public schools. By operating charter schools, religious institutions would be able to pay higher salaries and thus possibly attract better teachers. Finally, charter schools have so far proven to be a more widespread opportunity for religious institutions to receive public funding for education than through school voucher programs. Thus, for the foreseeable future, charter schools provide religious institutions with a more likely option to receive public funds for education.

This chapter examines the legal issues involving religion that are raised by charter schools. First, federal and state statutory provisions that limit the involvement of religious institutions are identified. The second and third sections of this chapter examine whether a charter school statute that permits religious institutions to participate in the charter school movement could survive facial and "as applied" challenges under the Establishment Clause. Fourth, the question of whether state constitutional provisions prohibit the involvement of religious institutions in charter schools is explored. Fifth, the chapter looks at whether a charter school statute that prohibits religious institutions and their members from participating in charter schools violates the Equal Protection Clause. Finally, the constitutionality of four charter school practices that may implicate the Establishment Clause are examined: (1) teaching ethics and morality; (2) teaching creationism; (3) providing released time for religious instruction; and (4) providing after-school religious instruction on the grounds of a charter school that is operated by a religious institution.

State and Federal Statutory Provisions That Limit the Involvement of Religious Institutions

Religious institutions and their members might attempt to participate in charter schools in a variety of ways that might implicate statutory provisions prohibiting charter schools from being affiliated with religious institutions. Religious institutions might submit proposals to operate new charter schools or try to convert sectarian schools into charter schools. Members of the same religious institution might attempt to open a charter school in their individual capacities. Churches might enter into partnerships with charter schools to provide educational services. Finally, churches might agree to lease space to charter schools.

The interest of religious institutions in charter schools has raised concerns regarding the separation of church and state. Some charter school sponsors have rejected proposals for schools operated by religious institutions on the ground that they violate federal and state constitutional provisions. In 1999, for example, the Aurora, Colorado, school board rejected a charter school proposal by the Heritage Christian Center. Even though the proposed school's curriculum would have been religiously neutral, the school board observed that the operating board would have been composed primarily of church officials.[3] In 2002, the Utah Board of Education unanimously rejected a proposal for a Waldorf charter school, in part, because of concerns that the school would cross the line between the separation of church and state.[4] Waldorf education is based on the view that "man is a threefold being of spirit, soul, and body whose capacities unfold in three developmental stages on the path to adulthood: early childhood, middle childhood, and adolescence."[5] In fact, a California charter school using the Waldorf curriculum was challenged on precisely this basis. The district court dismissed the case on the ground that the group of challengers, taxpayers and citizens, lacked standing to bring the case. The Ninth Circuit Court of Appeals disagreed and held that because the plaintiffs had challenged the curriculum as a whole instead of selected activities, and that substantial public funds supported the schools, they had standing to bring the claim and the case survived the motion to dismiss.[6]

Federal and state charter school statutes contain a variety of provisions designed to limit the participation of religious institutions. The Federal Public Charter School Program (PCSP), which provides financial assistance for the planning, design, and implementation of charter schools, defines a charter school as "not affiliated with a sectarian school or religious institution."[7] Additionally, several charter school states and the District of Columbia have statutes that contain provisions that restrict the involvement of religious institutions in charter schools. Table 9.1 identifies states with such provisions. Ten states and the District of Columbia prohibit charter schools from being affiliated with religious institutions. Five states and the District of Columbia do not allow religious institutions to operate charter schools. New York prohibits charter schools from being under the control of religious institutions. Finally, two states forbid sectarian private schools from converting to charter school status, while permitting nonsectarian institutions to convert.[8]

Table 9.1. Charter School Statutes That Restrict Involvement of Religious Institutions

Prohibit Charter Schools from Being Affiliated with Religious Institutions[9]	Delaware, District of Columbia, Idaho, Louisiana, Minnesota, Nevada, North Carolina, Oklahoma, Oregon, Rhode Island, Tennessee[10]
Prohibit Charter Schools from Being Operated by Religious Institutions[11]	Arkansas, Delaware, District of Columbia, Ohio, Pennsylvania, Tennessee[12]
Prohibit Charter Schools from Being under the Control of Religious Institutions	New York
Permit Only Nonsectarian Private Schools to Convert to Charter School Status	Wisconsin, Utah

In December 2000, the Department of Education (DOE) under President William J. Clinton issued nonregulatory guidance that clarified how religious institutions might be involved in the charter school movement without violating the Constitution.[13] The first section of the nonregulatory guidance applied only to charter schools that received funding under the PCSP, which prohibits funding to charter schools that are affiliated with religious institutions. According to this section, private schools that had converted into charter school status were ineligible for PCSP funds. This interpretation would also prohibit parochial schools that had converted into charter schools from obtaining funds. The non-regulatory guidance did not specifically address whether charter schools that were operated by religious institutions could receive financial assistance from the PCSP. A DOE official explained that under the Clinton Administration's interpretation of PCSP, such schools would have been ineligible for federal funds.[14]

The second section of the noregulatory guidance applied to all charter schools, regardless of whether they received funds under the PCSP. This section explained that leaders of religious institutions could participate in the designing, organizing, or running of charter schools in their individual capacities, but not as representatives of their religious institutions. Additionally, the guidelines recommended that charter school governing boards not be composed primarily of individuals from the same religious organization.

The second section also observed that a charter school could contract with religious institutions for the provision of secular educational services, such as tutoring or recreational services. Such partnerships could exist as long as the schools selected partners based on religiously neutral criteria, made sure that no public funds were used to advance religion, and did not encourage religious activity. The second section referenced a set of guidelines issued by then Secretary of Education Richard Riley, "Guidelines for School Officials, Volunteers and Mentors Participating in Public School Partnerships."[15] The Public School Partnerships guidelines explained that public schools should ensure that any space used for the partnership was free from religion symbols and select students without regard to religious participation. Furthermore, schools were advised to remind volunteers not to pray with students or encourage them to pray during volunteer sessions, or preach about their faith while conducting their educational activities.

Finally, the second section addressed leasing arrangements between charter schools and religious institutions. A charter school may lease space from a religious institution so long as the school remained secular in its programs and operations. The nonregulatory guidance further advised that: (1) the charter school should select space based on religiously neutral criteria; (2) the space should be free of religious symbols, and (3) the charter school should control the space during school hours and school activities.

The administration of President George W. Bush has yet to issue guidelines on the extent to which charter schools may be connected with religious institutions. It is safe to say that President Bush would be more supportive of charter schools that are operated by religious institutions than was President Clinton. This is because President Bush has advocated the idea of "charitable choice": the provision of federal funds to faith-based institutions for public services.

Facial Challenges under the Establishment Clause

A statute that permits religious institutions to participate in the charter school movement might be subject to a facial challenge under the Establishment Clause. A facial Establishment Clause challenge would require a court to examine whether the statutory text was constitutional. The Supreme Court has developed multiple approaches to evaluate Establishment Clause challenges. Two of these approaches would probably be used to analyze facial challenges to charter school statutes: (1) the *Lemon* and *Agostini* tests; and (2) the endorsement test. Under the *Lemon* test, which was developed in *Lemon v. Kurtzman*, a statute is constitutional if it: (1) has a legitimate, secular purpose; (2) does not have the primary effect of advancing or inhibiting religion; and (3) does not create excessive entanglement between government and religion.[16]

In *Agostini v. Felton*, the Court modified the *Lemon* test. Under the *Agostini* test, a statute must still have a secular purpose, and not have the primary effect of advancing religion.[17] The Court, however, collapsed the entanglement prong into its analysis regarding the effect on religion.[18] Three criteria are used to determine whether a statute has the effect of advancing or inhibiting religion: whether the statute (1) results in government indoctrination of religious beliefs; (2) defines its recipients on the basis of religion; or (3) creates an excessive entanglement between the government and religion.[19]

Under the endorsement test, state action is unconstitutional if it "sends a message to nonadherents that they are outsiders, not full members of the political community, and an accompanying message to adherents that they are insiders, favored members of the political community."[20] In *School District of the City of Grand Rapids v. Ball*, the Supreme Court cautioned that this examination must be performed with particular care when young children are involved because "[t]he symbolism of a union between church and state is most likely to influence children of tender years, whose experience is limited and whose beliefs consequently are the function of environment as much as of free and voluntary choice."[21]

The Supreme Court's analysis in *Bowen v. Kendrick*,[21] suggests that a statute that permits religious institutions to be involved in charter schools might withstand a facial constitutional challenge under the *Lemon* and *Agostini* tests. *Bowen* involved the constitutionality of the Adolescent Family Life Act (AFLA), a statute that authorized federal grants to public or nonprofit private organizations or agencies for services and research regarding premarital adolescent sexual relations and pregnancy. The AFLA observed that the complexity of the problem required the involvement of a variety of services, including those provided by religious and charitable organizations. A variety of recipients received federal funding under the AFLA, including organizations with institutional ties to religious denominations. Applying the *Lemon* test, the Court ruled that the AFLA did not facially violate the Establishment Clause. The Court found that the statute was motivated primarily by the legitimate purpose of eliminating or reducing social and economic problems caused by teenage sexuality, pregnancy, and parenthood.

The Court found that the AFLA did not have the primary effect of advancing or inhibiting religion. A wide variety of organizations were eligible for funding, and nothing on the face of the statute suggested it was anything but neutral with respect to the grantee's status as a sectarian or secular institution. Also, nothing on the face of the AFLA indicated that a significant proportion of federal funds would be dispersed to "pervasively sectarian" institutions: institutions in which religion was so pervasive that a substantial portion of their functions was subsumed by the religious mission. Three factors reduced the risk of pervasively sectarian institutions receiving direct governmental aid: (1) the AFLA's facially neutral grant requirements; (2) the wide variety of public and private organizations that were capable of satisfying the statute's requirements; and (3) the fact that many eligible religious institutions were not pervasively sectarian.

Finally, the Court found that the statute did not create an excessive governmental entanglement with religion. Because the religious institutions that received grants from the AFLA were not pervasively sectarian, the government would not have to become involved in their day-to-day operations. Sufficient grant monitoring would include reviews of the programs set up by AFLA grantees, reviews of the materials that grantees planned to use, and visits to the offices where AFLA activities were being conducted. This type of monitoring would not constitute excessive entanglement.

Bowen suggests that a statute that permits religious institutions to operate charter schools might withstand a facial constitutional challenge under the *Lemon* test. With regard to the first prong, charter school statutes were enacted for several legitimate secular purposes, including: (1) improving student learning, (2) increasing educational opportunities for all students by encouraging the development of innovative instructional methods, (3) increasing educational choices for students and parents, and (4) increasing educational opportunities for teachers.

The statute might pass the second prong of the *Lemon* test by showing that it does not have the primary effect of advancing religion. The statute might use religiously neutral criteria to award charters, including the educational programming of the school, the educational outcomes to be achieved, and the school's governance structure. The crucial issue would be whether, on the face of the statute, charters would be awarded primarily to pervasively sectarian institutions. If this were the case, then the statute would be in trouble under the primary effect and entanglement prongs of the *Lemon* test.

Recall that *Bowen* identified three factors that reduced the risk of providing direct governmental aid to sectarian institutions: (1) the statute's neutral grant requirements, (2) the wide variety of eligible public and private organizations, and (3) the large number of eligible religious institutions that were not pervasively sectarian. These three factors might also apply to the charter school context. The charter school statute might use religiously neutral criteria to grant charters. Also, the statute might permit a wide variety of non-religious groups, including parents, public-school teachers, and not-for-profit organizations, to start charters. Moreover, in the "as applied" analysis, this chapter will show that charter schools operated by religious institutions might not be pervasively sectarian.

Finally, the charter school statute might avoid creating excessive government entanglement with religion. Sufficient monitoring might include the application and review process, in which the educational programming and materials are reviewed. Sponsors might also make unannounced visits to guard against the indoctrination of religion.

The Supreme Court's decision in *Board of Education of Kiryas Joel v. Grumet*,[23] would probably not warrant a different conclusion. In *Kiryas Joel*, the Supreme Court ruled that a New York statute that carved out a separate public school district along the village lines of a religious enclave violated the Establishment Clause. The Court observed that it had upheld statutes that granted benefits to religious institutions on the ground that such benefits were distributed in a religiously neutral fashion. By contrast, the New York statute was unconstitutional because the aid flowed only to a single sect. This reasoning suggests that a statute that grants charters in a religiously neutral fashion would not violate *Kiryas Joel*.

A statute that permits religious institutions to be involved in charter schools might also withstand a facial challenge under the endorsement test. In *Bowen*, the Supreme Court rejected the assertion that the involvement of religious institutions in the AFLA created an impermissible symbolic link between government and religion. The Court argued that such reasoning would forbid all governmental aid to religious institutions, even if the aid were used only for secular purposes like religiously affiliated hospitals. The Court concluded that whatever symbolic linkage was in fact created by the AFLA's disbursement of funds was insufficient to justify declaring the statute facially unconstitutional.

As-Applied Challenges under the Establishment Clause

A charter school statute that permits the participation of religious institutions might also be subject to "as-applied" challenges in which plaintiffs claim that the funding of certain charter schools violates the Establishment Clause. Recall that religious institutions and their members might attempt to become involved in charter schools in at least five ways. First, a religious institution might wish to operate a charter school in its official capacity. Second, parochial schools might seek to convert to charter school status. Third, members of religious institutions might seek charters in their individual capacity as concerned citizens. Fourth, charter schools might contract out to religious institutions for secular services. Fifth, charter schools might enter into leasing agreements with religious institutions. An analysis of as-applied challenges to each of these possible arrangements follows below.

Charter Schools That Are Operated by Religious Institutions

It might be possible for a charter school that is operated by a religious institution to survive an as-applied challenge under the Establishment Clause. The sponsor might satisfy the first prong of the *Lemon* and *Agostini* tests by showing that its decision to grant the charter was based on the educational value of the proposal. To withstand the remainder of the *Lemon* and *Agostini* tests, the sponsor would have to demonstrate that the school was not pervasively sectarian.[24]

In the context of higher education, the Supreme Court has twice found that church-operated colleges were not pervasively sectarian because they were operated in a secular manner. In *Tilton v. Richardson*,[25] the Supreme Court upheld the direct federal funding of building projects to four institutions that were governed by religious organizations. A plurality of the Court found that the projects did not have the primary effect of advancing religion. All four schools were characterized by academic freedom instead of religious indoctrination. The plurality also ruled that there was no danger of excessive entanglement. Because religious indoctrination was not a substantial purpose of these universities, the necessity for intensive governmental monitoring was greatly reduced.

In *Hunt v. McNair*,[26] the Court upheld the constitutionality of a South Carolina statute insofar as it authorized a proposed financial transaction between a state governmental agency and a college operated by the South Carolina Baptist Convention. The proposal called for the issuance of revenue bonds that the college would use to refine capital improvements and complete a dining hall. The Court ruled that the proposed transaction did not have the primary effect of advancing religion. The college was not pervasively sectarian because its operations were conducted in a secular fashion. Moreover, there was little danger of excessive entanglement because the college did not place special emphasis on any particular religion, or use religious criteria with respect to student admissions or faculty hiring.

In the context of elementary and secondary education, courts have used the term "pervasively sectarian" to define parochial schools. The Supreme Court has never made clear whether a school is automatically pervasively sectarian because it is operated by a religious institution. In *Meek v. Pittenger*,[27] the Court has suggested that an elementary or secondary school is not pervasively sectarian merely because a church operates it. In *Meek*, the Supreme Court ruled that a program authorizing the direct loan of instructional materials to nonpublic elementary and secondary schools had the unconstitutional effect of advancing religion because many of the participating schools were pervasively sectarian.

It is important to recognize that *Mitchell v. Helms* overturned *Meek*'s holding that pervasively sectarian institutions cannot receive direct governmental aid in the form of instructional materials. Still, *Meek's* discussion of the qualities of pervasively sectarian elementary and secondary schools is instructive in light of the fact that direct governmental aid to such institutions in the form of money might still be unconstitutional. In striking down the program, the Court noted that "[t]he very purpose of many of those schools is to provide an integrated secular and religious education; the teaching process is, to a large extent, devoted to the inculcation of religious values and belief,"[28] and "'the secular education those schools provide goes hand in hand with the religious mission that is the only reason for the schools' existence.'"[29]

Courts might conclude that charter schools that are operated by religious institutions might be more similar to church-operated universities than to parochial schools. This is because charter school sponsors could specifically prohibit charter schools from using religious restrictions in their admissions process and hiring practices, inculcating religious values, or requiring students to attend religious instruction.

Under the endorsement test, the crucial issue would be whether the general public and children attending charter schools would perceive an impermissible symbolic link.[30] If the charter school sponsor employed religiously neutral selection criteria to select the charter school, the general public might conclude that the granting of the charter was not an endorsement of religion.

The question of how students might perceive the granting of charters to religious institutions would be more complex. In *City of Grand Rapids*, the Supreme Court applied the endorsement test to invalidate two programs that provided supplementary classes primarily to parochial school students. Public school teachers taught these classes on parochial school grounds. To address Establishment Clause concerns, the classrooms bore signs identifying them as public school classrooms while the supplementary classes were in session. Despite the presence of the public school signs, the Supreme Court held that the two programs created an impermissible symbolic link between government and religion. Students were unlikely to tell the difference between the religious school classes and the supplementary public school classes, even if the latter did not have religious indoctrination.

In *Agostini*, the Supreme Court stated that it had rejected the presumption in *Grand Rapids* that the presence of public employees on parochial school premises, without more, created an impermissible symbolic link between church and state. Lower courts had uniformly permitted Title I remedial services to parochial school students off-campus. This notion presumed that the danger of a symbolic link disappeared once the services were provided off-campus. Therefore, the Supreme Court reasoned that there was no logical basis for finding that such services created an impermissible symbolic link when offered on-campus, but not when offered off-campus.

It is important to recognize that neither *Agostini* nor *Grand Rapids* addressed the question of whether children attending a church-operated public school would perceive an impermissible symbolic link between church and state. Because the schools in the *Grand Rapids* case were pervasively sectarian, students had a difficult time separating the sectarian from the secular. Children attending church-operated charter schools might not endure the same level of confusion if religion did not pervade the curriculum, and the classroom space was devoid of religious symbols.

The examination of a symbolic union would be more complex for charter schools than the Title I programs that were found constitutional in *Agostini*. One complicating factor would be the interplay between the age of the students and the location of the school. Elementary school children might perceive a symbolic union if the charter school were located in the same building that religious services were conducted, because they would have a difficult time differentiating between the building as a place for worship and a place for education. This confusion might still exist, even if the classroom within the building had no religious symbols. By contrast, elementary school children might be less likely to perceive an impermissible symbolic link if classes took place in a building separate from the place of worship. Such separation might enable children to distinguish more easily between the church's secular and sectarian roles. There would probably be less concern for older students. Because older students are more sophisticated, they might be less likely to perceive an impermissible symbolic link, even if the school were located on the premises.

Another complicating factor would be the composition of the teachers and administrators. Elementary school children might perceive an impermissible symbolic link if the teachers and administrators were also officers of the religious institution that was operating the charter school, because they might be unable to perceive a difference between the teachers' and administrators' secular and sectarian roles. Older students, on the other hand, might not have such difficulty.

Parochial School Conversions to Charter Schools

Parochial schools that convert to charter schools might survive an as-applied analysis. Under the *Agostini* and *Lemon* tests, the school would have to get rid of its sectarian status. A converted parochial school might accomplish this task by adopting a secular curriculum, admitting students without regard to religion, and keeping a separate accounting system. A school that undergoes this process might survive the *Agostini* and *Lemon* tests because the school could then be operated in a secular manner and have sufficient separation from the operation of the parent church.

Converted parochial schools might have a more difficult time surviving the endorsement test. Elementary school children might be unable to distinguish between the old parochial school and the new charter school. This issue would be especially problematic if the student body of the school remained relatively unchanged, even with a student lottery. Conversions that involve older children might withstand the endorsement test because they might be able to distinguish between the old parochial school and new charter school.

Converted parochial schools might also consider changing their names, so as not to include the identity of the religious institution. This act might signal to the general public and to students that the government was not sponsoring religion.

Charter Schools That Are Operated by a Majority of Members from One Religious Institution

A charter school with a governing board consisting primarily of members of the same religious institution might survive an as-applied challenge. If the governing board operates the school in a secular fashion, then under the *Agostini* and *Lemon* tests, such a school would not violate the Establishment Clause. A charter school whose majority membership comes from one religious institution might also survive an as-applied challenge under the endorsement test. If the board carries out its duties in a secular fashion, it would be improbable that either the general public or children would perceive governmental support of religion.

If a chartering authority were to refuse to grant a charter on the ground that the majority of the school's board consisted of members from a religious institution, it might also be vulnerable to a Free Exercise Clause challenge. As the Supreme Court explained in *Kiryas Joel*: "[G]roups of religious people . . . cannot be denied the opportunity to exercise the rights of citizens simply because of their affiliations or commitments, for such a disability would violate the right to religious free exercise."[31]

Partnerships for the Provision of Secular Services

It has been noted earlier in this chapter that the DOE has provided guidelines for school-community partnerships. The guidelines state that public schools should use neutral criteria to select organizations with which to contract, make sure that any space used for the partnership is free from religion symbols, and select students without regard to religious participation. Furthermore, schools are advised to remind volunteers not to pray with students or encourage them to pray during volunteer sessions, or preach about their faith while conducting their educational activities.

A contract between a charter school and a religious institution that follows the DOE guidelines might withstand the *Agostini* and *Lemon* tests. Such a contract would probably not advance religion because the charter school would have used religiously neutral criteria to select the institution. Also, the charter school would have taken steps to protect against religious indoctrination. The secular nature of the activity would probably not require excessive monitoring. By following the DOE guidelines, the contract might also survive an endorsement test challenge because the general public and children would probably not perceive governmental support of religion.

Leasing Agreements between Charter Schools and Religious Institutions

Porta v. Klagholz[32] shows that leasing agreements could probably withstand an as-applied analysis based on the *Agostini* and *Lemon* tests. Applying the *Agostini* test, the United States District Court of New Jersey upheld the constitutionality of a lease arrangement between the Soaring Heights Charter School, a K–4 school, and the Riverside Assembly of God Church. The court ruled that the lease agreement did not result in governmental indoctrination of religious beliefs. There was no evidence of religious symbols in the classroom area or in other areas used by the charter school. Also, the charter school's entrance was on the opposite side of the building from the only sign that identified the building as a church and contained religious messages. Furthermore, the church restricted the religious messages on the sign from noon to 1 P.M. on Sundays.

Second, the district court ruled that the charter school did not lease the space for religious reasons. On the contrary, the charter school leased the church space after engaging in an extensive search for affordable housing. Third, the lease arrangement did not create an excessive government entanglement with religion. The court found that the lease did not require pervasive monitoring to prevent religious indoctrination. The court also observed that the school's location in a church placed no real restrictions upon the normal operation and independence of the school. For example, the school had exclusive use of its space during all school functions, the pastor's office was off limits and unidentified, and the church made no use of the premises for worship services when the school was in session.

Leasing agreements between charter schools and churches might withstand the endorsement test as well. If a charter school used religiously neutral criteria to select the location, the general public might not view the charter school's location as support for religion. Charter schools could also take steps to ensure that the children attending the school would not perceive an impermissible symbolic link between church and state. First, charter schools could remove all religious iconography from school space. Second, the church should place no restrictions on school use of the building during school hours and during school functions. Third, the charter school should not use the name of the church from which it is renting the facilities.

State Constitutions

The constitutions of thirty-three states contain "Blaine Amendments," which prohibit state governments from providing governmental aid to sectarian institutions.[33] *Wilson v. State Board of Education*[34] indicates that courts might interpret these provisions to provide greater restrictions to religious participation in charter schools than the Establishment Clause. In *Wilson*, the California Court of Appeal stated that charter schools that were operated by churches would violate Article XVI, § 5 of the state constitution, which prohibits the funding of schools that are controlled by sectarian organizations. Additionally, the court found that a charter school that was merely associated with a religious institution would violate Article XVI, § 5.

Two Georgia attorney general opinions also suggest that state constitutional provisions might prove to be an effective bar to religious participation in charter schools. In 1969, the attorney general concluded that a contract in which a county paid a YMCA for the use of recreational facilities would violate Article I, § 2, Paragraph 7, of the state constitution, which forbids religious institutions to receive public funding.[35] Nineteen years later, in 1988, the attorney general advised that a contract in which a school system paid a sectarian institution for the provision of after-school care would also violate the state constitution.[36] These opinions are significant because they suggest that in Georgia, contracts that paid religious institutions for the provision of secular services to charter schools would violate the state constitution.

It is important to recognize that state courts might interpret these constitutional provisions in a more lenient fashion. The state high courts for Illinois,[37] and Wisconsin[38] have ruled that their state constitutions' Establishment Clause provisions are similar to that of the U.S. Constitution, even though the state provisions appear to prohibit religious institutions from receiving public funds. Furthermore, courts in states with restrictive constitutional provisions would probably not interpret their constitutional provisions to forbid members of a religious institution to operate a charter school in their individual capacity as concerned citizens. Courts might refuse to assume that members of a religious institution could not carry out their secular duties merely because they are members of a church.[39]

Equal Protection Clause

In the two previous sections, this chapter asserted that religious institutions might participate in the charter school movement without violating either the Establishment Clause or state constitutional provisions. Thus, if a charter school sponsor were to prohibit erroneously the participation of a religious institution on these grounds, the sponsor might be in violation of the Equal Protection Clause.

Bagley v. Raymond School Department[40] supports this assertion. In *Bagley*, plaintiffs claimed that a Maine education tuition statute violated the Equal Protection Clause by explicitly excluding private schools with religious affiliations. The state's sole justification for the classification was to comply with the Establishment Clause. The Supreme Judicial Court of Maine found that: "[i]f the State's justification is based on an erroneous understanding of the Establishment Clause, its justification will not withstand any level of scrutiny."[41] Applying the *Agostini* test, the court ruled that the participation of religious private schools would have had the primary effect of advancing religion because religious schools would have received direct monetary subsidies from the state.

Bagley suggests that the denial of the participation of a religious institution in a charter school might violate the Equal Protection Clause if the chartering authority's justification was to comply with

federal and state Establishment Clause provisions. It has been argued in this chapter that state and federal Establishment Clause
provisions might permit such participation. Thus, if a chartering
authority were to deny an application because it incorrectly concluded that the application violated federal or state Establishment
Clause provisions, it might violate the Equal Protection Clause.

By contrast, religiously neutral statutory provisions that have the
effect of restricting the involvement of religious institutions—such
as prohibitions of private school conversions—are less vulnerable to
Equal Protection Clause challenges. Chapter 2 points out that twenty-
seven states prohibit private schools to convert to charter school status. Such provisions would be subject to the rational basis test, which
requires the state to demonstrate that they are rationally related to a
legitimate governmental purpose. The state could probably demonstrate that these policies were rationally related to the legitimate governmental policy of promoting public education.

Practices That Might Face
Establishment Clause Challenges

Teaching Ethics and Morality

Several charter schools have academic themes that emphasize
the development of ethics and character. For example, California's
Westwood Charter Elementary School states that:

> The teaching of social and community ethics and values is an es-
> sential part of the curriculum and will be a part of every child's
> school day. . . . Teachers, students, and parents will discuss the
> need for good health and work habits and the importance of feel-
> ing successful. Children will have opportunities to show respon-
> sibility and leadership. . . . The instruction will also encourage stu-
> dents to respect diversity.[42]

The teaching of secular ethics does not implicate the Establishment Clause. However, the teaching of ethics and character from a
religious standpoint would violate the Establishment Clause. In
Daugherty v. Vanguard Charter School Academy,[43] the United States
District Court for the Western District of Michigan analyzed a claim
that a K–8 charter school was teaching ethical values in a religious
manner. The charter of the Vanguard Charter Academy included
the goals of fostering moral character development and good citizenship. To accomplish these goals, Vanguard employed a "Moral
Focus Curriculum," based on the four Greek cardinal virtues that
embodied certain transcendent moral principals: prudence, temper-

ance, fortitude, and justice. The school identified nine elements that were derived from these four virtues. "Prudence" included respect and wisdom. "Temperance" included gratitude, self-control, and encouragement. "Fortitude" embodied courage and perseverance. "Justice" included compassion and integrity. Vanguard teachers emphasized one of these nine elements each of the nine months of the school year.

The district court found that the Moral Focus Curriculum did not violate the Establishment Clause on its face. In analyzing the case, the court merged the *Lemon* and endorsement tests. The curriculum satisfied the first prong of the merged *Lemon* test because it had the secular purposes of promoting moral character development and good citizenship. The curriculum did not violate the merged *Lemon*/endorsement test at face value because it did not convey to a reasonable observer that the statute supported religion. The fact that the curriculum used concepts in the development of character that coincided with religious beliefs would not lead a reasonable person to conclude that the curriculum endorsed religion. Also, Vanguard's policies indicated neutrality, rather than endorsement of religion. Vanguard's Declaration of Moral Purpose stated that the school's moral purpose was not religious in nature, but was rather based on commonly held, historic values that were not based on religious beliefs. The board's policies recognized the legitimacy of teaching about the role of religion in society, but cautioned against the indoctrination of religion, or promotion of any particular view.

Next, the district court examined whether Vanguard Academy could be held liable for the teachers' alleged violations of school policies. The court found that Vanguard could be held liable only if (1) the teachers had violated school policies in such a way as to be viewed as an endorsement of religion; and (2) the school had tacitly approved "such abuses through their deliberate indifference."[44] The court refused to hold the school liable for an incident in which a fifth- or sixth-grade student offered an animated videotape around Christmas time, which recounted the origins of Christmas and the birth of Jesus. The videotape was not an ordinary part of the curriculum, but was provided by a student. The teacher did not use the tape as a catalyst for indoctrination and made no comment about the tape in class. Additionally, there was little risk that the students would perceive the school of endorsing Christianity because the viewing of the film took place in a world religion class in conjunction with materials concerning other religious traditions.

The court also refused to hold the school liable for parent volunteers' reading aloud Bible stories during the lunch recess while students were in the classroom. Although reading aloud Bible stories was a questionable practice, this did not justify a reasonable perception of religious endorsement by the school because parents, not teachers, did the reading during noninstructional time when children were free to listen. Moreover, there was no evidence that school administrators were aware of the parents' practice and had rejected or ignored any complaints. Furthermore, the court refused to hold Vanguard liable for a substitute teacher's reading two stories to a student relating to Jesus' birth. There was no deliberate indifference because the principal, upon learning of this, instructed the substitute teacher not to read religious stories in the future.

Finally, the court ruled that the Moral Focus Curriculum did not create an excessive entanglement between government and religion. The court observed that "the Moral Focus Curriculum demands vigilance and diligence . . . to ensure that Vanguard's policy on Teaching About Religion is carefully adhered to. There are risks that the line between teaching virtue or 'teaching about religion,' on the one hand, and 'teaching religion,' on the other hand, will not always be perfectly observed."[45] However, the school's Declaration of Moral Purpose, the Moral Focus Curriculum, and the board's policies regarding the teaching of religion and First Amendment issues provided sufficient guidelines for monitoring.

The *Daugherty* case illustrates the importance of providing parental volunteers with instruction regarding the First Amendment rights of students in carrying out the dictates of a character-building curriculum. The district court in *Daugherty* ruled that a reasonable student in the K–8 charter school would not view the volunteers' reading Bible stories as school endorsement of religion because (1) parents, not teachers did the reading; and (2) the reading took place during noninstructional class time. Other courts might find, however, that elementary school students are unable to make these distinctions, and thus conclude that the actions of the volunteers reflect the views of the school. Therefore, charter school administrators should remind volunteers not to preach about their faith or engage in prayer during their volunteer work.

Teaching Creationism

Several charter schools teach creationism as a scientific theory that competes with evolution. For instance, Excel Charter Academy permits teachers to teach evolution and creationism in fourth-grade science classes.[46] The leading case that addresses the teaching of creationism as an alternative to evolution is *Edwards v. Aguillard*.[47] Applying the *Lemon* test, the Supreme Court held that Louisiana's Creationism Act, which forbade the teaching of evolution unless accompanied by "creation science," violated the Establishment Clause. The Court found that there was no legitimate, secular purpose for the statute. Outlawing the teaching of evolution or requiring the teaching of creation science did not further the goals of providing a more comprehensive curriculum or promoting academic freedom. Instead, the Court ruled that the Creationism Act's primary purpose was to endorse the theory of creationism. By ruling in this manner, the Court "did not imply that a legislature could never require that scientific critiques of prevailing scientific theories be taught. . . . [T]eaching a variety of scientific theories about the origins of humankind to schoolchildren might be validly done with the clear secular intent of enhancing the effectiveness of science instruction."[48] *Edwards* suggests that a charter school could teach creationism along with a variety of theories regarding the origin of life, including evolution, without violating the Establishment Clause. The school would also have to be sure to teach only what creationism says. Teaching creationism as a fact or to compel belief would be unconstitutional.

In *Daugherty*, the Western District Court of Michigan rejected the plaintiffs' claim that the Vanguard Academy was teaching creationism in violation of the Establishment Clause. Plaintiffs referred to incidents in which a visiting teacher answered science questions by referring to God and another teacher suggested that evolution was not true. The court found that neither episode indicated that creationism was taught as an accepted scientific theory in Vanguard Academy. In both instances, the court found that the complained of "teaching" was triggered by particular circumstances arising in the classroom and not an official policy compelling or permitting the teaching of creationism.

Providing Released Time for Religious Instruction

Several charter schools have provided students with the opportunity to leave school grounds during the school day to obtain religious instruction. In *Zorach v. Clauson*,[49] the Supreme Court found that such release time programs do not violate the Establishment Clause. *Zorach* involved a New York City program that permitted public schools to release students during the school day to go to religious centers. Students had to obtain written permission from their parents to be released from class. The Court found that the released time program violated neither the Establishment Clause nor the Free Exercise Clause because school authorities acted neutrally and did not coerce students to participate. The Court went on to explain that the Establishment Clause permitted public schools to adjust their schedules to accommodate the spiritual needs of their students. In providing these accommodations, however, the government must refrain from advocating any particular religious belief, or coercing students to act in a religious manner.

Finally, the Court distinguished *Zorach* from a previous case, *Illinois* ex rel. *McCollum v. Board of Education of School District No. 71, Champaign County, Illinois.*[50] In *McCollum*, the Court had ruled that a released time program in which religious groups came into public school classrooms to provide religious instruction violated the Establishment Clause. The *McCollum* Court found that the public school system actually promoted religion. By contrast, in *Zorach*, the public schools did no more than adjust their schedules to a program of outside religious instruction. *Zorach* suggests that charter schools may provide released time for religious instruction as long as (1) the instruction takes place outside school grounds; (2) the schools act in a neutral fashion; and (3) the schools do not coerce students to attend religious services.

Providing After-School Religious Instruction

A charter school that is operated by a religious institution might consider providing after-school religious instruction in the school's facilities. Under the *Lemon* and *Agostini* tests, the critical question would be whether such instruction would advance religion. This chapter has asserted that charter schools that are operated in a secular fashion might not be considered pervasively sectarian. Under this logic, it would follow that the charter school and the religious institution were separate entities. Thus, the church's provision of after-school religious instruction on school grounds might be permissible under the *Agostini* and *Lemon* tests because the instruction would not be attributable to the school.

It might be argued that a church's after-school religious instruction in the facilities of its charter elementary school would violate the endorsement test. *Good News Club v. Milford Central School,*[51] raises doubts about this argument. In *Good News Club*, the Supreme Court held that a public school's exclusion of a Christian children's club from meeting after hours because of the religious nature of the club violated the club members' free speech rights. The school argued that its prevention of the club from using its facilities was necessary to avoid an Establishment Clause violation because elementary school children would perceive that the school was endorsing the club. The Court observed that avoiding an Establishment Clause violation may justify content-based discrimination. However, the school had no valid Establishment Clause interest because:

> [w]hatever significance we may have assigned in the Establishment Clause context to the suggestion that elementary school children are more impressionable than adults, . . . we have never extended our Establishment Clause jurisprudence to foreclose private religious conduct during nonschool hours merely because it takes place on school premises where elementary school children may be present.[52]

It is important to recognize that a church-operated charter elementary school adds a level of complexity not contemplated by *Good News Club*. This chapter has already pointed out that children attending such a school might have a difficult time distinguishing between a religious institution's secular and sectarian activities. Thus, children might be unable to tell the difference between religious and secular activities that the church is conducting on school grounds. This confusion might be compounded if the same persons who run the charter school provide after-school religious instruction. To avoid such confusion, a charter elementary school that is operated by a religious institution should consider conducting religious activities outside of school facilities. Also, employees of the school should consider not providing this instruction.

A finding that the religious institution and the charter school that it operates are separate entities has important implications for other organizations that wish to use the school's facilities for after-school purposes. By providing after-school religious instruction on the grounds of its charter school, the religious institution might convert the charter school into a limited public forum under the First Amendment. Consequently, the school might not be able to prohibit organizations from using the facilities because it disagrees with their viewpoints.

Conclusion

This chapter has examined the legal issues regarding religion that arise in the charter school context. A statute that permits such participation might survive a facial constitutional challenge under the Establishment Clause if the statute selects participants in a religiously neutral fashion, does not result in a significant number of charters being awarded to pervasively sectarian institutions, and contains sufficient monitoring provisions. Also, under certain circumstances, religious institutions that participate in the charter school movement might be able to withstand as-applied Establishment Clause challenges. Although the constitutions of a number of charter school states appear to place more restrictions on the involvement of religious institutions in the charter school movement than the Establishment Clause, state courts might interpret these constitutional provisions in a more lenient fashion.

A charter school sponsor might be vulnerable to Equal Protection Clause challenges if it prohibits religious institutions and their members from participating in the charter school movement. If the sponsor's rationale is based on an incorrect understanding of the Establishment Clause or state constitutional counterpart, then its action might be unconstitutional. On the other hand, religiously neutral restrictions that have the effect of preventing religious institutions from operating charter schools could probably withstand Equal Protection Clause challenges.

Moreover, several charter schools may engage in activity that implicates the Establishment Clause. Charter schools may use curricula that have a moral focus as long as their instruction does not have a religious viewpoint. Charter schools may provide instruction on creationism as long as they teach a variety of theories regarding the origins of life in an evenhanded manner. Charter schools may provide released time for religious instruction as long as the instruction takes place outside school grounds; the schools act in a neutral fashion; and the schools do not coerce students to attend religious services. Charter schools that are operated by religious institutions might be able to provide after-school religious instruction on school grounds without violating the Establishment Clause. However, the constitutionality of this practice with respect to church-operated charter elementary schools is debatable. Furthermore, providing after-school religious instruction on charter school grounds might convert the church-operated charter school into a limited public forum. Such a finding would prevent the school from denying the use of facilities to other organizations because the church disagreed with their viewpoints.

Endnotes

[1] William Anderson, Jr., *Religious Groups in the Educational Marketplace: Applying the Establishment Clause to School Privatization Programs*, 82 Geo. L.J. 1869 (1994).

[2] 122 S. Ct. 2460 (2002).

[3] Andrew Guy Jr., *Church Set to Appeal Denial of Charter School*, Denver Post, Dec. 23, 1999, at B2.

[4] Ronnie Lynn, *Charter Proposals Rejected*, Salt Lake Tribune, Nov. 5, 2002, at B8.

[5] Henry Barnes, *Waldorf Education . . . An Introduction,* available at http://www. awsna.org/education-intro.html (viewed Jan. 25, 2003).

[6] PLANS, Inc. v. Sacramento City Unified Sch. Dist., 319 F.3d 504 (9th Cir. 2003).

[7] 20 U.S.C.S. § 7221i(1)(E).

[8] It is also important to observe that a number of states prohibit charter schools from being sectarian schools. Such prohibitions raise the question of whether charter schools become sectarian merely because religious institutions operate these schools. This chapter's discussion on the components of pervasively sectarian schools indicates that it might be possible for charter schools to be run by religious institutions without being sectarian.

[9] Michigan's statute forbids charter schools to be affiliated with religious institutions to the same extent that such affiliations are forbidden by the U.S. Constitution.

[10] Tennessee's statute prohibits charter school sponsors from "promot[ing] the agenda of any religious denomination or religiously affiliated entity." Tenn. Code Ann. § 49-13-104(7).

[11] Michigan's statute forbids charter schools to be organized by religious institutions to the same extent that these organizations are forbidden by the U.S. Constitution.

[12] Tennessee's statute prohibits charter school sponsors from being a "religious or church school." Tenn. Code Ann. § 49-13-104(7).

[13] U.S. Dep't of Educ., Office of Elementary and Secondary Educ., Public Charter Schools Program: Nonregulatory Guidance available at http://www.uscharterschools.org/lpt/uscs_docs/49.

[14] Telephone Interview with Alex Medler, Charter School Consultant, U.S. Dept. of Educ. (May 25, 2001).

[15] U.S. Dep't. of Educ., *Guidelines for School Officials, Volunteers and Mentors Participating in Public School Community Partnerships* (last modified Dec. 15, 1999), available at http://www.ed.gov/inits/religionandschools/v-guide.html.

[16] 403 U.S. 602, 612–613 (1973).

[17] 521 U.S. 203, 222–223 (1997).

[18] *Id*. at 232–233.

[19] *Id*. at 234.

[20] Lynch v. Donnelly, 465 U.S. 688 (O'Connor, J., concurring).

[21] 473 U.S. 373, 390 (1985).

[22] 487 U.S. 589 (1988).

[23] 512 U.S. 687 (1994).

[24] In Mitchell v. Helms, 530 U.S. 793 (2000), the Supreme Court indicated that the pervasively sectarian doctrine is in jeopardy, but is still applicable. In *Mitchell*, the Court upheld the constitutionality of Chapter 2 of the Educational Consolidation and Improvement Act of 1981, which provides federal funds to elementary and secondary public and private schools in the form of instructional materials and educational equipment. A plurality of four justices declared that it would no longer apply the pervasively sectarian doctrine in determining the constitutionality of a governmental funding program. However, Justice O'Connor, in a concurring opinion joined by Justice Breyer, limited her holding

to the false differences between direct aid in the form of instructional materials and educational equipment.

[25] 403 U.S. 672 (1971).

[26] 413 U.S. 734 (1973).

[27] 421 U.S. 349 (1975).

[28] *Id*. at 366.

[29] *Id*. (quoting *Lemon*, 403 U.S. at 616–617).

[30] *See* Anderson, *supra* note 1, at 1892 (analyzing the constitutionality of school privatization statutes).

[31] 512 U.S. at 698.

[32] 19 F. Supp. 2d 290 (D.N.J. 1998).

[33] Toby J. Heytens, Note, *School Choice and State Constitutions*, 86 Va. L. Rev. 117, 123 n.32 (2000). These states are as follows: Alaska, Arizona, California, Colorado, Delaware, Florida, Georgia, Hawaii, Idaho, Illinois, Indiana, Kentucky, Massachusetts, Michigan, Minnesota, Missouri, Montana, Nebraska, New Hampshire, New Mexico, New York, North Dakota, Oklahoma, Oregon, Pennsylvania, South Carolina, South Dakota, Texas, Utah, Washington, Wisconsin, and Wyoming.

[34] 89 Cal. Rptr. 2d 745 (Ct. App. 1999).

[35] 1969 Ga. Op. Att'y Gen. No. 69-136.

[36] 1988 Ga. Op. Att'y Gen. No. U88-6.

[37] People *ex rel*. Klinger v. Howlett, 305 N.E.2d 129 (Ill. 1973).

[38] Jackson v. Benson, 578 N.W.2d 602 (Wis. 1998).

[39] *See, e.g.*, Grumet v. Cuomo, 625 N.Y.S.2d 1000 (S. Ct. 1995) (finding that a school district whose board of education consisted of entirely members from one religious sect did not violate state constitutional provision prohibiting public funding of any school wholly or in part under the control or direction of a religious institution); *rev'd on other grounds*, 647 N.Y.S.2d 565 (A.D. 1996).

[40] 728 A.2d 127 (Me. 1999).

[41] *Id*.

[42] Westwood Charter Elementary School, Social And Community Ethics and Values, available at http://www.westwoodcharter.org/ethics.html (last visited on Jan. 21, 2003).

[43] 116 F.Supp. 2d 897 (W.D.Mich. 2000).

[44] *Id*. at 914.

[45] *Id*. at 915.

[46] The Evaluation Ctr., Western Michigan University, *The Impact of Charter Schools on Public and Parochial Schools: Case Studies of School Districts in Western and Central Michigan* (2000) 13, available at http://www.wmich.edu/evalctr/charter/michigan/district_impact_report.pdf (last visited Jan. 23, 2003).

[47] 482 U.S. 578 (1987).

[48] *Id*. at 593–594.

[49] 343 U.S. 306 (1952).

[50] 333 U.S. 203 (1948).

[51] 533 U.S. 98 (2001).

[52] *Id*. at 115.

Chapter 10

Charter Schools and the Rights of Parents and Students

Charter schools have adopted a variety of strategies to maximize the educational benefits for their students and parents. This chapter explores some of the legal issues surrounding these policies. First, the constitutionality of mandatory uniform policies will be examined. Second, this chapter analyzes whether charter schools that serve chemically dependent students or court-adjudicated youth may implement random urinalysis testing as a condition of enrollment. Third, the legality of parental involvement contracts is examined. Finally, this chapter looks at the legal implications that arise from charter school discipline policies.

Mandatory Uniform Policies

In recent years, many public schools have adopted mandatory uniform policies. According to the Educational Resources Information Center (ERIC) Clearinghouse on Educational Management, proponents have advanced four arguments for the adoption of mandatory uniform policies.[1] First, mandatory uniform policies may enhance safety. For instance, such policies protect against the dangers of gang-style clothing. Students who wear such clothing in school may be targets for violence. Gang-style clothes are often loose-fitting, thus providing students with the opportunity to bring weapons and drugs into school. Second, mandatory uniform policies may improve student performance. Students may be able to focus on their academic work instead of on what other students are wearing. Uniform policies might also increase respect for teachers, improve school attendance, and improve classroom behavior. Third, uniform policies may enhance self-esteem for students by concealing their socioeconomc status, and encouraging students to find more productive ways to express their individualism. Finally, mandatory uniform policies might reduce stress on the family by relieving the economic strain caused by buying expensive clothes.

A number of charter schools have followed this trend by adopting mandatory uniform policies for their students. For example, the

Pocatello Community Charter School, a K–7 school located in Idaho, argues that "[s]chool uniforms help keep the focus in the school on academics—not fashion. Uniforms provide a sense of pride and unity among school participants as well."[2] Because charter schools are public schools, their uniform policies must adhere to the Constitution. Such policies might be subjected to Free Speech Clause, and substantive due process challenges. Plaintiffs might also try to mount hybrid challenges to mandatory uniform policies that combine substantive due process and the Free Exercise Clause. An analysis of each of these possible challenges follows below.

Free Speech Clause

Plaintiffs might argue that a mandatory uniform policy violates their First Amendment right to free speech by preventing student expression. The Supreme Court has issued three decisions regarding student speech restrictions. In *Tinker v. Des Moines Independent Community School District*,[3] the Court held that school officials may restrict the expression of particular viewpoints only upon demonstrating that the expression would substantially interfere with the operation of the school. In *Bethel School District v. Fraser*,[4] the Court found that school officials may restrict lewd or obscene speech. In *Hazelwood School District v. Kuhlmeier*,[5] the Court held that school officials may regulate school-sponsored activities such as student publications, as long as their actions were reasonably related to legitimate pedagogical concerns.

In two cases, the Fifth Circuit upheld mandatory uniform policies. In each case, the court declined to use the analyses developed in *Tinker*, *Bethel*, or *Hazelwood*. In *Canady v. Bossier Parish School Board*,[6] the Fifth Circuit held that a Louisiana school board's uniform policy did not violate the Free Speech Clause. The policy did not fit under *Tinker* because it was viewpoint-neutral on its face and as applied. *Bethel* was inapplicable because school officials had not punished students for wearing clothing with lewd or obscene words or pictures. *Hazelwood* did not apply because a student's decision to wear certain clothing to school was neither an activity that was sponsored by the school nor was related to the school curriculum.

Instead, the Fifth Circuit applied the framework established by the Supreme Court in *United States v. O'Brien* for content-neutral restrictions of speech. Under the *O'Brien test*, a content-neutral restriction would be constitutional if (1) it was within the constitutional power of the government; (2) it furthered an important or substantial governmental interest; (3) the interest was unrelated to the suppression of student expression; and (4) the incidental restrictions on First Amendment activities were no more than was necessary to facilitate that interest.[7] Applying the *O'Brien* test, the Fifth Circuit upheld the uniform policy. The policy furthered the governmental interests of improving student behavior and test scores and was unrelated to the suppression of student speech. Furthermore, the policy did not prevent students from wearing what they wanted after school hours or expressing their views through non-clothing-related mediums during the school day.

In *Littlefield v. Forney Independent School District*,[8] the Fifth Circuit applied the *O'Brien* test to uphold a Texas school district's mandatory uniform policy. First, the court found that the school district had the power to pass the policy under state law. Second, the policy satisfied the important and substantial interests of improving student performance, instilling self-confidence, fostering self-esteem, increasing attendance, decreasing disciplinary referrals, and lowering drop-out rates. Third, the policy was adopted for reasons unrelated to the suppression of expression, such as increasing safety, decreasing socioeconomic tensions among students, and increasing attendance. Finally, the restrictions pertained only to student attire during school hours and did not affect other means of communication.

Canady and *Littlefield* suggest that a charter school's mandatory uniform policy is likely to withstand a free speech challenge. The policy might satisfy the first prong of the *O'Brien* test because enabling statutes give charter schools a lot of flexibility in developing educational programming. As for the second prong, the charter school might be able to demonstrate that the uniform policy advances several legitimate interests, such as increasing attendance and lowering drop-out rates. These asserted educational interests would probably satisfy the third prong of *O'Brien* because they are unrelated to student expression. Finally, the uniform policy would probably satisfy the last prong of *O'Brien* if the policy applied only to student attire during school hours and did not affect other means of communication.

Substantive Due Process

A charter school's mandatory uniform policy might be subject to two substantive due process claims: (1) the liberty interest of children to wear the clothing of their choice while at school and (2) the rights of parents to direct the upbringing and education of their children. *Littlefield* suggests that these claims might fail. In this case, a Texas school district adopted a policy that limited students' choice of clothing during school hours. Boys were required to wear khaki or navy blue pants or shorts, along with a white-, red-, yellow-, or blue-collar shirt. The policy afforded girls with similar color choices, and permitted them to wear skirts or "jumpers" of a prescribed length. Denim, leather, and suede were prohibited, except as an outer garment such as a jacket or coat. Students were prohibited from wearing any clothing in a manner suggesting gang affiliation, and manufacturer logos were limited in size.

The United States District Court for the Northern District of Texas rejected the claim that the uniform policy deprived students of their liberty interest to wear the clothing of their choice while at school. Although children had a general liberty interest in wearing the clothing of their choice while at school, the court found that strict scrutiny was inapplicable because this right did not rise to the level of fundamental significance. Applying the rational basis test, the court upheld the uniform policy. It served the legitimate educational objective of improving the learning environment. The policy also caused minimal intrusion upon the students' liberty interest because they could take off their uniforms after school.

The district court also rejected the claim that the uniform policy violated the parents' substantive due process right to direct the upbringing and education of their children. It found that *Wisconsin v. Yoder*,[9] a case in which the Supreme Court invalidated a compulsory education law as applied to Amish children, did not mandate the application of strict scrutiny analysis. The district court observed that heightened scrutiny was applied in *Yoder* because the parents' substantive due process claim was made in conjunction with a free exercise claim under the First Amendment. *Yoder* also made clear that the substantive due process claim, standing alone, would have warranted only rational basis review. Applying the rational basis test, the district court concluded that the policy was rationally related to the governmental interest of furthering education.

Hybrid Constitutional Claims

In *Employment Division, Department of Human Resources v. Smith*,[10] the Supreme Court held that facially neutral laws that incidentally burdened religiously motivated conduct would not be subject to strict scrutiny. However, *Smith* also suggested that strict scrutiny would apply to "hybrid" situations, such as *Yoder*, in which the parents' free exercise claim was made in conjunction with a parental substantive due process claim. Plaintiffs might attempt to make a hybrid-rights challenge to a charter school's mandatory uniform policy, thus subjecting it to strict scrutiny. If strict scrutiny were applicable, a charter school would have to demonstrate that the uniform policy was narrowly tailored to satisfy a compelling governmental interest.

Circuit courts have developed three approaches to hybrid-rights claims. The Sixth Circuit[11] has refused to recognize hybrid-rights claims until the Supreme Court instructs it to do so. The First Circuit[12] has held that the hybrid-rights exception applies only in situations where an independently viable claim was made in conjunction with the free exercise claim. The Ninth[13] and Tenth[14] Circuits have adopted a "colorable-claim" approach to hybrid-rights cases, which requires plaintiffs to show an infringement of recognized constitutional rights.

Two federal district courts have examined whether mandatory uniform policies fall under the *Smith* hybrid-rights exception. In *Hicks v. Halifax County Board of Education*,[15] the Eastern District of North Carolina used colorable-claims analysis to find that *Smith's* hybrid-claims exception was applicable and that the policy should be subject to strict scrutiny. A great-grandmother alleged that a school district's uniform policy violated her free exercise right because adherence to the policy demonstrated support of the Anti-Christ, a being that required enforced conformity and absence of diversity. She also asserted that the policy violated her right to direct the religious upbringing of her great-grandchild. The Eastern District rejected the defendants' motion for summary judgment because the great-grandmother's claim fell within *Smith's* hybrid-rights exception and was entitled to strict scrutiny. The court found that the plaintiffs had made a genuine claim of a constitutional infringement that was supported by the record.

In *Littlefield*, however, the Northern District of Texas employed independently viable claims analysis to hold that the school district's uniform policy did not fall under *Smith's* hybrid-rights exception. In refusing to apply strict scrutiny, the court found that the plaintiffs' free exercise claims were substantially weaker than the claims considered in *Yoder*. In *Yoder*, the Amish parents had made a convincing showing that the compulsory attendance law would undermine their way of life. By contrast, plaintiffs in *Littlefield* failed to show how the uniform requirement would have appreciably affected their religious practices. Applying the rational basis test, the court concluded that the policy was rationally related to the legitimate governmental interest of improving the learning climate in the district's schools.

Submission to Random Urinalysis
as a Condition of Attendance

According to the Association of Recovery Schools,[16] seventeen schools in eight states and the District of Columbia serve students who are recovering from chemical dependency. Given the country's concern with chemical dependency among its youth, it is foreseeable that charter schools will be developed to serve this population. Such charter schools might require students to submit to random urinalysis testing as a condition of enrollment. Attendent policies might be subject to challenges under the Fourth Amendment of the U.S. Constitution, which guards against unreasonable governmental searches.

A constitutional search usually requires the government to obtain a warrant issued upon probable cause. However, random urinalysis tests might be permissible under the "special needs doctrine," which excuses a search from the probable cause and warrant requirements if special needs make these prerequisites impracticable. First, a court determines whether there is a special need for the policy. If such a need exists, the court then determines the constitutionality of the search by balancing the government's interests with the individual's privacy interests. Several factors are used to conduct this analysis: (1) the nature of the privacy interest upon which the search intruded, (2) the character of the intrusion on the individual's privacy interest, (3) the nature of the governmental concern at issue, (4) the immediacy of the governmental concern, and (5) the efficacy of the particular means in addressing the problem.

In *Vernonia School District No. 47J v. Acton*,[17] the Supreme Court applied the special needs doctrine to uphold the random drug testing of the student-athletes at a high school and a middle school. The schools required all students wishing to participate in interscholastic sports to sign a consent form assenting to the drug testing. Students' names were chosen at random to undergo urinalysis. During the test, a monitor stayed in the restroom to listen for signs of tampering as the student produced the sample. The Court found that there was a special need for the elimination of the warrant and probable cause requirement. The school district had presented evidence of a sharp increase in drug use in its schools, which resulted in an increase in disciplinary problems, and that the athletes were the leaders of the drug culture.

The Court then conducted a balancing inquiry between the schools' interests with the student-athletes' privacy interests. The

Court found that student-athletes had less of a privacy interest than regular students because they shared locker rooms and showers and voluntarily assented to regulations to participate in a sport. With respect to the character of the intrusion, the Court found that collecting urine was relatively unintrusive because it was nearly identical to conditions encountered in public restrooms. With respect to the immediacy of the district's concern, the Court observed that deterring student drug use was important because the negative effects of drugs were most severe during the school years, and student drug use disrupted the educational process. The Court found that the immediacy of the school district's concern was unquestionable given the fact that a large segment of the student body, particularly student athletes, had posed serious disciplinary problems. Finally, with respect to the efficacy of the means, the Court found that random drug testing solved the problem of rampant drug use among athletes by ensuring that they did not use drugs.

In *Board of Education of Independent School District No. 92 of Pottawatomie County v. Earls*,[18] the Supreme Court applied the special needs doctrine to uphold a school district's random drug testing policy of all students involved in competitive, nonathletic extracurricular activities. Notably, the Court rejected the assertion that students participating in nonathletic extracurricular activities had a greater privacy interest than the *Vernonia* athletes. This was because participants in nonathletic curricular activities voluntarily subjected themselves to many of the same intrusions on their privacy as did athletes. With respect to the immediacy of the district's concerns and the efficacy of the policy in addressing them, the Court concluded that the drug testing policy effectively served the school district's interest in protecting the health and safety of its students. The district was not required to provide evidence of a particularized or pervasive drug problem to justify the suspicionless drug testing because of the potential danger of childhood drug use and the nationwide epidemic of drug use.

In *Tannahill* ex rel. *Tannahill v. Lockney Independent School*,[19] which was decided before the *Earls* decision, a federal district court applied the special needs doctrine to invalidate a school district's mandatory drug testing policy, which applied to the entire student population of junior and senior high schools during the school year. Students who refused to participate in the drug testing program were subject to "suspension from participation in all extracurricular activities for 21 days and removal to in-school suspension for a minimum of three days."[20] Refusal to participate in the program would "result in escalation of the aforementioned punishments, up to placing the child in an alternative school and disqualifying him from participating in any activity or receiving any honors for that year."[21] The court declared the drug testing policy unconstitutional. It found that the student body within the district had a higher expectation of privacy than the student-athletes in *Vernonia*. The court also held that the district had failed to demonstrate a compelling interest for the drug testing policy because drug use had not increased prior to its implementation, and drug use within the district was generally lower in the district than in other schools in the state.

Vernonia, *Earls*, and *Tannahill* suggest that charter schools that serve chemically dependent students should be able to justify the use of random urinalysis as a condition for attendance under the special needs doctrine. These schools could probably establish a special need for an exception to the warrant and probable cause requirements because of their students' demonstrated record of substance abuse. Students with records of abuse have the potential of negatively impacting on the operation of the school and injuring themselves.

Because charter schools that serve chemically dependent students could establish a special need for drug testing, a court would then engage in a balancing test between the concerns of the school and the privacy concerns of students. Students with records of drug and alcohol abuse have arguably a lesser expectation to privacy than student-athletes or students participating in competitive, nonathletic extracurricular activities. Many students who are looking to attend charter schools for chemically dependent students would have probably already gone through the juvenile justice system because of their chemical abuse and have been required to submit to random testing as part of their sentence. With respect to the character of the intrusion, *Vernonia*, *Earls*, and *Tannahill* indicate that random urinalysis would impose minimal intrusion if conducted in a manner similiar to the policies in those cases.

With respect to the immediacy of the problem and the efficacy of the policy, a court would have to address the level of evidence that the charter school would have to provide to justify the urinalysis policy. Recall that in *Earls*, the Supreme Court held that the district was not required to provide evidence of a pervasive drug problem among students who participated in nonathletic, extracurricular activities because of the potential danger of childhood drug use and the national epidemic of drug use. However, because requiring students to submit to urinalysis testing as a condition of attendance is more extreme than the policy upheld in *Earls*, it would not be sur-prising for a court to adopt the approach in *Tannahill* and require the schools to provide particularized evidence in support of this policy. Charter schools that serve chemically dependent students should be able to satisfy this requirement. As explained above, many of these students would probably have criminal records resulting from their chemical dependency. With respect to the efficacy of the drug testing policy, the school could argue that given the high com-position of drug and alcohol abusers, random urinalysis tests might be the most effective means of stopping drug use in the school and reducing the possibility of harm to students and employees.

A number of charter schools serve court-adjudicated youth.[22] If these schools required students to submit to random urinalysis test-ing as a condition of attendance, they might also be able to meet the requirements of the special needs doctrine. Because many of the students who attend such schools might be in the criminal system because of behavior stemming from chemical dependency, these students would have a lesser privacy interest than was the case for the students in *Vernonia* and *Earls* because they would have already engaged in drug testing. Also, such students, if under the influence of drugs and alcohol, pose a danger to themselves and the school. Therefore, random urinalysis tests might be the most effective means of ensuring the safety of students and employees.

Parental Involvement Contracts

Many charter schools have tried to encourage parental involve-ment by requiring parents to sign contracts promising to partici-pate in the operation of the school. These contracts can require par-ents to commit to volunteer hours to the school, participate in school meetings, or serve on school advisory councils. Thirteen of the twenty-three parental involvement contracts analyzed in a study of California charter schools contained "fail-to-comply" clauses, which stated that children could be expelled if their parents did not fulfill the terms of the contract. For example, one contract analyzed in the study stipulated: "Parents, by signing their child's registration form, commit themselves to a least 2 hours of school service per month. . . . Any students accepted on an above mentioned agreement will meet a prescribed written contract and will understand, if the contract is broken, said agreement will be revoked and the student will be disenrolled."[23]

Substantive Due Process

Parents may argue generally that having to sign parental involvement contracts as a condition for enrollment violates their substantive due process right to direct the upbringing and education
of their children. Courts have applied rational basis review when
analyzing such challenges to school regulations. Under rational basis
review, a court may conclude that parent involvement contracts are
rationally related to the legitimate interest of encouraging parents
to be involved in the operation of the school.

Children who are expelled because of their parents' failure to
fulfill the terms of the contracts might assert that such expulsions
violate their substantive due process right to continued enrollment
in the charter school. Because a fundamental right recognized under the U.S. Constitution would not be implicated, courts would
analyze whether expelling children because of their parents' failure
to satisfy the provisions of the contracts was rationally related to a
legitimate governmental interest.[24] Charter schools would probably
argue that such punishments are rationally related to the purpose
of encouraging parents to participate in the schools' operation. The
schools would have to convince courts to view parents and children as a holistic unit, instead of separate entities, and that the
schools need the engagement and participation of the entire unit to
fulfill their educational mission.

Equal Protection Clause—Freedom of Association

Parents might assert that parental involvement contracts with
fail-to-comply clauses requiring them to join school advisory councils or perform in-school duties violate the Equal Protection Clause.
Such fail-to-comply clauses might be subject to strict scrutiny because they implicate the fundamental First Amendment right to freedom of association. *Gavett v. Alexander*[25] supports this assertion.
Gavett involved an equal protection challenge under the Fifth
Amendment to a federal statute that directed the Department of
the Army to sell firearms at a discount to members of the National
Rifle Association (NRA).[26] The federal District Court of the District
of Columbia found that the statute impinged upon freedom of association because "[i]t directs that a person, in order to receive a
government benefit, the purchase of a rifle at a discount, must join
the National Rifle Association, contribute dues to that organization,
and pledge loyalty to its political goals."[27] Therefore, the court found
that the classification was subject to strict scrutiny analysis. Selling

rifles to NRA members at a discount violated strict scrutiny because it was not the least restrictive means of achieving the legitimate end of developing a pool of trained marksmen of military age. As the court observed:

> [I]t is possible to encourage and improve civilian marksmanship by means other than the requirement of membership in the NRA. One such means . . . is the continuation or expansion of what the Army is already doing: providing rifles, ammunition, targets, and awards to junior rifle clubs; helping to coordinate, administer, and support rifle matches; providing financial support to junior shooters attending competitions; and instructing civilians in marksmanship through the Small Arms Firing School. Alternatively, if it be deemed undesirable to involve the government more deeply in this activity, rifle sales might be held as at present, but without the requirement of NRA membership. Such a change would not dilute the quality of the potential rifle customers.[28]

Gavett suggests that a parental involvement contract that required parents to join a charter school's advisory council for their child to be enrolled in the charter school would infringe upon freedom of association, thus subjecting this requirement to strict scrutiny. In fact, such a requirement would seem directly analogous to *Gavett*: parents must join and contribute their time to an organization (the school advisory council) to receive a governmental benefit (their child's enrollment in the charter school). It would also appear that a contractual provision that required parents to devote time to the charter school would have to survive strict scrutiny under *Gavett*. Having to devote time to the charter school arguably requires as much or greater "association" to the school than joining an advisory council.

A charter school might argue that requiring parents to join school councils or provide in-school service is narrowly tailored to satisfy the compelling governmental interest of encouraging parents to participate in the operation of the school. A court might conclude that encouraging service to the school is a compelling interest. However, a charter school might have a difficult time satisfying the narrow tailoring requirement because less restrictive means might be just as effective in obtaining parental participation. The California study identified several such practices, including paying a parent to coordinate parental participation and having a professional make home visits. Also, a number of contracts without fail-to-comply clauses stated that they understood the value of "unique family talents." This language indicates that these schools would work with families to find alternatives by which they could contribute to the operation of the charter school.

State Constitutions and Statutory Provisions

Parents might assert that parental involvement contracts with fail-to-comply provisions mandating service to the charter school violate statutory and state constitutional provisions that prohibit public schools to charge tuition. Chapter 2 has pointed out that most enabling statutes prohibit charter schools from charging tuition and fees. Also, many state constitutions prohibit public schools from charging tuition. According to the California Supreme Court, the common understanding of tuition is "payment for instruction in a school curriculum and for materials incident thereto."[29] Under this definition, it would be reasonable for courts to conclude that the requirement of parents to perform duties for the school in exchange for their children's enrollment might be considered "tuition" in violation of charter school enabling statutes and state constitutions.

Charter School Discipline Codes

Chapter 1 observed that charter schools are exempt from certain state laws and regulations in exchange for the schools' commitment to achieve educational outcomes that are spelled out in the charter. Such exemptions may include the disciplinary provisions of state statutes and regulations. Some charter schools have responded to these exemptions by adopting their own discipline codes. Before taking on this task, it is important for charter schools to understand that designing discipline codes is a labor-intensive process. Charter schools should also be aware that state statutes and regulations generally provide extensive administrative procedures for students to challenge disciplinary decisions. Students might have to exhaust these remedies before going to court. By refusing to adopt the disciplinary provisions of state statutes and regulations in their disciplinary codes, charter schools might lose this layer of administrative protection, thus enabling students to get to court more easily. These considerations might cause charter schools to stipulate in the charter that they have adopted the state statutory and regulatory provisions pertaining to discipline.

Charter school disciplinary codes that refuse to adopt the disciplinary provisions of state statutes and regulations might also have consequences for the substantive and procedural due process rights of charter school students. For example, many states have abolished corporal punishment as a means of discipline in the public schools. If a charter school has received exemptions from these disciplinary provisions, it would instead have to adhere to constitutional substantive due process guidelines. In *Ingraham v. Wright*,[30] the Supreme Court held that ordinary corporal punishment did not violate the substantive due process rights of students. However, the Court failed to state whether corporal punishment could be so severe as to infringe upon their liberty interests. The Third,[31] Fourth,[32] Eighth,[33] and Tenth[34] Circuits have ruled that excessive corporal punishment can violate substantive due process.

Also, if charter schools choose not to adopt the disciplinary provisions of state statutes, they would have to adhere to constitutional procedural due process standards for suspensions and expulsions. In *Goss v. Lopez*,[35] the Supreme Court ruled that public schools must provide students facing short-term suspensions of ten days or less with procedural due process: They must have notice of the charges against them, a hearing, and an opportunity to be heard. However, students facing short-term suspensions are not entitled to a delay between the time of notice and the time of the hearing. Furthermore, such students are not entitled to an attorney or the opportunity to cross-examine their accusers. The Supreme Court has not set out procedural due process guidelines for students facing expulsion, but it is clear that the level of due process varies with the severity of the penalty facing the student.[36]

Conclusion

Charter schools have adopted several strategies to encourage educational innovation and maximize the educational benefits for their students and parents. Mandatory uniform policies might be subject to substantive due process, freedom of speech, and hybrid constitutional challenges that combine substantive due process and Free Exercise Clause claims. Relevant case law suggests that charter schools might survive substantive due process and freedom of speech claims. It is unclear whether plaintiffs could succeed on hybrid constitutional claims.

Charter schools that serve chemically dependent or court-adjudicated youth might be able to require their students to submit to random urinalysis testing without violating the Fourth Amendment. Charter schools might also be able to require parents to sign a parental involvement contract as a condition of enrollment without violating the substantive due process rights of parents and students.

However, contractual provisions that call for the expulsion of a child if the parents fail to join school advisory councils or volunteer time to the charter schools might be vulnerable to Equal Protection Clause and state constitutional challenges.

Finally, many charter schools have responded to the exemptions provided by enabling statutes to state laws and regulations by designing their own disciplinary codes. Before embarking on such a task, charter schools should be aware that designing disciplinary codes is labor-intensive and that substantial departures from state laws and regulations might enable students to get to court more easily. Moreover, charter school disciplinary codes that refuse to adopt state laws and regulations have implications for the substantive and procedural due process rights of students. These charter schools would have to follow federal constitutional law tenets.

Endnotes

[1] Educational Resources Info. Ctr., *Why Dress Codes and Why Now?*, available at http://eric.uoregon.edu/publications/policy_reports/dress_codes/whynow. html (visited Jan. 26, 2003).

[2] *See* www.uscharterschools.org, available at http://www.uscharterschools.org/cs/uscsp/view/s/669 (visited Jan. 26, 2003).

[3] 393 U.S. 503 (1969).

[4] 478 U.S. 675 (1986).

[5] 484 U.S. 260 (1988).

[6] 240 F.3d 437 (5th Cir. 2001).

[7] 391 U.S. 367, 377 (1968).

[8] 108 F.Supp.2d 681 (N.D.Tex. 2000), *aff'd*, 268 F.3d 275 (5th Cir. 2001).

[9] 406 U.S. 205 (1972).

[10] 494 U.S. 872 (1990).

[11] Kissinger v. Board of Trustees of Ohio State Univ., 5 F.3d 177 (6th Cir. 1993).

[12] Brown v. Hot, Sexy and Safer Productions, Inc., 68 F.3d 525 (1st Cir. 1995).

[13] Miller v. Reed, 176 F.3d 1202 (9th Cir. 1999).

[14] Swanson v. Guthrie Indep. Sch. Dist., 135 F.3d 694 (10th Cir. 1998).

[15] 93 F. Supp. 2d 649 (E.D.N.C. 1999).

[16] *Association of Recovery Schools*, available at http://www.recoveryschools.org/ (site visited Jan. 29, 2003).

[17] 515 U.S. 646 (1995).

[18] 122 S. Ct. 2559 (2002).

[19] 133 F. Supp. 2d 919 (N.D.Tex. 2001).

[20] *Id*. at 922–923.

[21] *Id*.

[22] Twelve percent of the charter schools responding to a 2000-2001 survey of charter schools conducted by the Center for Educational Reform served court-adjudicated youth. Center for Educ. Reform, *Survey of Charter Schools (2000-01) Executive Summary* 5, available at http://edreform.com/charter_schools/report/exesumm.pdf (site visited Jan. 29, 2003).

[23] *Id.* at 3. Henry J. Becker et al., *Parental Involvement Contracts in California's Charter Schools: Strategy for Educational Improvement or Method of Exclusion?* 3 (1995), on microfiche at ERIC ED384120 (Educational Resources Information Center).

[24] In C.B. v. Driscoll, 82 F.3d 383 (11th Cir. 1996), the Eleventh Circuit rejected a student's substantive due process claim challenging his suspension and transfer to an alternative school because the suspension and transfer were executive acts and the right infringed was not a fundamental right under the U.S. Constitution. This holding suggests that children attending charter schools under the Eleventh Circuit's jurisdiction cannot challenge decisions to expel them because of their parents' failure to comply with the provisions of a parental involvement contract.

[25] 477 F. Supp. 1035 (D.C.D.C. 1979).

[26] Federal statutes are not subject to the Equal Protection Clause of the Fourteenth Amendment, which applies to state action. However, courts have construed the Due Process Clause of the Fifth Amendment to require the federal government to provide equal protection.

[27] *Gavett*, 477 F. Supp. at 1045.

[28] *Id.* at 1046.

[29] Hartzell v. Connell, 201 Cal. Rptr. 601, 624 (Cal. 1984).

[30] 430 U.S. 651 (1977).

[31] Metzger v. Osbeck, 841 F.2d 518 (3d Cir. 1988).

[32] Hall v. Tawney, 621 F.2d 607 (4th Cir. 1980).

[33] Wise v. Pea Ridge Sch. Dist., 855 F.2d 560 (8th Cir. 1988).

[34] Garcia v. Miera, 817 F.2d 650 (10th Cir. 1987).

[35] 419 U.S. 565 (1975).

[36] *See* McClain v. Lafayette County. Bd. of Educ., 673 F.2d 106 (5th Cir. 1982) (holding that the requirements of due process vary with the severity of the penalty).

Chapter 11

Concluding Thoughts

State charter school laws raise a number of interesting legal and policy issues that span the life of a charter school, from establishment, to operation, to revocation. It is also clear that each policy decision made by state legislatures marks the schools as more or less similar to traditional public schools. As the foregoing description and analysis detail, state policy decisions regarding certain issues on charter schools may push the boundaries of what characterizes public schools. Figure 11.1 illustrates a series of continuums that illustrate some of those issues.

Figure 11.1. Continuums of Public/Private Nature of Charter Schools

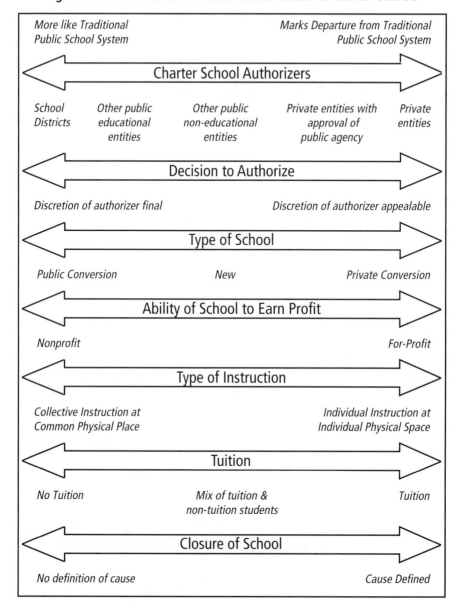

Each continuum depicted in Figure 11.1 demonstrates a potential policy decision regarding how charter schools will become established and how they will operate. States such as Arizona, Minnesota, and Texas, for example, have created systems with significant departures from traditional public schools, since they allow a variety of charter school authorizers and all three types of charter schools. In essence, they have more liberally embraced the free market principles embodied by school choice advocates. States such as Mississippi and Oklahoma have crafted charter school laws that reflect more cautious approaches to the charter school movement, since they limit authorizers to public school districts and the types of charter schools that can be created. Issues such as the ability of a school to earn a profit, the type of instruction delivered, and cause to close a school also show variation from state to state. Only the matter of charging students tuition seems to have escaped variance, although even that was at least nominally tested by the City of Milwaukee in its exercise of charter-granting authority.

Controversies resulting in the litigation reported here indicate that the definition of "charter school" is evolving as courts become involved in construing charter school legislation. This development should not be surprising. Because charter schools have been designed to innovate, it follows that legislators cannot anticipate every new approach that might be conceived under the charter school banner (for example, cyber education), or what resistance might develop in response to various uses of charter schools. That charter schools would be scrutinized regarding issues of equity and access likewise seems unsurprising, given the history that created those rights to access in traditional public schools. Litigated controversies also raise questions about whether the legislature has struck the proper balance between a charter school's public accountability and its operational autonomy.

It is also interesting to note that some jurisdictions have spawned far more litigation than others. In particular, Pennsylvania school districts and charter schools have frequently requested judicial assistance in determining how charter schools should operate. Although this increased activity is without doubt a function of the state's statutory provisions, it may also stem from the fact that Pennsylvania statutes require that school districts relinquish both state and local funds to charter schools enrolling children[1] and that parents have discretion to enroll their children in schools without regard to district boundaries.[2] Accordingly, the competition created by charter schools causes greater impact on existing schools than occurs in states where only state funds are at risk and local funds remain the province of local school district decision-making.

It is not remarkable that charter schools have raised numerous questions and drawn the attention of numerous interest groups.[3] What seems remarkable is that the rapid expansion of the charter school movement has occurred in the absence of research that demonstrates the veracity of the central claims of the concept, that freedom from regulation, coupled with parental choice and contractual accountability for student results will produce better educational environments.[4] Research is just now beginning to be produced that examines those central issues.[5] Similarly, research regarding the implications of the policy choices reviewed here has just begun. In the absence of such guidance, charter schools, their sponsors, state policy makers, teachers, parents, and others have turned to the judiciary to define more clearly the relationships that exist between each of the parties in the charter school movement. State legislatures, too, have revised laws, sometimes expanding the availability of charter schools[6] and sometimes responding to controversies with additional regulation. In so doing, each state has engaged in a complex process of defining what "charter school" means in its public education system. As one author concludes, "The verdict is still out on whether charter schools will serve our students well, and on whether they will serve primarily as a privatizing or as a democratizing force in public education reform."[7] Only by careful examination of the legislative choices made in each charter school statute, however, can that verdict be rendered with any accuracy. For as the adage has long advised, the devil (if there is one to be found) is in the details.

We began this book by noting that understanding law is all about understanding relationships. The preceding chapters have explored the legal relationships created under the title "charter schools." We have examined statutory variations, reported case law, and identified legal questions that may spark future litigation.

But charter schools are a relatively new phenomenon in public education. As such, the legal issues associated with them have only begun to evolve. Some litigation has already prompted lawmakers to revise charter statutes in much the way legal issues in traditional schools have spurred legislative activity since the inception of public education. As such, we are witnessing the redefinition of public education and a new and fascinating focus for legal scholars who study schools. The variation created by the interplay between federal, state, local, and contract law can be staggering. And understanding the legal context created by charter schools poses a challenge to all those interested in charter schools: their operators, their authorizers, the children who learn there, the parents who elect charter schools for their children, the employees who work there, academics who study them, policymakers at all levels, and the public at large.

Will other legal issues arise? Most likely. Will charter schools escape vulnerability to legal challenge? Most unlikely. And that is as it should be. For judicial review is just another way the public holds schools and policymakers accountable. Therefore, if this new form of public education is to be fully accountable, the new relationships created by the laws and contracts that define charter schools' existence must be able to withstand judicial scrutiny. And by examining what charter schools may do and must do—the only questions legal analysis can address—the public and the policymakers that serve them can better reflect on what charter schools, indeed all public education, should do.

Endnotes

[1] *See* 24 Pa. Cons. Stat. Ann. § 17-1725-A(a)(5).

[2] *See id.* § 17-1723-A(c).

[3] There are strong interest groups on both sides of this debate. *See generally* Thomas L. Good & Jennifer S. Braden, *The Great School Debate: Choice, Vouchers and Charters,* 120 (2000). Proponents of school choice, such as conservative political groups and business interests, see charter schools as a means to demonstrate the efficacy of the central premise that parental choice benefits schooling. The American Federation of Teachers and the National Education Association, large stakeholders in public education, have voiced suspicions that charter schools are designed to blunt or even bust union influence over education.

[4] Others have made the same observation. *See, e.g.,* Seymour B. Sarason, *Charter Schools: Another Flawed Educational Reform?* 112 (1998).

[5] *See, e.g.,* Bruce Fuller, Inside Charter Schools: The Paradox of Radical Decentralization (2000) (addressing the central assertions supporting the creation of charter schools).

[6] *See, e.g.,* Joe Nathan, *Minnesota and the Charter Public School Idea, in* The Charter School Landscape 17, 22 (Sandra Vergari ed., 2002).

[7] *See e.g.,* Lee Sensenbrenner,"Online School Has 500+ Applicants." The Capital Times (February 28, 2002). Available at http://www.madison.com/archives/read. php?ref=tct:2002:02:28:40954:COMMUNITIES>; (last visited Feb. 2003).

[8] Stacy Smith, The Democratic Potential of Charter Schools 212 (2001).

Appendix A

Public Charter Schools Program: Nonregulatory Guidance (December 2000)

U.S. Department of Education, Office of Elementary and Secondary Education

On May 4, 2000, President Clinton issued a Memorandum for the Secretary of Education concerning additional guidelines for charter schools. The President instructed the Secretary to develop guidelines "to help faith-based and other community-based and business institutions understand the role they can play in the charter school movement." In many communities, faith-based and other community- based and business institutions are an integral part of the community and a key resource for improving public education. This nonregulatory guidance responds to the President's Memorandum by incorporating additional questions and answers into the Department's March 1999 nonregulatory guidance addressing a wide range of issues facing charter schools. Charter schools are now an integral part of the educational landscape with approximately 2,000 in operation, and 36 states, the District of Columbia, and Puerto Rico having passed legislation to enable charter schools. Charter schools promote public school choice by allowing local innovators, community groups, teachers, and other entities to start publicly accountable schools. The Public Charter Schools Program (PCSP) was authorized in October 1994, under Title X, Part C of the Elementary and Secondary Education Act of 1965 (ESEA), as amended, 20 U.S.C. 8061-8067. In October 1998, the program was amended by the Charter School Expansion Act of 1998. The program, which provides support for the planning, program design, and initial implementation of charter schools, is intended to enhance parent and student choices among public schools and give more students the opportunity to learn to challenging standards. Enhancement of parent and student choices will result in higher student achievement, however, only if sufficiently diverse and high-quality choices, and genuine opportunities to take advantage of those choices, are available to all students. Every student should have an equal opportunity to attend a public charter school.The nonregulatory guidance in Section I of this document applies only to charter schools receiving Federal start-up grants under the PCSP. It addresses questions the Department has received regarding various provisions of the PCSP statute, including those related to student admissions to public charter schools, the use of lotteries, private school conversions, and the involvement of for-profit organizations in charter schools. These guidelines do not contain all of the information you will need to comply with PCSP requirements, but are intended to provide guidance on the PCSP and on examples of ways to implement it. For additional information about the PCSP, please contact the PCSP Office, U.S. Department of Education, 400 Maryland Avenue, S.W., Room 3E122, Washington, D.C. 20202-6140. Telephone: (202) 260-2671. The nonregulatory guidance in Section II applies to all public charter schools. Section II of the guidance is intended to answer questions about how businesses, faith-based and other community-based organizations and the individuals associated with them can be involved in charter schools. Questions and answers 14 through 19 address issues that are affected by laws applying to all public schools, including public charter schools. Questions and answers 20 and 21 address programmatic issues and reflect the Department's recommendations for addressing potential issues emerging in the field.

SECTION I: PUBLIC CHARTER SCHOOLS PROGRAM

This section of the guidance applies to charter schools receiving start-up grants under the PCSP. It addresses issues related to admissions, the use of lotteries, private school conversions, and the involvement of for-profit entities in charter schools.

1. **What is the purpose of the PCSP?**
   The purpose of the PCSP is to expand the number of high-quality charter schools available to students across the Nation by providing financial assistance for their planning, program design, and initial implementation; and evaluating the effects of charter schools, including the effects on students (in particular, student achievement), staff, and parents.

2. **In addition to Title X, Part C of the ESEA, what other Federal statutory and regulatory authorities apply to the PCSP?**
   Recipients of funds under this program should be aware of the following statutory requirements in addition to those in Title X, Part C of the ESEA: (a) the definitions set out in Title XIV of the ESEA, which establishes general provisions for all programs authorized under the ESEA; (b) Title VI of the Civil Rights Act of 1964, which prohibits discrimination on the basis of race, color, and national origin; (c) Title IX of the Education Amendments of 1972, which prohibits discrimination on the basis of sex; (d) Section 504 of the Rehabilitation Act of 1973, which prohibits discrimination on the basis of disability; (e) the Age Discrimination Act of 1975, which prohibits discrimination on the basis of age; (f) Title II of the Americans with Disabilities Act of 1990, which prohibits discrimination on the basis of disability by public entities, including public charter schools and public school districts, regardless of whether they receive Federal financial assistance; and (g) Part B of the Individuals with Disabilities Education Act, which requires States to make available a free appropriate public education to children with disabilities. The Education Department General Administrative Regulations (EDGAR), Parts 75, 76, 77, 79, 80, 81, 82, 85, and 86 also apply to this program.

3. **Who is eligible to apply for a PCSP grant?**
   State educational agencies (SEAs) in States with a specific State statute authorizing the establishment of charter schools are eligible to apply for PCSP grants. An "eligible applicant," defined as an authorized public chartering agency in partnership with a charter school developer, in such States may apply to the SEA for a subgrant. If a State elects not to participate in the PCSP or is denied funding, an eligible applicant may apply directly to the Department for a grant.

4. **How may PCSP planning and implementation grant funds be used?**

SEAs may use PCSP funds to award subgrants to charter schools in the State, and charter schools may use the funds only for post-award planning and design of the educational program, and for initial implementation of a charter school. SEAs may also reserve up to 5 percent of PCSP grant funds for administrative expenses related to operating the charter school grant program, and up to 10 percent of the PCSP grant funds to support dissemination activities. These dissemination activities are carried out through separate dissemination grants to charter schools.

5. **What are dissemination grants?**
   Dissemination grants are awarded to charter schools to support activities that help open new public schools (including public charter schools) or share the lessons learned by charter schools with other public schools. The following activities may qualify as dissemination activities: (a) assisting other individuals with the planning and start-up of one or more new public schools, including charter schools, that are independent of the assisting charter school and its developers and that agree to be held to at least as high a level of accountability as the assisting charter school; (b) developing partnerships with other public schools designed to improve student performance; (c) developing curriculum materials, assessments, and other materials that promote increased student achievement and are based on successful practices within the assisting charter school; and (d) conducting evaluations and developing materials that document the successful practices of the assisting charter school that are designed to improve student performance in other schools.

   A charter school may not use dissemination grant funds, either directly or through a contractor, for marketing or recruitment activities designed to promote itself or the programs offered by it or by a contractor to parents or the community. In particular, grant funds may be used to develop materials documenting successful practices of the charter school for the educational purpose of assisting other schools in improving student achievement, but not for the purpose of recruiting students or promoting the program of the school or its contractor. Any charter school receiving a dissemination grant should provide thorough and high-quality information that meets the needs of other schools trying to learn from the charter school's experience.

6. **Who is eligible to apply for a dissemination grant?**
   A charter school may apply for a dissemination grant, regardless of whether it has applied for or received a planning or implementation grant under the PCSP, if the charter school has been in operation for at least three (3) consecutive years and has demonstrated overall success, including the following: (a) substantial progress in improving student achievement; (b) high levels of parent satisfaction; and (c) the management and leadership necessary to overcome initial start-up problems and establish a thriving, financially viable charter school. For more information about dissemination grants, see section 10304(f)(6) of the ESEA, 20 U.S.C. 8064(f)(6).

7. **Is a for-profit entity that holds a legal charter eligible to apply for a PCSP grant or subgrant?**

A for-profit entity does not qualify as an eligible applicant for purposes of the PCSP. A charter school receiving PCSP funds may enter into a contract with a for-profit entity to have the for-profit entity manage the charter school on a day-to-day basis. However, it should be emphasized that if the charter school enters into such a contract, the charter school must be held by the State and the cognizant chartering authority to the same standards of public accountability and requirements that apply to all public charter schools, including State student performance standards and assessments that apply to all public schools; and the charter school must supervise the administration of the PCSP grant and is directly responsible for ensuring that grant funds are used in accordance with statutory and regulatory requirements (see EDGAR, Part 75, Subpart F).

8.   **a. Is a private school eligible to receive PCSP funds?**
Only charter schools that meet the definition of a charter school under the ESEA are eligible to receive PCSP funds. Section 10310(1) defines a charter school as, among other things, a "public school" that is created by a developer as a public school, or adapted by a developer from an existing public school, and operated under public supervision and direction. See section 10310(1) of the ESEA, 20 U.S.C. 8066(1), for the definition of a charter school for purposes of the PCSP.

8.   **b. Can a private school be converted into a public charter school?**
As stated above, the ESEA defines a charter school as a newly created public school or one adapted from an existing public school. There is no provision or mechanism in the law for converting private schools into public charter schools. The ESEA does not foreclose a newly created public school from using resources previously used by a closed private school or from involving the parents and teachers who may have been involved in the closed private school. However, any newly created public school must be just that; it cannot be a continuation of a private school under a different guise. The public charter school must be separate and apart from any private school. It must be established as a public school, and comply with applicable State and federal laws regarding public schools.

In its creation, development, and operation, a charter school receiving PCSP funds cannot have any affiliation "with a sectarian school or religious institution." 20 U.S.C. 8066(1)(E). (For information on issues relating to religion and charter schools in general, including charter schools not receiving PCSP funds, see Q&A Nos. 14-18.) Because a newly created public school would not have any "previously enrolled" students, all students would need to apply for admission and would have to be selected by lottery if there are more applicants than spaces available. Similarly, the charter school must inform the community of its public school status and have a fair and open admissions process. Outreach and recruitment efforts, such as radio advertisements or community meetings, should be designed to reach all segments of the parent community. The charter school must recruit in a manner that does not discriminate against students of a particular race, color, national origin, religion, or sex, or against students with disabilities; but the charter school may target additional recruitment efforts toward groups that might otherwise have limited opportunities to participate in the charter school's programs. In its programs or activities, the charter school may not discriminate on the basis of race, color, national origin, religion, sex, or disability.

9. **What is a lottery for purposes of the PCSP?**
    A lottery is a random selection process by which applicants for admission to a public charter school are admitted to the charter school.

10. **Under what circumstances must a charter school use a lottery?**
    A charter school receiving PCSP funds must use a lottery if more students apply for admission to the charter school than can be admitted. A charter school with fewer applicants than spaces available does not need to conduct a lottery.

11. **Are weighted lotteries permissible?**
    Weighted lotteries are permitted only when they are necessary to comply with Title VI of the Civil Rights Act of 1964, Title IX of the Education Amendments of 1972, the Equal Protection Clause of the Constitution, or a State law requiring desegregation.

12. **May a charter school exempt certain categories of applicants from the lottery and admit them automatically?**
    A charter school that is oversubscribed and, consequently, must use a lottery, generally must include in that lottery all eligible applicants for admission. A charter school may exempt from the lottery only those students who are deemed to have been admitted to the charter school already and, therefore, do not need to reapply. Specifically, the following categories of applicants may be exempted from the lottery on this basis: (a) students who are enrolled in a public school at the time it is converted into a public charter school; (b) siblings of students already admitted to or attending the same charter school; (c) children of a charter school's founders (so long as the total number of students allowed under this exemption constitutes only a small percentage of the school's total enrollment); and (d) children of employees in a work-site charter school (so long as the total number of students allowed under this exemption constitutes only a small percentage of the school's total enrollment). When recruiting students, charter schools should target all segments of the parent community. The charter school must recruit in a manner that does not discriminate against students of a particular race, color, national origin, religion, or sex, or against students with disabilities; but the charter school may target additional recruitment efforts toward groups that might otherwise have limited opportunities to participate in the charter school's programs. Once a student has been admitted to the charter school through an appropriate process, he or she may remain in attendance through subsequent grades. A new applicant for admission to the charter school, however, would be subject to the lottery if, as of the application closing date, the total number of applicants exceeds the number of spaces available at the charter school.

To be eligible for Federal start-up grants, a charter school's admissions practices must comply with State law and applicable Federal laws. Accordingly, the exemptions discussed above are permissible only to the extent that they are consistent with the State's charter school law, State law regarding desegregation, the school's charter, and any applicable Title VI desegregation plans or court orders requiring desegregation. A charter school's admissions practices must also comply with Part B of the Individuals with Disabilities Education Act and Federal civil rights laws, including, but not limited to, Title VI of the Civil Rights Act of 1964; Section 504 of the Rehabilitation Act of 1973; and Title II of the Americans with Disabilities Act of 1990, as applicable.

13. **May a charter school receiving PCSP funds set minimum eligibility criteria for admission to the charter school?**

The ESEA does not specifically prohibit charter schools from setting minimum qualifications for determining who is eligible to enroll in a charter school and, thus, to be included in the lottery. Charter schools receiving PCSP funds are required, however, to inform students in the community about the charter school and give them an "equal opportunity to attend the charter school." Thus, a charter school may set minimum qualifications for admission only to the extent that such qualifications are: (a) consistent with the statutory purposes of the PCSP; (b) reasonably necessary to achieve the educational mission of the charter school; and (c) consistent with civil rights laws and Part B of the Individuals with Disabilities Education Act. A major purpose of the PCSP, for example, is to assist "educationally disadvantaged" and other students to achieve to challenging State content and performance standards.

In light of this purpose, it is unlikely that an elementary charter school could justify establishing minimum qualifications for admission, regardless of the school's mission or purpose. On the other hand, a secondary charter school might be able to justify certain admission requirements. For example, an alternative secondary school might have admissions qualifications related to a purpose to serve students who have dropped out of school, or a secondary school for the performing arts might require that applicants for admission be able to demonstrate a minimum level of competence in the performing arts. Such requirements might measure the capacity of the student to benefit from and contribute to the purpose of the school.

In establishing any such admissions criteria, a secondary charter school should consider multiple measures of a student's ability to benefit from the educational program, and must ensure—consistent with Federal civil rights laws and Part B of the Individuals with Disabilities Education Act—that such factors are not used in a manner that inappropriately restricts access to the charter school. It should not, for example, use a test as a sole criterion to determine a student's ability to benefit from the school's program. The secondary charter school should target all segments of the parent community in its outreach efforts, and should recruit in a manner that does not discriminate against students of a particular race, color, national origin, religion, or sex; or against students with disabilities.

SECTION II: INVOLVEMENT OF COMMUNITY-BASED ORGANIZATIONS AND BUSINESSES IN PUBLIC CHARTER SCHOOLS

This section of the guidance applies to all charter schools, regardless of whether they receive funds under the PCSP. It addresses issues related to religion and the involvement of businesses and community-based organizations in charter schools. Questions and answers 14 through 19 address issues that arise from the application of laws that apply to all public schools, including public charter schools. Questions and answers 20 and 21 address programmatic issues and reflect the Department's recommendations for addressing potential issues emerging from the field.

14. **May a public charter school be religious in nature?**

No. As public schools, charter schools must be non-religious in their programs, admissions policies, governance, employment practices and all other operations, and the charter school's curriculum must be completely secular. As with other public schools, charter schools may not provide religious instruction, but they may teach about religion from a secular perspective. And though charter schools must be neutral with respect to religion, they may play an active role in teaching civic values. The fact that some of these values are also held by religions does not make it unlawful to teach them in a charter school. Furthermore, as discussed below, faith-based and religious organizations can be involved with charter schools in many ways, and religious expression by students is allowed in charter schools to the same extent as in other public schools.

15. **What are some examples of ways religious organizations and their members may partner with or be involved with charter schools?**

A faith leader may participate in designing, organizing, or operating a charter school in his or her individual capacity—as a member of the community, not as a representative of his or her religious organization. The Department recommends that diverse segments of the local community be included in the initial organization and operation of a charter school, and that charter school founders, operators, and governing boards not be comprised primarily of individuals from the same religious organization.

All activities of a charter school must be non-religious. Public funds may not be used for religious purposes or to encourage religious activity. In addition, even if funded by non-public sources, religious activity may not be conducted, promoted, or encouraged during charter school activities by charter school employees or by persons working with charter schools. However, to the extent that their involvement promotes academic learning and the mission of the charter school, religious organizations and their members may partner with and be involved with charter schools so long as the charter school's decision to partner with the religious organization is made without regard to the religious character or affiliation of the organization and is not otherwise reasonably perceived as an endorsement of religion.

Like other public schools, charter schools may enter into partnerships with community groups for secular purposes, such as tutoring or recreational activities. Religious groups may be partners for these types of activities so long as charter schools select partners without regard to their religious affiliation, ensure that no public funds are used for religious purposes, and do not engage in or encourage religious activity. Charter schools may not limit participation in the partnership to religious groups or certain religious groups, and they may not select students or encourage or discourage student participation with particular partners based on the religious or secular nature of the organization. The Secretary recently issued a new set of guidelines describing these types of partnerships in detail.

These guidelines can be found at http://www.ed.gov/inits/religionand
schools/v-guide.html.

16. **May charter schools use the facilities of a religious organization?**
A charter school may use the facilities of a religious organization to the
same extent that other public schools may use these facilities. Generally,
this means that a charter school may lease space from a religious organization so long as the charter school remains non-religious in all its programs and operations. Therefore, the religious landlord may not exercise
any control over what is taught in the charter school.Space constraints are
a major challenge facing charter schools. A charter school should select
space based on its logistical and educational needs, not because the space
is located in or near a religious school or institution or because officials of
the charter school are connected to a particular religious organization.
However, it is important that charter school operators examine a range of
options in their community. The Department strongly recommends that
any space used by a charter school be free of religious symbols and under
the full control of the charter school during school hours and during all
charter school activities.

17. **May charter schools conduct outreach activities in churches or through
religious organizations?**
A charter school's outreach and recruitment activities should be designed
to reach all segments of the parent community. Thus, a charter school may
conduct outreach or recruitment activities in churches or through religious
organizations as part of a broad-based and balanced effort to inform parents in the community about the charter school and to recruit a diverse
student body. In order to ensure that recruitment efforts reach all members of the community, these activities should not be conducted primarily
in or through religious organizations.

18. **Is religious expression allowed in charter schools?**
Religious expression is allowed in charter schools to the same extent as in
other public schools, consistent with the First Amendment. The Secretary
of Education has issued Religious Expression in Public Schools (http://
www.ed.gov/Speeches/08-1995/religion.html), guidelines that address
many of the issues facing public schools, including charter schools, with
respect to religion, including student prayer and religious discussion, teaching values, teaching about religion and student religious clubs. As public
schools, charter schools are subject to the responsibilities and limitations
outlined in the guidance. The guidance states that "two basic and equally
important obligations imposed on public school officials by the First
Amendment" are—

- [S]chools may not forbid students acting on their own from expressing their personal religious views or beliefs solely because they are
of a religious nature.

- [S]chools may not endorse religious activity or doctrine, nor may
they coerce participation in a religious activity. Among other things
. . . school administrators and teachers may not organize or encourage prayer exercises in the classroom.

As stated in the Secretary's guidelines, students have the same right to engage in individual or group prayer and religious discussion during the school day as they do to engage in other comparable activity. For example, "students may read their Bibles or other scriptures, say grace before meals, and pray before tests to the same extent that they may engage in comparable nondisruptive activities." In informal settings such as cafeterias and hallways, students "may pray and discuss their religious views with each other, subject to the same rules of order as apply to other student activities and speech." In addition, students may "participate in before or after school events with religious content, such as 'see you at the flag pole' gatherings, on the same terms as they may participate in other noncurriculum activities on school premises."The Secretary's guidelines also state that "[t]he right to engage in voluntary prayer or religious discussion free from discrimination does not include the right to have a captive audience listen, or to compel other students to participate. Teachers and school administrators should ensure that no student is in any way coerced to participate in religious activity" and "[t]eachers and school administrators, when acting in those capacities . . . are prohibited . . . from soliciting or encouraging religious activity, and from participating in such activity with students."

Charter schools are encouraged to consult the Secretary's guidelines when questions arise concerning religious expression and to ensure that teachers, administrators, students, and parents are fully informed about the contents of the guidelines.

19. **May work-site charter schools limit admission to children of employees at the worksite?**
Work-site charter schools receiving PCSP funds generally may not limit admission to children of employees at the worksite (see Q&A No. 12). In furtherance of its educational mission, however, it may be permissible for a work-site charter school that does not receive PCSP funds to limit admission to children of employees at the worksite. Like all charter schools, work-site charter schools that do not receive PCSP funds must comply with civil rights laws and Part B of the Individuals with Disabilities Education Act. Accordingly, when recruiting students, the Department encourages work-site charter schools to employ a broad-based recruitment strategy designed to reach all segments of the local parent community, including parents who are not employed at the worksite. When advertising or conducting outreach, work-site charter schools, like other public schools, may not discriminate on the basis of race, color, national origin, religion, sex, or disability.

20. **Can community-based organizations and business entities play a role in charter schools?**
Yes. Community-based organizations and businesses can play a positive role in creating and supporting charter schools. Examples of ways in which non-religious organizations can get involved in charter schools include helping to plan or design a new school, developing curriculum and assessment strategies, serving on governing boards, participating in the day-to-day management of charter schools, establishing partnerships with charter schools, and even creating work-site charter schools. A broad range of community-based organizations and businesses are currently involved

with charter schools, including plastics and automobile manufacturers; hospitals, museums and homeless shelters; and courts and social service agencies. Like all charter schools, charter schools operated by or affiliated with community-based organizations or business entities must be schools of choice, must be non-religious, and must operate in a nondiscriminatory manner.

Religious organizations may also be involved with charter schools. For questions and answers on how religious organizations and their members can partner with or be involved with charter schools, see Q&A Nos. 15-17.

The U.S. Department of Education has funded an initiative by the National Alliance of Business and Public Policy Associates to examine the role of employers in charter schools. This project has developed materials that may be useful to both employers and charter schools that are interested in establishing partnerships. For more information on the role employers may play with charter schools, you may visit the employer-linked charter schools project website at http://www.employercharter schools.com, or you can contact Public Policy Associates, Inc. by telephone at 517-485-4477.

21. **What should be done to prevent commercial exploitation of a charter school or its students?**
Charter schools frequently form partnerships and initiatives that involve businesses and other community organizations. These partnerships can expand the quality of programs and benefit both the charter school and the larger community. The unique nature of charter schools and the community alliances that they form, however, may also make charter schools susceptible to commercial exploitation. For example, a charter school developer or operator who owns a building leases the building to the charter school at an above-market rate; or a member of the governing board of a charter school influences the charter school to purchase substandard equipment or services from a company affiliated with the board member; or a business attempts to direct what students study or where they work, or to include advertising or promotional materials in the curriculum, for its own economic benefit.

Charter schools and, when appropriate, charter-granting entities should implement appropriate safeguards to prevent the commercial exploitation of the charter school and its students. In establishing a charter school, for example, the founding members should ensure that the charter school is designed to meet a specific educational need in the community and that the governing board of the charter school is comprised of [sic] individuals from diverse backgrounds. The charter school should not be established or operated for direct economic gain, and individuals with a personal or economic interest in a management or procurement decision should not be involved in making that decision. Management and procurement decisions involving the charter school should be made in accordance with applicable law and based on the terms of the charter, the educational mission of the charter school, the best interests of the school's students, and the long-term financial viability of the charter school. The charter-granting entity as well as the administrators and governing board of the charter school all must exercise sufficient oversight to protect the charter school and its students against exploitation.

Appendix B

Office for Civil Rights: Applying Federal Civil Rights Laws to Public Charter Schools: Questions and Answers

U.S. Department of Education

As part of the U.S. Department of Education's (ED's) and the U.S. Department of Justice's (DOJ's) efforts to support innovation and choice within the public school system, this publication provides important information on how public charter schools may be developed and operated consistent with federal nondiscrimination laws. The purpose of this publication is to answer civil rights-related questions that charter school developers and operators have raised. The civil rights principles that apply to charter schools are the same principles that apply to all public schools. This publication contains no new law. Rather, it is designed to assist charter school developers and operators by making available a summary of civil rights issues applicable to public schools. This publication provides general information that covers a broad range of federal civil rights issues. It does not seek to answer every question that may arise. In many cases, answers will turn on the particular facts of a given situation. In others, the law regarding the issue is evolving. Finally, other state or local civil rights requirements or other federal laws may apply. For additional information, we encourage you to contact ED's Office for Civil Rights (OCR) or visit OCR's Web site. A list of the addresses and telephone numbers of OCR offices is attached. DOJ contributed significantly to this document by preparing the portions where DOJ is featured. Contact information for DOJ and for other federal offices is included where appropriate. OCR and DOJ can provide technical assistance. Early consultation can help you understand and meet these requirements.

U.S. Department of Education
Office for Civil Rights
May 2000

Background

One of the fastest growing areas of public school reform is the charter schools movement. Charter schools are public schools under contract—or charter—between a public agency and groups of parents, teachers, community leaders, or others who want to create alternatives and choice within the public school system. Charter schools create choice for parents and students within the public school system, while providing a system of accountability for student achievement. Charter schools also encourage innovation and provide opportunities for parents to play powerful roles in shaping and supporting the education of their children. As a result, charter schools can spur healthy competition to improve public education. In exchange for increased accountability, charter schools are given expanded flexibility with respect to select statutory and regulatory requirements. Federal legislation provides support for the creation of charter schools as a means of promoting choice and innovation within public school systems. Of course, charter schools, like all public schools and other recipients of federal financial assistance, must operate consistent with civil rights laws.The U.S. Department of Education (ED), Office for Civil Rights (OCR) enforces a number of civil rights laws that apply to public schools, including charter schools. These laws include: Title VI of the Civil Rights Act of 1964 (Title VI), which prohibits discrimination on the basis of race, color, or national origin; Title IX of the Education Amendments of 1972 (Title IX), which prohibits discrimination on the basis of sex in education programs; Section 504 of the Rehabilitation Act of 1973 (Section 504), which prohibits discrimination on the basis of disability; and the Age Discrimination Act of 1975, which prohibits discrimination on the basis of age. These laws apply to programs and activities that receive federal financial assistance. OCR is also responsible for enforcing Title II of the Americans with Disabilities Act of 1990 (Title II), which prohibits discrimination on the basis of disability by public entities, including public schools. Title II applies to public entities, regardless of whether they receive federal financial assistance. OCR receives and resolves more than 5,000 complaints of discrimination each year and provides technical assistance on a wide range of issues.In addition, the U.S. Department of Justice, Civil Rights Division (CRD) works on a variety of legal issues involving elementary and secondary schools. DOJ enforces in the courts many of the same statutes that OCR enforces administratively, including Title VI, Title IX, Section 504, and Title II. DOJ also enforces Title IV and Title VII of the Civil Rights Act of 1964 and the Equal Educational Opportunities Act of 1974. DOJ may intervene in private suits that allege violations of education-related anti-discrimination statutes and the Fourteenth Amendment of the U.S. Constitution. CRD is also responsible for monitoring more than 400 school districts currently covered by desegregation court orders in over 200 desegregation cases where the United States is a party.ED and DOJ support the implementation of charter schools as a valuable way to enhance choice among public schools and to give more students the opportunity to learn to challenging standards. This guidance seeks to aid charter school developers and operators in their efforts to plan, develop, and deliver their important educational programs in a nondiscriminatory manner. To avoid distraction within this guidance, we have often used acronyms and abbreviations to substitute for the names of agencies and multiword concepts. The meaning of each is explained within the context. For your convenience, we also include the following key to the acronyms and abbreviation you will find in this publication.

- CRD—Civil Rights Division, U.S. Department of Justice
- DOJ—U.S. Department of Justice
- ED—U.S. Department of Education
- FAPE—Free appropriate public education
- IDEA—Individuals with Disabilities Education Act
- LEA—Local Educational Agency
- LEP—National-origin minority, limited-English proficient
- OBEMLA—Office of Bilingual Education and Minority Languages Affairs, U.S. Department of Education
- OCR—Office for Civil Rights, U.S. Department of Education
- OSEP—Office of Special Education Programs, U.S. Department of Education

- OSERS—Office of Special Education and Rehabilitative Services, U.S. Department of Education
- SEA—State Educational Agency
- Section 504—Section 504 of the Rehabilitation Act of 1973
- Title II—Title II of the Americans with Disabilities Act of 1990
- Title VI—Title VI of the Civil Rights Act of 1964
- Title IX—Title IX of the Education Amendments of 1972

Responsibilities for Civil Rights Compliance

Perhaps the most common image associated with education is the relationship between a child and his or her teacher. Of course, public education is that and more. It includes shared responsibility by many entities, including the school, the school district, and the state, acting in cooperation with parents. In much the same way, the responsibility for safeguarding the civil rights of the students, parents, and teachers in a public school, such as your charter school, is shared and does not fall exclusively on any one individual or agency.

1. **Who is responsible for making sure that my charter school is complying with federal civil rights laws?**

   Public schools, including your charter school, are responsible for complying with several federal civil rights laws, based on their status as recipients of federal financial assistance and as public entities. Other entities share responsibility for your school's compliance. If your charter school is part of a Local Educational Agency (LEA), such as a school district, the LEA is also responsible for ensuring that your school is complying. Furthermore, if your charter school receives federal funds through the State Educational Agency (SEA) or an authorized public chartering agency that receives federal funds, or is chartered by the SEA or its designee, the SEA is also responsible. The SEA is responsible in all cases for having methods of administration that are not discriminatory, including procedures for chartering schools.

   Sources of federal education funds include programs authorized under the Elementary and Secondary Education Act of 1965, as amended, including the Public Charter Schools Program.

2. **In general, what are the federal civil rights obligations that apply to public elementary or secondary schools, including my charter school?**

   Public schools, including charter schools, must not discriminate on the basis of race, color, national origin, sex, or disability in any of their programs or activities. The primary federal civil rights laws addressed in this publication include:

   - Title VI of the Civil Rights Act of 1964, which prohibits discrimination on the basis of race, color, or national origin;
   - Title IX of the Education Amendments of 1972, which prohibits discrimination on the basis of sex in education programs;
   - Section 504 of the Rehabilitation Act of 1973, which prohibits discrimination on the basis of disability; and
   - Title II of the Americans with Disabilities Act of 1990, which prohibits discrimination on the basis of disability.

   Other applicable federal civil rights laws not directly addressed in this publication include:
   • Age Discrimination Act of 1975;

- *Title IV of the Civil Rights Act of 1964;*
- *Title VII of the Civil Rights Act of 1964; and*
- *Equal Educational Opportunities Act of 1974.*

Recruitment and Admissions

Students attend charter schools by choice, but their admission might be subject to certain qualifications or selection procedures, including a lottery. This is one factor that may distinguish the operation of your charter school from many other public schools. Although your civil rights obligations are no different from those of other public school officials, the fact that your students are not simply assigned to attend your charter school underscores your need to be mindful of the rights of children and parents in your community when publicizing your school to attract students and when evaluating their applications for admission.

3. Do I have any responsibility regarding the recruitment of students in order to be in compliance with federal civil rights laws?

Yes. When announcing your charter school or conducting outreach, you may not discriminate against students of a particular race, color, or national origin, or against students with disabilities. If your charter school is co-educational, then you may not discriminate in recruitment on the basis of sex. If your charter school recruits students, you should recruit them from all segments of the community served by the school, including students with disabilities and students of all races, colors, and national origins. Also, you may target additional recruitment efforts toward groups that you believe might otherwise have limited opportunities to participate in your program.

> *Title IX allows single-sex programs, classes, and schools under certain conditions. For more information, see Question 9.*

4. What steps should I take when providing outreach information to parents who are limited-English proficient?

You must make sure that parents in your community who are not proficient in English have the opportunity to understand the outreach information provided to other parents. This information may need to be provided in a language other than English. For example, if outreach materials are made available to parents, you should provide the content of the materials to parents who do not understand English in a manner and form they understand. If you conduct public informational meetings with parents or community groups, you should make sure that limited-English proficient parents who can be reasonably expected to attend have a meaningful opportunity to understand what is being presented.

5. What steps should I take when providing outreach information to parents with disabilities?

You must make sure that a parent with a disability has a meaningful opportunity to understand the outreach information given about the charter school as effectively as other parents. Appropriate auxiliary aids and services must be made available whenever they are necessary to ensure effective communication with disabled parents. For example, if outreach materials are made available to parents, you need to make sure that parents with disabilities have appropriate access to the content of the materials. If requested, you may need to provide the materials using alternative formats, such as Braille, large print, or audio cassette. If you conduct public informational meetings with parents or community groups, those meetings must be physically accessible to individuals with disabilities. Qualified interpreters or another effective means of communication must be provided if requested.

6. What is my obligation to make sure that all students—regardless of race, color, or national origin—are treated in a nondiscriminatory manner in admissions?

You may not discriminate on the basis of race, color, or national origin in determining whether an applicant satisfies any admissions requirements. Students with limited-English proficiency must have the opportunity to meet any appropriate minimum eligibility criterion for admission, consistent with the mission of the charter school. Eligibility criteria must be nondiscriminatory on their face and must be applied in a nondiscriminatory manner. If such criteria have a disparate impact on the basis of race, color, or national origin, then the criteria should be examined to ensure that they are educationally justified and that no alternative criteria exist that would equally serve your goals and have a lesser disparate impact. It is important to understand that disparities alone do not constitute discrimination under Federal law. For more information and technical assistance, contact the OCR office that serves your state. If your charter school receives funds under the federal Public Charter Schools Program, you must use a lottery to admit students if the charter school is oversubscribed.

> For schools receiving funds under the federal Public Charter School Program, see the discussion on establishing minimum eligibility criteria for admission and other important information in Public Charter Schools Program: Non-Regulatory Guidance.

7. May my charter school consider race in admissions decisions?

A charter school may take race into account in making admissions decisions in limited circumstances. Race may be used only in a narrowly tailored way to meet a compelling interest, such as to remedy discrimination, to promote the educational benefits of diversity, or to reduce minority-group isolation. The state of the law in this area is undergoing close examination by the courts. The legal standard that applies to your state may vary, depending on State law and the federal circuit in which your state is located.

> For more information and technical assistance concerning the use of race in admissions, contact the OCR Office that serves your state and see, for example, the Federal Register notices on the Magnet Schools Assistance Program application notice.

8. What is my obligation to make sure that student applicants with disabilities are treated in a nondiscriminatory manner in admissions?

Under Section 504 and Title II, you may not categorically deny admission to students on the basis of disability. For example, you may not deny admission to a student with a disability solely because of that student's need for special education or related aids and services. Students with disabilities must have the opportunity to meet any appropriate minimum eligibility criterion for admission, consistent with the mission of the charter school and civil rights requirements.

> For more information on civil rights requirements regarding the educational needs of students with disabilities, see Questions 23 to 30 concerning Services to Students with Disabilities.

9. Does Title IX permit single-sex classes, programs, or schools?

An exemption in Title IX permits LEAs to establish single-sex elementary or secondary schools as long as they are not vocational schools. However, when an

LEA establishes a public school for one sex—unless it is necessary to remedy discrimination—any student excluded based on sex must have made available comparable courses, services, and facilities, pursuant to the same policies and criteria of admissions. The Title IX regulation generally prohibits single-sex classes or programs in co-educational schools. There are some exceptions, including contact sports, chorus, and portions of classes dealing with human sexuality. Separate classes may also be provided for pregnant students, but participation must be voluntary. Title IX also allows for single-sex classes and programs if they are necessary to remedy discrimination found by a court or OCR, or as a response to conditions that have limited participation by sex.

> *If you are thinking of establishing a single-sex class, program, or school, we encourage you to contact your LEA and the OCR office that serves your state for more guidance. ED is reviewing its Title IX regulation pertaining to single-sex programs and schools.*

Schools Affected by Desegregation Plans or Court Orders

Some school districts have desegregation obligations under plans or court orders that could affect or be affected by the establishment of your charter school, even if your charter school is its own LEA. Typically, desegregation plans and court orders are resolutions of past segregative discrimination by school districts determined by OCR or by the courts, in some instances with the participation of the U.S. Department of Justice, Civil Rights Division (CRD). If the jurisdiction in which your charter school is located is under a desegregation plan or order, there are steps you can take to ensure compliance and avoid unnecessary delays.

10. How do I determine whether my proposed charter school is in a jurisdiction with a duty to desegregate?

If you are uncertain whether your charter school is in a jurisdiction that is covered by an existing desegregation plan or court order, you may contact several entities for assistance. First, to determine if there is an applicable court order where the United States is a party to the case, you may contact the appropriate LEA, your SEA, or CRD. To assist you in this process, CRD has provided your chief state school officer with a list of the LEAs in the state that are subject to such a court order. Second, to determine if there is an applicable OCR Title VI desegregation plan, you may contact the appropriate LEA or the OCR office that serves your state. You should also know that there are other desegregation plans and orders that do not involve CRD or OCR. These desegregation plans and orders only involve private parties in state or federal courts, or state agencies that have ordered districts to desegregate. In some states and school districts there may also be other obligations under state or local laws or policies, such as those to promote integration or diversity, that could affect or be affected by your charter school. In these cases, you should consult your SEA or the appropriate LEA to determine whether the jurisdiction has a desegregation obligation.

> *If you have questions about a desegregation court order where the United States is a party to the case, you may contact CRD at 202-514-4092. If you have questions about a Title VI desegregation plan, you may contact the OCR office that serves your state. A list of OCR offices is attached.*

11. What steps should my LEA or I take in order to establish a school that complies with an existing desegregation plan or court order?

The establishment of any new public school, including a new charter school, in a jurisdiction with a duty to desegregate must be consistent with the LEA's obligations under its desegregation plan or court order. Alternatively, it is possible to seek a modification of the applicable plan or order. If you are establishing a charter school in a jurisdiction that is under an OCR Title VI desegregation plan, OCR should be consulted on any applicable Title VI obligations. Similarly, CRD should be contacted if you are establishing a charter school in a jurisdiction under a desegregation court order in which the United States is a party to the case. You, the appropriate LEA, or your chartering authority may contact these agencies. Early consultation will speed the process for your charter school proposal and can avoid unnecessary delay or disruption in the future. Review of any new school by a court or OCR involves a case-by-case, fact-bound determination that takes into account the particular charter school's impact on the ability of the appropriate LEA to comply with its unique desegregation obligations.

12. What information is needed for this consultation process to be effective?

As a first step, you should provide a copy of the charter school application to either OCR or CRD. In general, OCR and CRD are interested in the effect a new public school will have on the appropriate LEA's obligations. Your charter application will contain at least some of the information needed to make this determination, such as those items listed below.Because charter school applications vary from state to state, and because each court order and OCR Title VI desegregation plan is different, CRD or OCR may need more information than is included in your charter application. The information below is especially helpful to CRD or OCR in evaluating the impact of your school on the LEA's desegregation obligations, although additional information may be necessary:

- theme and target population;
- recruitment and admissions processes;
- proposed location;
- enrollment capacity of the school;
- projected racial composition of students, faculty, and staff for the coming school year; and
- impact on racial composition of students at other schools in the LEA.

13. In the case of a court order, what does CRD do with this information?

If your jurisdiction is under a desegregation court order where the United States is a party to the case, you should consult with CRD. When CRD receives information on your charter school, it will review your submission, its own files, and any other readily available information to see if these sources provide enough data to reach a position about the charter school's impact on compliance with the desegregation order. If more information is needed, CRD will contact you and the appropriate LEA to request the additional information. In many cases, the limited number of students enrolled in a charter school does not have a significant impact on the attendance patterns and enrollment in the appropriate LEA's other schools, and does not adversely affect compliance with the desegregation order. In such cases, and in other cases where CRD concludes there is no adverse impact, CRD will advise you and the appropriate LEA that it has no objection to the proposed operation of the charter school. If CRD's review of the information raises

concerns about compliance with the desegregation order, CRD may offer suggestions and modifications that address these concerns, where appropriate.

> *When an LEA is subject to a desegregation court order, it is the court, not DOJ, that*
> *determines whether or not to approve a new school. Where approval is required, the*
> *court will ask the other parties to the case, including DOJ, for their views.*

14. Who is responsible for notifying the court about a new charter school to obtain court approval when required?

If your jurisdiction is under a desegregation court order, the appropriate LEA
may need to have the court approve any new school, including a charter school.
Where court approval is required, charter school developers should contact their
LEA or SEA for information on how best to obtain the approval of the court. Where
appropriate, CRD may be able to make a joint motion with a charter school or
LEA to seek court approval for a new charter school. However, CRD can not represent charter school developers before the court, and can not submit motions on
their behalf.

15. In the case of a desegregation plan, what does OCR do with this information?

If your jurisdiction is under an OCR desegregation plan, you should consult
with the OCR office that serves your state. After OCR receives information on your
charter school, we promptly examine it along with the Title VI desegregation plan
and any other readily available information to determine if establishing the new
school would be consistent with the appropriate LEA's Title VI obligations. If OCR
needs more information, we will contact you and the appropriate LEA. In many
cases, a charter school does not adversely affect compliance with the OCR Title VI
desegregation plan because the limited number of students enrolled has a minimal
effect on the attendance patterns and enrollment in the LEA's other schools. In such
cases, and in other cases where OCR concludes there is no adverse impact, OCR
will advise you and the appropriate LEA that it has no objection to the proposed
operation of the charter school. If OCR's review of the information raises concerns
about compliance with the LEA's Title VI obligations, OCR may offer suggestions
and modifications that address these concerns, where appropriate.

Selection of Facilities to Provide Access to Students with Disabilities

For some people with physical disabilities, an otherwise outstanding program may as well not exist if it is located in an inaccessible facility. Section 504
and Title II require that persons with disabilities have access to the programs and
activities offered at public schools. Because charter schools often open in older
buildings that may lack attention to accessible design or in contemporary or reno-
vated buildings that were not originally designed for use as public schools, it is
important that you be aware of these requirements.

16. Are there requirements for physical access that apply when I select the facilities that will house my charter school?

Yes. An LEA (including your charter school if it is its own LEA) may not deny
persons with disabilities, including parents and students, the benefits of programs
and activities offered at its schools because of inaccessible facilities. The selection
of the facility for your charter school may not result in excluding or limiting enrollment of people with disabilities from any school program or activity.

The program accessibility requirements of Section 504 and Title II often involve complex issues. For technical assistance regarding accessible programs and facilities, please contact the OCR Office that serves your state.

17. Are there different legal requirements that apply to charter schools located in existing facilities as compared to newer facilities?

Yes. For existing facilities, a charter school's programs and activities, when viewed in their entirety, must be readily accessible to individuals with disabilities. Both the Section 504 and Title II regulations permit considerable flexibility in meeting this legal standard. For example, structural changes are not required in existing facilities if nonstructural methods are effective in achieving program accessibility. For new construction and alterations, Section 504 and Title II require that a new or altered facility (or the part that is new or altered) must be readily accessible to and usable by individuals with disabilities. The focus here is on providing physical access to buildings and facilities in addition to programs and activities. This means you must make sure that a child with a physical disability has access to every part of the new building or the parts that are newly altered. For example, if your charter school is in a new building, all parts of the building, including the third-floor chemistry labs, must be accessible for use by persons with disabilities. In contrast, if your charter school is in an existing facility, you might be able to meet the program accessibility requirement by locating at least one chemistry lab in an accessible location like the first floor.

18. How do I know if a building is considered an existing facility or new construction?

Any building or alteration by or on behalf of your LEA or your charter school for which construction began since June 1977, is considered new. Any construction or alteration that was not done by or on behalf of your LEA or charter school is likely to be considered an existing facility, regardless of its age.

Any construction that began before June 4, 1977, is considered existing. Any construction or alteration by or on behalf of your LEA or charter school that began after January 26, 1992, is considered new. Construction that began on or between those two dates is new under Section 504 and existing under Title II. In these cases, the more stringent standard for new construction would apply.

19. What should I consider when acquiring the space in which I operate my program?

In summary, when you purchase, take title to, lease, or rent a facility, you are encouraged to look for the most accessible space available. At a minimum, you must make sure that the educational program, when viewed in its entirety, is readily accessible to and usable by individuals with disabilities, in accordance with the requirements for existing facilities. Construction or alteration initiated by you or for your charter school must also meet standards for new construction.

Educating Students Who Are Limited-English Proficient

A growing number of students in the public school population are national-origin minority students who are limited-English proficient (LEP). These children include recent immigrants to the United States, and other children raised with languages other than English. Generally, these children's limited ability to speak, read, write, and understand English well enough to participate meaningfully is a barrier to their educational success. Federal civil rights law requires that public schools provide LEP children appropriate services designed to teach them English and the general curriculum.

20. What civil rights requirements apply if there are LEP students attending my charter school?

In *Lau v. Nichols*, the U.S. Supreme Court held that school districts must take affirmative steps to help LEP students overcome language barriers so that they can participate meaningfully in each school district's programs. Under Title VI, public schools and LEAs must identify LEP students and provide them educational services so they can learn English-language skills and acquire the knowledge and skills in academic content areas that all students are required to know. Public schools are not required to adopt any particular model of instruction for LEP students. However, where a program is necessary to ensure equal educational opportunity for LEP students, it must be based on a sound educational theory, adequately supported with qualified staff and adequate resources so that the program has a reasonable chance for success, and periodically evaluated and revised, if necessary.

21. Are there federal funds available to help me educate LEP students?

Yes. A wide variety of resources are available to help you serve your charter school's LEP students. In addition to receiving general educational funds and state and local funds appropriated for the education of LEP students, LEAs may qualify for Federal financial assistance. For example, like any public school, your charter school might qualify for funds from Title I, Title VII, or other titles of the Elementary and Secondary Education Act of 1965, as amended. These grant funds may be used to supplement the services that the LEA is required to provide using state and local educational funds. Title I is administered by ED's Office of Elementary and Secondary Education (OESE). There are specific requirements that you must meet in order to receive Title I funds. Contact your SEA to find out if your charter school is eligible for these funds. LEAs may apply for Title VII funds from ED's Office of Bilingual Education and Minority Languages Affairs (OBEMLA). Your charter school might also join with other charter schools or work with LEAs to share qualified staff and other resources. Keep in mind that the obligation to educate LEP students is the same regardless of whether special funds or resources are available.

> *Title I provides assistance to at-risk children in high-poverty schools. For further information on Title I, visit OESE's World Wide Web site. Title VII helps LEAs meet their needs and objectives related to improving the instruction of LEP students. For further information on Title VII, visit OBEMLA's Web site.*

22. What must I do to make sure that limited-English proficient parents of students in my school are provided with information about school activities?

Like operators of other public schools, you must ensure that language-minority parents who are not proficient in English receive the same information provided to other parents, in a manner and form they understand. This may include information about their children's program, progress, and disciplinary problems, as well as information about the school's rules, policies, and activities. This information may have to be provided in a language other than English for parents who are not proficient in English.

You may find assistance through real-time interpreting services, such as those provided by telecommunications companies.

Educating Students with Disabilities

Some children arrive at school with disabilities that affect their participation in the educational program. Sometimes, these disabilities are known; sometimes they remain hidden until a parent or teacher raises a concern. The challenge for all public schools is to identify children with disabilities, assess their individual needs, and provide appropriate educational services without undue delay.

23. What civil rights requirements apply to my charter school for the education of students with disabilities?

Under Section 504 and Title II, students with disabilities enrolled in public schools, including your charter school, are entitled to a free appropriate public education (FAPE). The Section 504 regulation includes several substantive and procedural requirements regarding the provision of FAPE. Among these requirements is that a student with a disability must receive appropriate regular or special education and related aids and services. The requirement is designed so that the individual educational needs of the disabled student are met as adequately as the needs of nondisabled students.

24. Are there federal funds available to help me meet my obligation to educate students with disabilities?

Yes. Your charter school might benefit from federal funds available under the Individuals with Disabilities Education Act (IDEA). The IDEA is a federal law that provides funds to SEAs, and through them to LEAs, to help schools serve students with disabilities. There are specific requirements of the IDEA that you must meet in order to receive these federal funds. Contact your SEA to find out if these funds are available to you.Like Section 504 and Title II, the IDEA has FAPE requirements. In general, if you satisfy the FAPE requirements under the IDEA, then you will be in compliance with the FAPE requirements of Section 504 and Title II. The IDEA, which has distinct requirements that are not discussed in detail in this publication, is administered by ED's Office of Special Education and Rehabilitative Services (OSERS).

For further information on the IDEA and its requirements, contact OSERS' Office of Special Education Programs (OSEP) at 202-205-5507; or visit OSEP's World Wide Web site.

25. Are there additional ways to help me meet my obligations under Section 504 and Title II?

Yes. In addition to providing federal funds to eligible entities, the IDEA allows a state the flexibility to designate some other entity as responsible for ensuring that the requirements of the IDEA are met for children with disabilities enrolled in public schools. Where you are meeting your charter school's Section 504 and Title II FAPE responsibilities through compliance with IDEA requirements, the IDEA's flexibility could help you meet your charter school's Section 504 and Title II FAPE responsibilities. Generally, if a state designates another entity as responsible for ensuring that all of the IDEA requirements are met for eligible disabled children enrolled in a particular charter school, that designated entity would ensure that FAPE is provided to each of those students, generally at the charter school site.

> *Contact your SEA to learn whether your state makes this flexibility available to your charter school.*

26. **Could a child be protected by Section 504 and Title II but not be eligible to receive services under the IDEA?**

   Yes. Some students with disabilities are protected by Section 504 and Title II, but are not eligible to receive services under the IDEA because they do not need special education. One example would be a child with juvenile rheumatoid arthritis who requires the periodic administration of medication during the school day, but who does not need any special education services. The child may have the right to FAPE under Section 504 and Title II, even though the child is not eligible for services under the IDEA.

   > *Under Section 504 and Title II, an individual with a disability is an individual who either has a physical or mental impairment that substantially limits one or more major life activities (such as learning), has a record of such an impairment, or is regarded as having such an impairment.*

27. **May I limit the participation of students with disabilities to certain aspects of my charter school's program?**

   No. Consistent with civil rights requirements, students with disabilities must be provided a range of choices in programs and activities that is comparable to that offered to students without disabilities. This includes an opportunity to participate in a range of nonacademic or extracurricular programs and activities offered at your charter school.

28. **Is a student with a disability required to be educated with students without disabilities?**

   A student with a disability must be educated with nondisabled students to the maximum extent appropriate for the disabled student. The education of students with disabilities must be designed to meet their individual needs. A student with a disability may be placed in a setting outside the regular classroom only if the regular educational environment—including using supplementary aids and services—cannot satisfactorily meet the student's educational needs. The group making placement decisions is responsible for selecting the setting that satisfies these requirements.

   > *The Section 504 regulation requires that any placement decision be made by a group of persons, including persons knowledgeable about the child, the meaning of the evaluation data, and the placement options.*

29. **What do I need to do when a student enrolled in my charter school is believed to have a disability?**

   When a student is believed to have a disability, your charter school, like any public school, must initiate the procedures established by your SEA or by your LEA (if your charter school is a part of the LEA) to identify and refer the student for evaluation in a timely manner.

30. **What other rights and responsibilities are included in the provision of FAPE regarding student identification, evaluation, and placement?**

   Under Section 504 and Title II, students with disabilities, and their parents or guardians, are entitled to due process from the LEA concerning student identification, evaluation, and placement. Simply stated, due process is procedural fairness. In the context of FAPE, due process includes notice, the opportunity for review of records, the right to request an impartial hearing with representation by counsel, and a procedure for review. In general, by complying with the relevant IDEA procedural-safeguard requirements, an LEA is complying with these Section 504 and Title II requirements.

Endnotes

The information provided in this document discussed the application of federal civil rights laws to charter schools. As stated above, the document discusses the application of existing law, and does not set forth new law. These same civil rights laws apply to all public schools, including charter schools. The following endnotes provide citations and background information to the major points addressed in this document. Numbers correspond to the answers in this document. These endnotes are not meant to be an exhaustive list of existing regulations or case law, but a brief, helpful summary and restatement of relevant federal civil rights laws. If you have further questions, please contact the OCR office that serves your state. A list of OCR offices is attached.

Responsibilities for Civil Rights Compliance

1. The federal civil rights laws and the implementing regulations that OCR enforces include: 42 U.S.C. § 2000d *et seq.*, 34 C.F.R. Part 100 (1999) (Title VI); 29 U.S.C. § 1681 *et seq.*, 34 C.F.R. Part 106 (1999) (Title IX); 29 U.S.C. § 794 *et seq.*, 34 C.F.R. Part 104 (1999) (Section 504); 42 U.S.C. § 12101 *et seq.*, 28 C.F.R. part 35 (1999) (Title II); 42 U.S.C. § 6101 *et seq.*, 45 C.F.R. Part 90 (1999) (Age Discrimination Act). (All subsequent citations in this document from the Code of Federal Regulations (C.F.R) are also from the 1999 edition.)

2. There are other federal civil rights statutes that apply to public schools, which are not addressed in this publication. These include, but are not limited to:
    - Title IV of the Civil Rights Act of 1964, 42 U.S.C. § 2000b *et seq.*, which authorizes the Attorney General to institute civil actions alleging discrimination on the basis of race, color, sex, religion or national origin by public elementary and secondary schools and public institutions of higher learning.
    - Title VII of the Civil Rights Act of 1964, 42 U.S.C. § 2000e *et seq.*, which prohibits employment practices that discriminate on the grounds of race, sex, religion, and national origin.
    - The Equal Educational Opportunities Act of 1974 (EEOA), 20 U.S.C. § 1701 *et seq.*, which prohibits specific discriminatory conduct, including segregating students on the basis of race, color or national origin, and discrimination against faculty and staff. The EEOA also requires school districts to take action to overcome students' language barriers that impede equal participation in educational programs.

Recruitment and Admissions

3. For regulations that generally address nondiscrimination in recruitment, see: 34 C.F.R. § 100.3(b); 34 C.F.R. § 106.23; 34 C.F.R. §106.36; 28 C.F.R. § 35.130; 34 C.F.R. § 104.4(b). For regulations which govern targeted recruitment, see: 34 C.F.R. § 100.3(b) (6) (i) (ii); 34 C.F.R. § 106.3 (a)-(b); 34 C.F.R. § 104.6(a)-(b); 45 C.F.R. § 90.49.

4. For documents supporting outreach to limited-English proficient parents, see: Identification of Discrimination and Denial of Services on the Basis of National Origin, 35 Fed. Reg. 11595 (1970) (hereinafter OCR 1970 memorandum) (requires adequate notice to LEP parents of school activities); Policy Update on Schools' Obligations Toward National Origin Minority Students with Limited-English Proficiency (9/27/91) (hereinafter OCR 1991 memorandum) at 8 (discussing notification to parents of LEP students in specialized programs). OCR's policy on the requirements for LEP students are encompassed in three documents: the 2 documents listed above along with The Office for Civil Rights' Title VI Language Minority Compliance Procedures (initially issued 12/3/85, reissued without change 4/6/90). These three documents should be read together and are available through your OCR office.

5. For regulations related to outreach for parents with disabilities, see: 28 C.F.R. § 35.160; 28 C.F.R. § 35.104 (1)-(2). See also 34 C.F.R. § 104.4(b).

6. For regulations regarding non-discriminatory treatment in admissions, regardless of race, color and national origin, see: 34 C.F.R. § 100.3(b) (1) (v); 34 C.F.R. § 100.3(b) (2). Also read Guardian's Association v. Civil Service Commission, 463 U.S. 582 (1983) (holding disparate impact standard as valid). Many courts use the term "equally effective" (see, for example, Georgia State Conf. of Branches of NAACP v. Georgia, 775 F.2d 1403, 1417 (11th Cir. 1985)) and "comparably effective" (see, for example, Elston v. Talladega County Bd. of Educ. , 997 F.2d 1394, 1407 (11th Cir. 1993)) when discussing whether alternative criteria serve the educational goals; the courts appear to use the terms synonymously. Also helpful is 34 C.F.R. 100, Appendix B, part K (Guidelines for Eliminating Discrimination and Denial of Services on the Basis of Race, Color, National Origin, Sex and Handicap in Vocational Education Programs). For admissions requirements concerning LEP students, see OCR 1991 memorandum at pages 8-9 (LEP students cannot be categorically excluded from specialized programs unless the particular program requires proficiency in English for meaningful participation).

7. The list of cases discussing the use of race is lengthy. For the general principles regarding the use of race, see, for example, Adarand Constructors, Inc. v. PeÒa, 515 U.S. 200 (1995) (holding that use of race must serve a compelling legal interest and be narrowly tailored to serve that interest). Elimination of discrimination is a compelling government interest that can justify race-conscious measures. See, for example, United States v. Fordice, 505 U.S. 717 (1992). The Supreme Court and other courts have recognized other compelling interests. See, for example, Regents of University of California v. Bakke, 438 U.S. 265, 311-14 (1978) (opinion of Powell, J.) (Promotion of educational benefits of diverse student body furthers a compelling state interest justifying use of race in university admissions). See, for example, Wittmer v. Peters, 87 F.3d 916, 919 (7th Cir. 1997), cert. denied, 117 S. Ct. 949 (1997) (finding a compelling interest in the use of use of race in maintaining the integrity of correctional facility's boot camp program). But see, for example, Hopwood v. State of Texas, 78 F.3d 932, 944-948 (5th Cir.), cert. denied, 518 U.S. 1033 (1996) (University interest in attaining diverse student body does not constitute a compelling governmental interest to justify use of race in law student selec-

tion). Other courts have assumed for the sake of argument that diversity is a compelling legal interest, but struck down the use of race in admissions on the grounds that the specific policy challenged was not narrowly tailored to meet the diversity interest. See, for example, <u>Wessmann v. Gittens</u>, 160 F.3d 790, 795-799 (1st Cir. 1998). Congress has also recognized that the elimination of racial isolation has significant benefits. See 20 U.S.C. §§ 7201-7213 (Magnet School Assistance Program). For additional helpful background information on this topic, see: <u>Adarand</u> Memorandum to General Counsels from Assistant Attorney General Walter Dellinger (6/28/95); 34 C.F.R. § 100.3(b) (6) (i) and (ii); 59 Fed. Reg. 8756 (02/23/1994) (Title VI and applicability to financial aid); Bakke Notice, 44 Fed. Reg. 58509 (10/10/79).

8. The regulations related to admissions of students with disabilities include: 34 C.F.R. § 104.4(a)-(b); 28 C.F.R. § 35.130(a); 28 C.F.R. § 35.104 (1)-(2).

9. The regulations that address single-sex courses, activities, programs and schools are: 34 C.F.R. § 106.34 (single-sex courses); 34 C.F.R. § 106.35 (single-sex schools); 34 C.F.R. § 106.3(a)-(b) (single-sex activities/programs). The Supreme Court has also addressed the legality of single-sex institutions. See, for example, <u>United States v. Virginia</u>, 518 U.S. 515, 531 (1996) (parties who seek to defend gender-based government action must demonstrate an "exceedingly persuasive justification").

Schools Affected by Desegregation Plans or Court Orders

10. For a discussion of de jure segregation in public schools, see generally, for example, <u>Swann v. Charlotte-Mecklenburg Board of Education</u>, 402 U.S. 1 (1971); <u>Green v. County School Board of New Kent County</u>, 391 U.S. 430 (1968); <u>Brown v. Board of Education</u>, 347 U.S. 483 (1954). See also: 34 C.F.R. § 100.4 (c) (2) (OCR plans); 34 C.F.R. § 100.4(c) (1) (court orders). To examine more recent Supreme Court school desegregation cases, in particular unitary status, see, for example, <u>Jenkins v. Missouri</u>, 515 U.S. 70 (1995); <u>Freeman v. Pitts</u>, 503 U.S. 467 (1992); <u>Board of Education of Oklahoma City v. Dowell</u>, 498 U.S. 237 (1991). If a charter school is its own LEA, it still could affect a desegregation plan or court order. Two Supreme Court cases which provide support are: <u>Wright v. Council of Emporia</u>, 407 U.S. 451, 460-462 (1972) (Even if there is no discriminatory intent, a new school district could not be created if its effect would be to impede progress of dismantling the existing dual system); <u>United States v. Scotland Neck City Bd. of Ed.</u>, 407 U.S. 484 (1972) (Whether action affecting dismantling of dual school system is by legislature or school district is immaterial, criterion is whether the dismantling of dual system is furthered or hindered).

11. For cases dealing specifically with charter schools and school desegregation, see, for example, <u>Berry v. School District of the City of Benton Harbor</u>, 56 F.Supp.2d 866, 872 (W.D. Mich 1999) (holding charter school has same burdens as other public schools in district subject to court's remedial order); <u>Beaufort County Board of Education v. Lighthouse Charter School et. al.</u>, 516 S.E.2d 655, 659 (S.C. 1999) (holding valid a school board finding that charter school applicant failed to adhere to same remedial requirements as other public schools in the district under OCR Title VI desegregation plan); <u>Davis v. East Baton Rouge Parish School Board, et al</u>, C.A. No. 56-1662 (M.D. La. 1999)

(stating that charter schools in district remain subject to court's orders relating to desegregation of district). Courts are guided by the general principle established in Wright and Scotland Neck, both discussed in note 10.

12. As stated before, it is the effect of the action, not the intent, that determines whether new schools comply with school desegregation decrees. See: Wright and Scotland Neck, both discussed in note 10. For more discussion on how charter schools can meet school desegregation requirements, see, for example, Benton Harbor, discussed in note 11 (court approved a charter school since it provided sufficient information; ordered it to undertake recruitment steps that would guarantee a population to approximate racial characteristics of district). Generally, see also: 34 C.F.R. § 100.3(b) (2); 34 C.F.R. § 100.3(b) (3).

13. See the endnote discussing the answer to question 12.

14. See the endnotes discussing the answers to questions 10-12.

15. See the endnote discussing the answer to question 12.

Selection of Facilities to Provide Access to Students with Disabilities

16. For requirements involving physical accessibility to schools, see: 34 C.F.R. § 104.21; 28 C.F.R. § 35.149.

17. For regulations involving existing facilities as opposed to new facilities, see: 34 C.F.R. §§ 104.22-23; 28 C.F.R. §§ 35.150-151. For additional background information, see: Uniform Federal Accessibility Standards; Americans with Disabilities Act Accessibility Guidelines; American National Standards Institute A117.1-1961 (R1971).

18. The regulations that distinguish new facilities from existing ones are: 34 C.F.R. § 104.23 (c); 28 C.F.R. § 35.151.

19. To assist you in choosing the space where you operate your charter school, you should read: 34 C.F.R. §§ 104.21-23; 28 C.F.R. §§ 35.149-151.

Educating Students Who Are Limited-English Proficient

20. The legal support for taking affirmative steps in educating LEP students are: Lau v. Nichols, 414 U.S. 563 (1974); 34 C.F.R. § 100.3(b) (2); OCR 1970 memorandum (35 Fed. Reg. 11595, 07/18/70) (cited with approval in Lau). For the legal standard regarding the instructional program for LEP students, see: Casteneda v. Pickard, 648 F.2d 989, 1009-1010 (5th Cir. 1981) (decided under EEOA framework and applied in OCR Title VI analysis, OCR 1991 Memorandum at 12-15).

21. The relevant statute is the Improving America's Schools Act of 1994, P.L. 103-382 (10/20/94), 108 Stat. 3518. 20 U.S.C. § 6301-6514 (Title I); 20 U.S.C. § 7401-7602. (Title VII).

22. The OCR 1970 memorandum, set out more fully in note 4, specifically addresses this issue. See also 34 C.F.R. § 100.3(b) (2).

Educating Students with Disabilities

23. For regulations dealing with the civil rights requirements of providing a free appropriate public education, read: 34 C.F.R. § 104.33; 28 C.F.R. § 35.130(b) (1) (iv).

24. The regulations of the IDEA are at: 34 C.F.R. Part 300. If a school satisfies the FAPE requirement under IDEA, it is in compliance with FAPE under 504 and Title II. See: 34 C.F.R. § 300.13; 34 C.F.R. § 104.33(b) (2).

25. The regulation discussing the flexibility of IDEA is 34 C.F.R. § 300.312.

26. For discussion of how a student could be protected under Section 504 and Title II, but not be eligible for IDEA services, see in general: 34 C.F.R. § 104.3(k) (2); 34 C.F.R. § 300.7. The definition of a person with a disability can be found at 34 C.F.R. § 104.3(j); 28 C.F.R. § 35.104.

27. For discussion of participation of students with disabilities in nonacademic services, see: 34 C.F.R. § 104.37; 34 C.F.R. § 104.34(b).

28. The regulations addressing the educational placement of students with disabilities are: 34 C.F.R. § 104.4(b) (2); 34 C.F.R. § 104.34(a).

29. The regulation that addresses when a student is believed to have a disability is 34 C.F.R. § 104.35(a).

30. Other rights and responsibilities included in the provision of FAPE are discussed at 34 C.F.R. § 104.36.

Appendix C

Nonregulatory Guidance: The Impact of the New Title I Requirements on Charter Schools, Draft Guidance (March 24, 2003)

U.S. Department of Education Office of Elementary and Secondary Education

A. Charter Schools and Accountability Requirements in NCLB

A-1. **Are charter schools subject to meeting adequate yearly progress (AYP)?**
Yes, charter schools, like all public schools within a State, are subject to the State's Title I accountability requirements. However, a State shall look to its charter school law to ascertain the entity responsible for overseeing charter school accountability for Title I purposes.

A-2. **Which entity in a State is responsible for ensuring that charter schools make adequate yearly progress and comply with other accountability provisions in Title I, Part A?**
Section 1111(b)(2)(K) of the Elementary and Secondary Education Act of 1965, as amended by the No Child Left Behind Act of 2001 (NCLB) and Section 200.49(f) of the final Title I regulations (67 Fed.Reg. 71710, 71727, to be codified at 34 C.F.R. pt. 200) require accountability for charter schools to be overseen in accordance with State charter school law. Thus, a State's charter school law determines the entity within the State that bears responsibility for ensuring that charter schools comply with the Title I, Part A accountability provisions, including AYP. The charter authorizer is responsible for holding charter schools accountable for Title I, Part A provisions unless State law specifically gives the SEA direct responsibility for charter school accountability. We do not expect the LEA in which the charter school is located to be this entity, unless it is also the charter authorizer.

A-3. **Must charter school authorizers now insert state plans for meeting AYP into individual charter contracts?**
NCLB requires that authorizers monitor their charter schools to ensure they are meeting the State's AYP definition. If authorizers wish, they may choose to incorporate the AYP definition into charter contracts, especially for new schools, but NCLB does not explicitly require this step.

A-4. **Given the important role for charter authorizers in many States under NCLB, should authorizers be assured resources from SEAs to discharge their accountability oversight responsibilities effectively?**

Yes, pursuant to State charter laws, NCLB empowers many charter authorizers with the oversight responsibilities for this Act. In States where the charter law defers to charter authorizers for accountability oversight, SEAs should consult with authorizers, especially in States that permit alternate authorizers such as public universities and/or municipal governments, to ensure they have the resources necessary to perform the duties assigned to them under NCLB.

A-5. Will eligible charter authorizers now be responsible for allocating Title I and other federal formula funds to their charter schools?
No. If a charter school is authorized by an entity other than a traditional (school-district) LEA, the SEA will still be responsible for allocating Title I funds directly to the charter school, pursuant to federal and state laws. In allocating these funds, SEAs will still comply with Section 5206 of ESEA and ensure that funds are allocated in a timely and efficient manner for new and expanding charter schools. If a charter is, under State law, part of an LEA, the LEA will allocate Federal funds to the school on the same basis that it provides funds to its other schools.

A-6. Should State Title I accountability plans specifically address charter schools and reflect input from charter authorizers and operators?
Yes. Charter schools are public schools subject to the accountability requirements of NLCB. In accordance with congressional intent, Title I state accountability plans may not "replace or duplicate the role of authorized chartering agencies" in overseeing accountability requirements for charter schools. State Title I accountability plans should respect the unique nature of charter schools and should reflect input from charter operators and authorizers.

A-7. Are charter schools subject to the same Title I accountability requirements as other public schools under NCLB?
Yes. In general, State charter laws currently require charter schools to participate in a State's assessment system for public schools in the State. Charter schools are subject to the same Title I accountability requirements as other public schools in a given State, including AYP (see A-1 and A-2).

A-8. What if a charter school fails to meet AYP requirements but meets its contractual requirements with its authorizer?
If a charter school fails to meet AYP requirements, then the charter school authorizer must take actions as required by NCLB.

A-9. Does NCLB prohibit more rigorous accountability requirements than the requirements of a State's Title I accountability plan in an existing charter contract or a future charter contract?
No. Nothing in NCLB prohibits the continuation of existing charter contracts, nor prohibits the development of future contracts that meet or exceed the Title I accountability requirements of NCLB. If a charter school's contract with its authorizer imposes more immediate consequences than a State's Title I accountability plan, the Department believes the authorizer should continue to ensure that the school abides by the charter contract under state law, not withstanding the fact that the school may have made AYP.

B. Charter Schools and the Title I Public School Choice Provisions

B-1. May an eligible charter school that is part of an LEA be listed as a choice option for parents who wish to transfer their child to a higher-performing school?

Yes. LEAs should list charter schools that have not been identified for improvement, corrective action, or restructuring as choice options. Section 200.44(a)(3)(B)(ii) of the Title I regulations (67 Fed. Reg. 71710, 71724, to be codified at 34 C.F.R. pt. 200) also discusses charter schools as choice options.

B-2. If a charter school is its own LEA but falls within the boundaries of a larger LEA, should eligible students from the larger LEA be able to transfer to it?

Yes. An LEA should work with charter school LEAs within its geographic boundaries to reach agreements allowing students to transfer to these schools. Also, allowing eligible students to transfer to a charter school LEA within its boundaries does not lift the requirement that the LEA provide choice options in schools that it operates.

B-3. Do charter schools that admit students using a lottery have to give priority to eligible students transferring under the public school choice provisions of NCLB?

No. Nothing in the statute requires that students transferring under the Title I public school choice provisions be granted preference in these lotteries. State law determines how and if lotteries operate for oversubscribed charter schools. Also, to be an eligible charter school under the Federal charter school grants program, a charter school must use a lottery to admit students if there are more applicants than openings; however some State laws allow other methods for determining admission to oversubscribed charter schools.

B-4. Must parents be notified if a charter school is identified as in need of improvement, corrective action, or restructuring?

Yes. If a charter school is identified for improvement, parents of students enrolled at the school must be notified of its status before the beginning of the school year following identification, just as parents of students enrolled in other public schools are notified. If a charter school is part of an LEA, then the LEA should notify parents of their options. If the charter school is an LEA itself, then the authorizer or the charter school itself should notify parents of the school's status and their options, including returning children to their "home" public school.

B-5. Are charter schools that are parts of LEAs under State law, required to provide choice options and offer transportation for students to other higher-performing schools in the LEA if the charter school is identified by the State as in need of improvement, corrective action, restructuring?

Yes, consistent with the statute, LEAs that authorize charter schools must provide choice options and offer transportation to other public schools of choice within the LEA, even if a State's charter law does not require that transportation funds be made available for charter schools.

B-6. Are charter schools that are their own LEAs under State law required to provide choice options and offer transportation for students to other higher-

performing schools in another LEA if the charter school is identified by the State as in need of improvement, corrective action, or restructuring?

No. As noted above, if the charter school is an LEA itself, then the authorizer or the charter school itself should notify parents of the school's status and their options, including returning children to their "home" public school.

However, according to Section 200.44(h)(1) of the Title I regulations (67 Fed. Reg. 71710, 71725, to be codified at 34 C.F.R. pt. 200), if all public schools to which a student may transfer within an LEA (including charter school LEAs) are identified for school improvement, corrective action, or restructuring, the LEA must, to the extent practicable, establish a cooperative agreement with one or more other LEAs in the area. Therefore, a charter school LEA must, if it is practicable, establish such agreements with other LEAs.

Also, according to Section 200.44(h)(2) of the final Title I regulations, LEAs (including charter school LEAs) which have no eligible schools to which qualifying students may transfer, are allowed to offer supplemental educational services to parents of eligible students in the first year of school improvement.

B-7.   **Are there Department resources one can use to find more information on NCLB's public school choice provisions?**

Yes. For more information please consult the Department'sTitle I regulations at: http://www.ed.gov/legislation/FedRegister/finrule/2002-4/120202a.html. You may also wish to consult the non-regulatory guidance on public school choice at: http://www.ed.gov/offices/OESE/SASA/schoolchoiceguid.doc

C. Charter Schools and Supplemental Educational Services Provisions

C-1.   **Can charter schools provide supplemental educational services to students enrolled in low-performing Title I schools?**

Yes, charter schools that are not identified for improvement are eligible to become supplemental educational service providers pursuant to the Title I requirements.

C-2.   **Are students who attend charter schools that are parts of LEAs under State law eligible for supplemental educational services?**

Yes. As with other public schools, if a charter school is identified as in need of improvement for two or more years, then Title I students in the school are eligible to receive supplemental educational services. The LEA must pay for such services on the same basis as it would pay for supplemental services for eligible students in any other school.

C-3.   **Are students who attend charter schools that are their own LEAs under State law eligible for supplemental educational services?**

Yes. As with other public schools, if a charter school is identified as in need of improvement for two or more years, then Title I students are eligible to receive supplemental educational services. A charter school that is its own LEA must pay for such services on the same basis as any other LEA. Also, charter school LEAs that are identified for improvement but are unable to enter into cooperative agreements with other LEAs to accept transferring students may make supplemental services available in the first year of school improvement to eligible students.

C-4. How much must an LEA pay for supplemental educational services?
The law establishes a combined funding requirement for choice-related transportation and supplemental educational services. Unless a lesser amount is needed to meet demand for choice-related transportation and to satisfy all requests for supplemental educational services, an LEA must spend up to an amount equal to 20 percent of its Title I, Part A allocation, before any reservations, on:
   (1) Choice-related transportation;
   (2) Supplemental educational services; or
   (3) A combination of (1) and (2).
These funds may come from Title I, other federal programs such as Title V, Part A of ESEA, funds moved into these programs under the "transferability" authorization, or State or local sources. This flexible funding approach means that the amount of funding that an LEA must devote to supplemental educational services depends in part on how much it spends on choice-related transportation.

If the cost of satisfying all requests for supplemental educational services exceeds an amount equal to 5 percent of an LEA's Title I, Part A allocation, the LEA may not spend less than that amount on those services. An LEA may also spend an amount exceeding 20 percent of its Title I, Part A allocation if additional funds are needed to meet all demands for choice-related transportation and supplemental educational services. This funding mechanism applies to both charter schools that are parts of LEAs and charter schools that are their own LEAs under State law.

C-5. Are there Department resources one can use to find more information on the Title I supplemental educational services provisions?
Yes. For more information please consult the Department's Title I regulations at: http://www.ed.gov/legislation/FedRegister/finrule/2002-4/120202a.html. You may also wish to consult the non-regulatory guidance on supplemental educational services at: http://www.ed.gov/offices/OESE/SASA suppsvcguid.doc.

D. Charter Schools and Corrective Action

D-1. Does NCLB give either States or authorizers the authority to reorganize a charter school's management and enforce other corrective actions?
Yes. As with other public schools, charter schools that are unable to make AYP by the end of the second full school year after identification are placed under corrective action according to Section 1116(b)(7)(C) of ESEA. NCLB gives the appropriate entity under state law (see A-2) the responsibility to reorganize a charter school's management and enforce other corrective actions, consistent with State charter law and the State's accountability plan for its charter schools. State charter law shall determine if this requires the charter school to modify its charter contract.

D-2.   **Under the "corrective action" provisions, NCLB allows States to convert low-performing Title I schools into charter schools. How might a State explain the manner in which this provision would be implemented?**
If a State's charter school law allows public schools to convert to charter status, a State's Title I accountability plan may explain how the process of converting schools identified for corrective action to charter schools would work. The accountability plan might also identify the entities that will be expected to authorize such charters and explain whether these entities have discretion in extending the contracts for these charter schools.

E. Qualifications of Teachers and Paraprofessionals

E-1.   **What qualifications do teachers in Title I charter schools have to meet under NCLB?**
Charter school teachers who teach core academic subjects must comply with any requirement in a State's charter school law regarding certification or licensure. A teacher in a charter school does not have to be licensed or certified by the State if the State's charter law does not require such licensure or certification.

However, teachers of core academic subjects in charter schools must meet the other requirements that apply to public school teachers, including holding a four-year college degree and demonstrating competence in the subject area in which they teach. According to Section 9101(11) of NCLB, the term "core academic subjects" includes English, reading or language arts, mathematics, science, foreign languages, civics and government, economics, arts, history, and geography. For more information on the highly qualified teacher requirements, please consult the Title I regulations, Section 200.56 (67 Fed. Reg. 71710, 71730, to be codified at 34 C.F.R. pt. 200) and the Department's non-regulatory draft guidance on Title II, ESEA, Improving Teacher Quality State Grants, available at: http://www.ed.gov/offices/OESE/SIP/TitleIIguidance2002.doc.

E-2.   **When do charter school teachers have to meet these highly qualified requirements?**
Newly hired teachers of core academic subjects in Title I charter schools are teachers that are hired after the 2002-2003 school year. These teachers must meet the highly qualified teacher requirements applicable to charter school teachers before entering the classroom. Teachers of core academic subjects hired before the start of the 2002-2003 school year must meet the requirements by the end of the 2005-2006 school year. For more information on how teachers can demonstrate competence in their subject area(s), please refer to Appendix A of the Department's draft Title II non-regulatory guidance: Improving Teacher Quality State Grants, available at: http://www.ed.gov/offices/OESE/SIP/TitleIIguidance2002.doc

E-3.   **What qualifications do charter school paraprofessionals have to meet?**
Paraprofessionals with instructional support duties in charter schools receiving Title I funds need to meet the same requirements as paraprofessionals in traditional Title I public schools. This requirement applies only to paid paraprofessionals and not parents or other volunteers.

According to Section 1119(c) and (d) of ESEA, paraprofessionals hired after enactment of NCLB (January 8, 2002) and working in Title I programs must complete at least two years of study at an institution of higher education, possess at least an associate's degree, or demonstrate subject matter competence through a formal State or local assessment.

E-4. **When do paraprofessionals employed prior to the enactment of NCLB need to meet these requirements?**
Paraprofessionals hired before enactment of NCLB (before January 8, 2002) and working in Title I programs must meet these same requirements by January 8, 2006. For more information, please see the draft non-regulatory guidance on paraprofessionals at: http://www.ed.gov/office/OESE/SASA/paraguidance.doc

E-5. **If a charter school does not accept Title I funds, must it comply with these requirements for paraprofessionals?**
No, these requirements are applicable only to Title I schools and to paraprofessionals working in Title I programs.

E-6. **Must charter school LEAs reserve a portion of their Title I funds for professional development if they currently meet the "highly qualified" requirements for charter school teachers and the new requirements for paraprofessionals, do they still need to?**
No. Section 1119(l) of ESEA requires all LEAs, including charter school LEAs, to spend between 5 and 10 percent of their Title I allocations on professional development to help all teachers meet the new requirements by the end of the 2005-06 school year. If all teachers and paraprofessionals in a charter school LEA have met these requirements, the funds do not need to be reserved for professional development. However, even though existing staff may meet these requirements, care should be taken to ensure that all teachers and paraprofessionals (including those who transfer in from other schools in the LEA) meet the requirements on schedule.

E-7. **Which entity is responsible for ensuring that charter schools comply with NCLB's charter school teacher quality requirements?**
Section 1111(b)(2)(K) of ESEA is clear that accountability oversight for charter schools shall be determined by individual State charter laws. The charter authorizer bears primary responsibility for holding charter schools accountable for Title I, Part A provisions (including the Part's teacher quality requirements) unless State law specifically gives the SEA direct responsibility for charter school accountability. We do not expect the LEA in which the charter school is located to be this entity, unless it is also the charter authorizer.

Appendix D

Summaries of Selected Cases
Involving Charter Schools

Acad. of Charter Sch. v. Adams County Sch. Dist. No. 12, 32 P.3d 456 (Colo. 2001).

In this case, the Colorado Supreme Court was asked to determine whether a charter school had standing to sue its sponsoring agent, the local school district, for enforcement of provisions of the charter contract. The court read Colorado's charter school statute to allow such enforcement with regard to the service provisions of the contract (e.g. commitments by the school district to provide services to the charter school) but did not allow the school to sue over policy decisions (e.g., oversight, revocation, or renewal).

Apple Valley Unified Sch. Dist. v. Vavrinek, Trine, Day & Co., 120 Cal.Rptr.2d 629 (Cal. Ct. App. 2002).

A school district sued an accounting firm for malpractice, alleging that the firm misrepresented the number of students enrolled in a charter school, resulting in inflated payments to the school. The court never reached the merits of the claim dismissing on the grounds that the statute of limitations had run out and precluded suit at the time it was filed, more than two years after the district discovered the alleged wrongdoing.

Bacon v. The Leona Group, LLC, No. 219900, 2000 WL 33415004 (Mich. App. 2000).

In this unpublished per curium decision, a Michigan appellate court was asked to determine whether the records held by about a charter school by a for-profit management organization hired to administer the school were subject to the Freedom of Information Act. The school had argued that as a private entity, the management company records were not subject to such a request. The court rejected this thinking and affirmed the lower court's grant of a motion to join the management company to the plaintiff's complaint against the school.

Beaufort County Board of Education v. Lighthouse Charter School, 516 S.E.2d 655 (S.C. 1999).

A South Carolina school board denied a charter based on the failure of the application to meet the Charter Schools Act's requirements. The charter school applicant appealed and the State Board of Education reversed. In June 1999, the Supreme Court of South Carolina affirmed, for the most part, a circuit court's decision to reverse the State Board of Education's decision. The court found the county board to be correct in denying the charter on the grounds that the application did not meet health and safety requirements, as it lacked specifics about proposed buildings. As well, it failed to meet civil rights requirements in not addressing the district's desegregation agreement, which required approval of new school buildings from the United States Department of Education Office for Civil Rights. The application also failed to address the issue of racial composition, which by law could vary by no more than ten percent from the composition of the district. The county board was also within its discretion in finding the economic plan of the school unsound and was reasonable in requiring the school to identify prospective students so as to gauge the financial and racial impact of the school. While the court saw the board as correctly following the charter law, it did remand the case to the lower court to rule on the constitutionality of the racial composition requirement. The Court directed that strict scrutiny should be applied to consider the constitutionality of the provision.

Berkley Elementary School Advisory Council v. School Board of Polk County, 826 So.2d 364 (Fla. App. 2 Dist. 2002).

A school advisory council asked a court to rule on the issue of whether it had standing to make an appeal with respect to the denial of a charter school application by a county school board. The court ruled that the council was a voluntary association and not a legal entity within Florida statutes and as such lacked standing to make any claim. The group failed "to amend its notice of appeal to include any individual or group of individuals it believed had standing to contest" the school board's action (at 365).

Berry v. School District of the City of Benton Harbor, 56 F. Supp. 2d 866 (W.D.Mich. 1999).

In July 1999, a United States District Court in Michigan ruled on whether the funding of a charter school could be denied due to its impact on the district's capacity to carry out a remedial order to eliminate the remnants of discrimination. Potential charter schools, attempting to establish themselves in a district under desegregation orders, petitioned the court to allow state funding of their schools. The state itself had so petitioned the court in 1996, with the case leading to the original court supervision of the district beginning in 1967. While the court reiterated its lack of authority regarding the political decisions concerning charters, it saw a legitimate concern in evaluating the impact of charter schools on existing court orders. It saw the burden on charters of analyzing their effects on the re-segregation of the district reasonable in light of a similar burden on the rest of the district. The court asked for information on transportation, recruitment, curriculum, and on the potential diversity of students, staff, and board. The court was also concerned about which existing schools would lose students to the charters. As well, the court looked at the financial impact on the district's attempts to provide the quality of education required by the court order.

The court was satisfied that the schools had adequate transportation plans to attract a diverse student body. However, the court refused to consider granting one school's petition because it failed to provide enough information on its future student body, thus not allowing the court to judge the school's impact on the district. The other school did provide adequate information, which indicated it would be virtually all African-American. Such a re-segregation was in violation of the desegregation decree. Consequently the judge granted this school's petition with the restriction that its recruitment effort achieve a student body that was 90% African American, as was the case overall in the district. The school was also to routinely report to the court and district information on all student applicants and enrollees, allowing the district to adjust and the court to monitor. Finally, the court ordered the school to continue to recruit a diverse staff and board, implement diversity training, and report on its special education population. The judge was satisfied that the economic impact on the district would not appreciably impede the district's obligations under the decree. While concerned about a draining of resources, the judge did see potential positive impacts from charter schools on the decree's goals, in that they would lower class sizes in the district and provide alternative choices.

Blumenthal v. Barnes, 804 A.2d 152 (Conn. 2002).

When the Attorney General of Connecticut became concerned that a charter school official had breached her fiduciary duty to the school by enriching herself by entering into a lease and two employment contracts with the school, he filed a three part complaint against her. The issue before the Connecticut Supreme Court was whether he had the authority to do so. The court concluded that the attorney general lacked the authority either expressly or on a "common-law" basis. The court reviewed the history of the office and the grant of authority by the state legislature and reasoned that powers of the attorney general were limited by statutory authority. Since the court determined that the "attorney general is 'a creature of statute'" there existed no basis for the actions he took against the charter school official and those complaints were properly dismissed by the lower court.

Board of Education of the Riverhead Central School District v. Board of Regents of the University of the State of New York, 754 N.Y.S.2d 437 (A.D. 3 Dept. 2003).

A school district challenged the granting of a charter by the Board of Regents of the University of the State of New York. The court found no error in the grant of the charter noting that the Board of Regents had made the requisite finding that the charter school was "likely to improve student learning and achievement." The court also noted that the Board of Regents had also given consideration to the financial effects of granting the charter on the existing school district. Finding no error, the court upheld the grant of the charter.

Board of Education of School District No. 1 v. Booth, 984 P.2d 639 (Colo. 1999).

In September 1999, the Supreme Court of Colorado ruled on a constitutional challenge to the state's Charter Schools Act. Charter school applicants had sought to have the courts compel a local board to comply with instructions from the State Board of Education to grant them a charter. The school board argued that the Act's second-appeal procedure violated the state constitution and that the State Board exceeded its authority when it directed a local district school board to approve a charter the local board had rejected twice. The second rejection came after an initial appeal by the applicants to the State Board had led to revisions in the application. After the applicants' second appeal resulted in the State Board ordering the local board to grant the charter, a series of court actions ensued, leading to the case at hand. The court weighed the balance between local control and state's interest in educational policy, in determining that the State Board only overstated its authority in requiring status reports from the negotiating parties. The court supported the State Board's decision to override the local board, as it was for the good of the community. The justices ruled that the second-appeal procedure was constitutional.

Board of Education of Cmt. Consol. Sch. Dist. No. 59 v. Ill. State Board of Education, 740 N.E.2d 428 (Illinois App. Ct. 2000).

A foundation submitted a charter school proposal to an Illinois school district, which denied the charter on the basis that the proposal lacked a proper budget or proposed facility. The foundation appealed to the Illinois State of Education which reversed the school board's decision. The State Board concluded that the proposal largely met the requirements of the charter statute and that the charter should be granted if the foundation could submit a viable budget and facility plan. The school district appealed. The appellate court affirmed the State Board's decision finding that the agency had the authority to conditionally reverse local board's denial of a charter and finding nothing clearly erroneous in its decision to do so in this instance.

Board of Education of Roosevelt Union Free School District v. Board of Trustees of State University of New York, 723 N.Y.S.2d 262 (A.D. 3 Dept. 2001).

In April 2001, the Appellate Division of the Supreme Court of New York partially affirmed a trial court's finding that a school board had the "capacity to challenge" the granting of a charter, but not the constitutionality of the Charter Schools Act. The school board and others brought suit questioning the application on grounds it failed to adequately address the fiscal impact of the charter school on the district. As to one governmental entity suing another, the court saw the district as having a concrete interest and read the charter school act, while prohibiting a rejected charter school from seeking review, to permit a school board or district to seek administrative and judicial review of the granting of a charter. The court did agree that the Board of Regents essentially rubber-stamped the application and was correctly dropped from the case as a distant party to any possible injury. The remaining defendant was the chartering entity, the Trustees of the State University of New York. The school board's status as a state entity, in the court's view, did prohibit it from challenging the constitutionality of legislation. The school board had argued it had a proprietary interest in the funds that would be diverted to the charter, allowing it to sue. The court saw the monies as linked to the student and not to a right of the district.

Board of Education of Roosevelt Union Free School District v. Board of Trustees of the State University of New York, 731 N.Y.S.2d 524, 527 (App. Div. 3 Dept. 2001).

In October 2001, a New York Appellate court overturned the dismissal of a petition by a school board and others challenging the granting of a charter on the grounds that the chartering entity had failed, as required by law, to make a finding that the charter school was "likely to improve student learning and achievement" and had adequate community support, and to consider the fiscal impact on school districts of the charter school. The court accepted only the first premise, remitting the case on the grounds that the chartering authority presented no explicit findings on the potential impact on students. The court also found that, as well as the board, other affected parties, namely students, parents, taxpayers and residents of the district, had standing to sue.

Boyertown Area School District v. Department of Education, 797 A.2d 421 (Pa. Cmwlth.Ct. 2002).

A number of school districts sued the Pennsylvania Department of Education after the agency withheld payments of state funds to the school districts. The funds were withheld because each district refused to forward funds to "cyber" charter schools as directed by state law. The district maintained that the Department should not have withheld funds without first allowing the districts an opportunity to be heard on the issue. The court agreed, finding that the decision of the Department was an "adjudication" and should only have occurred after the districts had an opportunity to be heard. Accordingly the court vacated the deductions made by the Department and ordered that it re-consider the issue in a manner consistent with the courts opinion.

Brackbill v. Ron Brown Charter School, 777 A.2d 131 (Pa. Cmwlth. Ct. 2001).

In May 2001, the Commonwealth Court of Pennsylvania upheld the granting of a charter by the Charter School Appeal Board. The state board had issued the charter after a local school district board had denied the charter without regard to the procedures prescribed by law. The district failed to provide written notice of its original denial and, when it took no action on a revised application within the allotted time frame, the charter school appealed to the state board. When the state board granted the charter, the district board and taxpayers filed appeals. The district contended that it was not required to act on the resubmitted application because it was not actually revised and that the state board should rule on the original denial. The court found many revisions in the reapplication and read, in the Charter School Law, a clear district responsibility to act on the reapplication. The court also saw the charter law as permitting charter schools to contract services for school operations from for-profit companies, and for those companies to be involved in the planning and establishment of the school, so long as the charter was granted to a non-profit entity that maintained true authority and the school itself does not make a profit. The court also found that the state board had correctly applied the charter law in finding that the charter school had adequate community support. The court even found support from teachers, when the state board had not, by citing the teaching credentials of the board members who testified. Finally, the court also saw proposed facilities as satisfying the charter law, with no need for the school to have facilities under contract, especially given that the originally proposed facilities had been lost to the school by the delaying actions of the district. In addition, the court agreed with the state board in denying the taxpayers' petition to intervene.

Butler Area Sch. Dist. v. Einstein Acad. No. E.Q. No. 2001-50031 (Pa. Com. Pl. Sept. 10, 2001).

School districts unhappy with a "cyber" charter school authorized by another Pennsylvania school district challenged the school on four grounds (1) the constitutionality of cyber charter schools under the Pennsylvania Constitution; (2) the authorization of the cyber schools as inconsistent with the state charter school law; (3) the process by which the school was chartered; and (4) the non-compliance of the school with the charter school statute. As to the last two issues, the plaintiffs complained that even if cyber charter schools were constitutional and within the scope of the charter school statute, irregularities in the process of obtaining the charter rendered it out-of-compliance with the law. The group made a number of specific allegations but was especially troubled that the "non-profit entity" that received the charter was operated by the same two persons that owned and operated the "for-profit" group hired to manage the school. The group also alleged that students were not receiving the materials or instruction promised. The court determined that sufficient evidence existed to warrant the issuance of an injunction against the charter school prohibiting it from enrolling students who were residents of the challenging districts or collecting funds from them.

Council of Organizations about Parochiaid v. Governor. 566 N.W.2d 208 (Mich. 1997).

In July 1997, the Supreme Court of Michigan ruled that the state's charter school law was constitutional. In overturning the lower court rulings, the Supreme Court did not find that the state had relinquished the level of control and guidance of public schools called for in the state constitution. The appellees and a majority of the lower courts saw the lack of a public board as evidence of the private nature of charter schools, making them ineligible for public funds. The Supreme Court found charter schools to fit the constitutional definition of public schools by virtue of the ultimate control retained by the state, via the application, revocation, funding, and regulatory procedures in the law and applicable school codes. In addition, the will of the legislature was fulfilled by this definition of terms. In regards to the lack of the local public's selection of the board, the court traced their legitimacy through the legislature to the state body of voters. Again disagreeing with the plaintiffs' definitions, the court ruled that the schools at issue were not parochial schools, which were prohibited by the amended charter school law. A dissent warned that the legislature could not arbitrarily designate where the public sphere transformed to the private, and had in fact strayed across this divide in directing the state to cede direct control of individual board members and to abandon other regulatory functions.

Daugherty v. Vanguard Charter School Academy, 116 F.Supp. 2d 897 (W.D.Mich. 2000).

In September 2000, a U.S. District Court in Michigan granted a motion for summary judgment to a charter school accused by plaintiffs of violating state and federal constitutional protections regarding the establishment of religion. Parents brought the suit on behalf of their children, who they alleged had been subjected to religious influences at the school. The court found that the parents had standing to claim constitutional violations when their children were directly affected. This removed from contention plaintiff's complaints about religious aspects of the staff in-service training and Christmas party, as no students were present. The use of a parent room for prayer was also seen as not directly influencing the elementary school students. On the remaining items, upon which the parents had standing, the court found a lack of evidence that isolated expressions of religion, by parents and staff outside the classroom, had excessively entangled the school in religion. Clearly written school policies on religion's place in the curriculum allowed the Court to view prayer meetings on campus, bible readings at recess, and religious materials in student handouts as parental involvement accepted by the school in a manner neutral to religion. In the most serious matter, the classroom reading of stories about Jesus by a substitute teacher, the Court saw the corrective response by the principal as demonstrating that the school was not endorsing religion. The Court also dismissed claims that the use of the "Moral Focus Curriculum" was a gateway to religious indoctrination or that religious remarks by science teachers constituted a creationist curriculum. Overall, without evidence of direct school-supported indoctrination usurping parental rights to instill their own views, the Court found no injury to the children from the presence of religious activities on the school campus.

Fairfield Area Sch. Dist. v. Einstein Acad., No. 01-S-1008 (Pa. Com. Pl. Dec. 11, 2001), rev'd, 804 A.2d 762 (Pa. Cmwlth. Ct. 2002).

A court granted a preliminary injunction to a group of school districts challenging the existence of cyber charter schools in the state of Pennsylvania. Although reversed in later proceedings, the court in the initial hearing of the case found sufficient evidence to grant plaintiff's motion based on allegations that the cyber charter schools were improper given the intent of the charter school statute.

Francine Delany New School for Children, Inc. v. Asheville City Board of Education, 563 S.E.2d 92 (N.C. Ct. App. 2002).

This dispute between a charter school and it local school district occurred over the issue of funding and whether a proportion of certain monies collected by the county through a supplemental school tax, penal fines and forfeitures should be provided to the charter school. The school district had provided the charter school with funds collected through the annual appropriation, but not through the other revenue measures used by the county and provided to the school district. The trial court ruled in favor of the charter school and the school district appealed. The appellate court affirmed, finding that the requirement in North Carolina's charter school statute that charter schools receive a per pupil share of the "local current expense appropriation to the local administrative unit for the fiscal year" (N.C.G.S. '115C-238.29H(b)(2001)) included revenues from the disputed sources.

In re Abbott v. Burke Implementing Regulations, 792 A.2d 412 (N.J. Sup. A.D. 2002).

As part of an ongoing challenge to New Jersey's system of funding, a group a children who attend districts designated by the state and court as "special needs" or "Abbott" districts challenged the exclusion of charter schools physically located within such districts from compliance with the regulatory provisions for "special needs districts." The plaintiffs maintained that charter schools located within special needs districts should have available the fiscal benefits that flow from that designation and should also be required to comply with the same rules as other traditional public schools in the district. They further asserted that charter schools' exclusion from these districts violated the state's constitution. The court rejected this argument finding that New Jersey's charter school law was an alternative reform measure enacted in addition to the special needs districts, charter schools require flexibility in order to offer the innovative programs consistent with legislative intent, no history of charter school failure exists to make them analogous to the special needs districts, and parents may choose but are never compelled to send their children to charter schools. Therefore, the court found no constitutional barrier to excluding charter schools from "Abbott" reform measures.

In re Charter School Appeal of Greater Brunswick Charter School, 332 N.J.Super. 409, 753 A.2d 1155 (N.J.Super.A.D. 1999).

In May 1999, the Superior Court of New Jersey affirmed a lower court ruling upholding the approval of a charter school by the Commissioner of Education and the State Board of Education. In general, the court deferred to the Commissioner's discretion in the application process. The judges found little need in the application for the specificity argued for by the district board of education, which brought the appeal. In regards to procedure, the court found that the Commissioner had the power of final approval and had acted on specific criteria. Furthermore, the judges accepted the Commissioner soliciting addenda to the school's application, as they did not see the application process as an adversarial one in which an insufficiently presented case should be rejected. As the school had begun operation, the court passed on curriculum issues and only ordered a remedy to the one argument of the district it accepted, when it directed that, starting in the new school year, the leader of the school, by whatever title addressed, was to be properly certified. The court approved of the charter school being regional, seeing such a development as a logical expression of the law. Claims of financial harm to the district were dismissed as an issue more appropriate for the legislature. The court also rejected the district's contention that the Commissioner should be required to consider the impact of the charter school on the school district's racial balance. Overall, in speculative matters, the court suggested objections were best dealt with when they actually occurred.

In re Grant of the Charter School Application of Englewood on the Palisades Charter Sch., 753 A.2d 687, 697 (N.J. 2000).

This consolidated opinion, by the Superior Court of New Jersey, was decided in March 1999 in favor of the defendant charter schools who were challenged by their local school boards. The three charter schools (Englewood on the Palisades, Classical Academy Charter School of Clifton, and Franklin Charter School) filed for approval from the New Jersey Department of Education in August 1997. In each case, the charter school received approval after revisions and additions to their application, as called for by state reviewers. The local boards opposed the charter schools by, in Englewood's case, passing a resolution stating its opposition, and, in Clifton and Franklin Township, by writing to the Commissioner of Education. After the Commissioner granted approval, the boards appealed to the State Board of Education, which upheld the Commissioner's decisions in all three cases, on April 3, 1998. The school boards appealed to the Superior Court which addressed the three cases together. The boards challenged the schools by asserting that they did not meet the "informational requirements of the Act or regulations." In Englewood's case, the board's complaint argued that the founders of the charter school did not meet the Act's criteria requiring some number of the founders being teachers and/or parents of attending students. The court agreed with the charter school's interpretation of the statutes, allowing that one parent was adequate and that teachers could be from out-of-state. Additionally, the board said the lack of specifics concerning facilities and the composition of the charter school's Board of Trustees invalidated the application. The Court found the issue of facilities moot, as the school had subsequently opened, the board's request for a stay having been rejected, and it did not read the regulations concerning Trustees in the board's favor. As well, it dismissed the board's contention that the charter school's adoption of the district's calendar as lacking innovation, a key requirement of the Act.

International High School: A Charter School at LaGuardia Community College v. Mills, 715 N.Y.S.2d 490 (App. Div. 3 Dept 2000).

In November 2000, a New York Supreme appellate court affirmed a lower court's dismissal of a petition by charter schools attempting to retain their previous status in another category of alternative schools so as to retain their exemptions from state testing. Each of the schools were existing public schools that had converted to charter school status. The schools' previous status as "twenty-first century schools" allowed them to assess students without the statewide Regents exams. The court ruled that the schools had voluntarily relinquished their original status and any accompanying variances when they converted to charter schools. Furthermore, as contractual corporations separate from the school district, they were not eligible for "twenty-first school" status. Consequently, as charter schools they were bound by the state's education law requirements that charter schools administer Regents exams. The court read the charter law as prescribing that inconsistencies between the governing statutes be decided in favor of the charter law.

Keystone Central School District v. Sugar Valley Concerned Citizens, 799 A.2d 209 (Pa. Cmwlth. 2002).

A school district appealed Pennsylvania's Charter School Appeal Board's (CAB) decision to reverse its denial of a charter school application. The CAB first voted 3–3 with regard to the appeal, but later voted again 4–1 to reverse the decision of the school district denying the charter school application. The school district filed suit maintaining that the first CAB vote having resulted in a tie should be considered an affirmance of its decision to deny. The court disagreed finding the CAB's first vote amounted to "no action." In addition, the court found the CAB's later reversal of the school district's action was a proper *de novo* review under the charter school law and that the CAB had based its vote on ample evidence.

Megan C. v. Independent School District No 625, 30 IDELR 132 (D.Minn. 1999).

In a dispute over the appropriateness of the programming provided to a child with a disability, a federal district court based its decision in favor of the defendant school district on the fact that the mother withdrew her child from a district school and enrolled her at a charter school. When she did so, the charter school became responsible for the development and implementation of an appropriate individualized educational program (IEP), not the previously attended school district.

Milwaukee Teacher's Education Association v. Milwaukee Board of School Directors, Case No. 97-2110, (Wis. Ct. App. 1998).

A teachers union challenged the propriety of Wisconsin's charter school statute. At the time, the law prohibited the board of directors of Milwaukee Public Schools from engaging in collective bargaining over the issue of the conversion of an existing school to a charter school or the reassignments of employees at the time of conversion They also asserted that the law was unconstitutional as it was passed as part of the state's budget bill. The trial court had issued a temporary restraining order which prohibited Milwaukee Public Schools from chartering any additional charter schools until the decision on the merits of the claim could be resolved. The trial court was persuaded that the plaintiffs were likely to prevail on at least one of their claims, that of the method of the bill's enactment. In an unpublished opinion, the appellate court determined that the matter was better resolved by the Wisconsin Supreme Court and certified for appeal.

Montessori Regional Charter School v. Millcreek Township School District, 810 A.2d 718 (Pa. Cmwlth. 2002).

A group wished to begin a regional charter school and applied to the thirteen school districts it wished to draw students from. All thirteen denied the application at which point the group re-applied to five of the school districts. Having been denied a second time, the group decided to appeal, but only within two of the districts. As required by the charter school law, the group obtained signatures of two percent of the residents of each of the two districts and appealed to Pennsylvania's Charter School Appeals Board (CAB). The school districts challenged the appeal in state court on the grounds that the group that wished to operate the charter school needed the requisite number of signatures from all five school districts. The trial court ruled in the school districts' favor. On appeal, the court determined that nothing in the charter school law required that appeal be taken on all the denials received. Rather, the group was required to obtain signatures in support of its appeal only in those districts it sought to operate. Since the group had abandoned its original goal of operating in the other districts, the appeal could go forward with respect to the two districts from which it had sought and obtained signatures of support.

Mosaica Academy Charter School v. Pennsylvania Department of Education, 813 A.2d 813 (Penn. 2002).

A charter school sued in order to have the court compel a school district to pay the per capita required allotment for each resident of the district enrolled in the charter and to provide transportation of resident students to the charter school. The trial court entered a judgment for the charter school and ordered the school district to pay attorneys fees and costs in addition to providing the funding and transportation at issue. The school district appealed. The Pennsylvania Supreme Court affirmed the decision with respect to per pupil funding and transportation, finding the charter school law clear on each of these points. However, the court reversed the holding of the lower court determining that the award of attorney fees and costs was not proper in this instance as it amounted to "ancillary relief."

Nuffer v. Molalla River School District, 65 P.3d 1111 (Or. App. 2003).

A school administrator was dismissed by the school district. She challenged her dismissal on the grounds that she was the director of a charter school and therefore, only the charter school's governing body could dismiss her. However, the court concluded that the school had never been properly constituted as a charter school since it had never established as a nonprofit organization under Oregon law and therefore, the school never operated as a charter school within the meaning of the act. Accordingly, the school district acted within its discretion when it dismissed her. The court did not rule on whether her dismissal would have been proper had the school actually operated as public charter school.

Orange Ave. Charter Sch. v. St. Lucie County Sch. Bd., 763 So.2d 531 (Fla. Dist. Ct. App. 2000).

A charter school was denied a renewal of its charter by a local school board. The charter school appealed to the Florida State Board of Education. The state board ruled in favor of the charter school and, consistent with Florida statutes, remanded the matter to the local school board for re-consideration. The school board then held a public hearing on the matter and took evidence on the issue of the school's contract renewal. It then made a finding that the school failed to show that students enrolled performed to standards or made sufficient progress toward them. Based on this finding, the school board again denied renewal of the charter. The school appealed to state court. The court found that the school district's second finding was consistent with its discretion under the appeals procedure, that the hearing provided the charter school was proper, and that the school district had sufficient evidence upon which to base its decision. Thus the court upheld the school district's determination not to renew the school's charter.

Pa. Sch. Bds. Ass'n v. Zogby, 802 A.2d 6 (Pa. Cmwlth. Ct. 2002).

In June 2002, the Commonwealth Court of Pennsylvania denied a petition by school districts to restore state education subsidies withheld by the Secretary of

Education. The state monies had been rerouted to cyber charter schools that had been refused tuition payments by the districts. The districts asked the court to rule that cyber charters were illegal. While finding several issues beyond their immediate jurisdiction, a majority of the judges did rule that cyber schools were reasonable interpretations of the Charter School Law. As well, the court found the interests of the districts too distant to allow them to challenge the legality of a charter school, with such standing being limited to the participants—the chartering school district and the State Charter School Appeal Board. The court saw the Charter School Law as limiting the extent of a non-chartering district's involvement to making tuition payments. Furthermore, the court also saw the Secretary as a "stranger" to the process, having no authority to rule on the legality of cyber schools. The Secretary was following the law in withholding the funds, and though the court directed the Department of Education to allow the districts to challenge that action, the legality of cyber schools was not to be an issue in the process. The limited view of who had standing to challenge a charter school drew a dissent in which the withholding of subsidies was seen as an adverse affect of state action that conferred standing on the non-chartering, yet paying, districts.

PLANS, Inc. v. Sacramento City Unified School District, 319 F.3d 504 (9th Cir. 2003).

A group of California citizens and taxpayers, People for Legal and Non Sectarian Schools (PLANS) sued two school districts for sponsoring schools that employed a Waldorf curriculum. One of the two schools in question was the Yuba City Charter School. PLANS objection stemmed from the relationship between the Waldorf curriculum and Anthroposophy, a religion founded by the creator of the Waldorf curriculum, Rudolf Steiner. PLANS maintained that Anthroposophy infused the Waldorf curriculum such that the two were inseparable and challenged the public support of the schools as a violation of the Establishment of Religion Clause of the First Amendment to the U.S. Constitution. The district court dismissed the complaint on the grounds that the organization lacked taxpayer standing to bring the suit. The Ninth Circuit Court of Appeals reversed holding that because the group challenged the curriculum as a whole, not a single activity or set of activities, and because substantial public funds supported the schools in question, PLANS had standing to assert its complaint.

Porta v. Klagholz, 19 F.Supp.2d 290 (D.N.J. 1998).

A challenge was brought against the New Jersey charter school law; in particular the operation of a charter school in a building owned by a church, alleging that the law violated the Establishment of Religion Clause of the First Amendment. By the time the case went before the court, the specific charter school in question had moved out of the church. As such the court determined that the plaintiff, a taxpayer, had failed to advance a justiciable issue." The court also found the fact that the school had moved rendered the issue moot. The court then examined the charter school statute on its face and found nothing to suggest that merely leasing church property without more violated the Establishment Clause of the First Amendment. Finally the court found nothing in the specific lease agreement in question provided evidence of an Establishment Clause violation.

Pry v. Spartz, 1997 WL 718673 (Del.Super. 1997).

In August 1997, the Superior Court of Delaware, in an unpublished opinion and without ruling on the merits of the case, denied a request for a Writ of Prohibition barring the State Board of Education from proceeding on an application for a charter school. The plaintiff argued that it was not proper for the board to consider the reapplication by an Edison school, because it had earlier rejected the application, time had elapsed, and that the Charter School Act and state constitution prohibited the board from granting charters to for-profit corporations. The judge saw no harm, which could not be remedied later, in the application hearing proceeding and suggested the issues be addressed if and when the board approved the charter.

Richard Milburn Public Charter Alternative High School v. Cafritz, 798 A.2d 531 (D.C. 2002).

In May 2002, the District of Columbia Court of Appeals decided that two charter schools did not have the right to a contested case hearing in the process leading to their charter revocations. In the consolidated case, the court found no requirement for a trial-like hearing in District of Columbia statutes. The schools had also argued that their Fifth Amendment rights to due process required a contested hearing, allowing them to cross-examine witnesses and present a fuller case. The judge found adequate safeguards, in the revocation procedure used to protect the private interests of the charter schools. Thus these private interests did not outweigh the governmental interests in regulating charter schools. The court upheld the District Board of Education's procedures and decisions in revoking the charters.

Riester v. Riverside Community School, 257 F.Supp.2d 968 (S.D.Ohio 2002).

A teacher complained to the principal of the charter school in which she worked about what she alleged to be its failure to appropriately provide services for a child with an emotional disability. She also complained about the delivery of special education services generally. The principal fired her for insubordination and the teacher sued, alleging she was wrongfully dismissed for exercising her rights to freedom of speech under the First Amendment. The school was managed by a for-profit management organization. The school, the management company, and the principal filed motions to dismiss on the theory that the principal was a private and not a public employee and therefore not a state actor within the meaning of the First Amendment. The court rejected this argument concluding that the school's status as a public charter school meant that the actions of the school principal and management company constituted state action. Accordingly, the court refused to dismiss the case.

Salt River Pima-Maricopa Indian Community School v. Arizona, 23 P.3d 103 (Ariz. Ct. App. 2001).

In May 2001, the Court of Appeals of Arizona affirmed a lower court finding in favor of the state and its method of calculating funding for charter schools. Charter schools receiving funding from the Bureau of Indian Affairs (BIA) argued that their state equalization funding should not be eliminated because of the BIA funding. The contested statute calls for the reduction of funding equal to any monies from federal or state agencies, so that taxpayers did not pay twice for education. The court saw the statute as a reasonable classification that did not violate the state or federal Equal Protection Clauses. Native American students were not being adversely harmed or denied an education since the net funding, with the BIA monies, was equal to what the schools would have received from the state. Without disproportionately negative effects, no violation of Title VI was established and the right to an education, under the state constitution, was fulfilled. Finally, the court did not accept that charter schools met the definition of "state" under the Pastor Amendment and were thus not bound by the Amendment, which prohibits the deduction of federal funds in state aid formulas.

School District of the City of York v. Lincoln-Edison Charter School, 772 A.2d 1045 (Pa. Cmwlth. Ct. 2001).

In April 2001, a Commonwealth Court of Pennsylvania ruled on a petition, by a school district, asking the court to review a decision by the Charter School Appeal Board, which reversed the district's denial of a charter. The district had cited 25 reasons for denying the charter to an organization attempting to convert an existing elementary school. The court found the state board to be well within its authority in overriding a district's decision and in accepting additional evidence in the process. In regards to a challenge to the legitimacy of the signatures on the petition, the court found that addresses were not necessary and that the burden of proof fell on the district to show that signators were not parents or teachers. However, the management agreement between the proposed charter school and the Edison Corporation failed to pass muster with the court, which read the law as proscribing the employee relationship proposed and which did not allow the state board's recognition of a tentative model. Thus, the court remanded the case for further review by the state board.

School District of Philadelphia v. Independent Charter Sch., 774 A.2d 798 (Pa. Cmwlth. Ct. 2001).

In May, 2001, a Pennsylvania court upheld an order by the Charter School Appeal Board directing a school district to grant a charter. The district had failed to vote in a timely fashion on the school's application, which the court saw as clearly allowing the appeal and the assumption of jurisdiction by the state board. The only original objection given any weight by the court, the lack of a facility, was made moot by a site having been identified and backed financially, during the pendency of the proceedings. The court continued to defer, as it felt was proper in these matters, to the administrative agency in ruling that the state board had made the findings necessary to grant the charter and order the district to issue the charter contract.

Shelby School v. Arizona State Board of Education, 962 P.2d 230, 244 (Ariz. Ct. App. 1998).

In June 1998, a Court of Appeals of Arizona affirmed and reversed in parts, and remanded a case in which a private school had gone to court to seek a review of the state Board of Education's denial of a charter. The court found the state board's actions skirted the line of acceptability, but were for the most part reasonable expressions of its authority, only failing to act in line with statute when not accepting amendments by the charter school sponsors to their application. The court found the state board's request for financial records from the proposed school's board members sound, even if awkwardly administrated; as well, the board's denial of the charter based on the sponsors' creditworthiness was well within its authority. Given the need to review credit reports in private, the board had also acted properly in deliberating in executive session, before voting in open session, though the court found this issue suspended in tension within the law's requirements. But while it agreed that the state board could add requirements midstream, it saw a similar power and responsibility on its part to accept amendments to the application. The court saw no merit in the argument that a property interest, triggering Fifth and Fourteenth Amendment grounds, existed in the potentiality of a school. The sponsors were not entitled to a school charter or due process. Nor did the court find constitutional violations of the school sponsor's rights to free association, religious affiliation, or privacy in the board's investigative practices, in that it was reasonable for the board to examine whether the proposed school had successfully distanced itself from its predecessor school, the Church of Immortal Consciousness. As well, the court found no violation of equal protection rights, as it was sensible for the state to treat charter schools in a different manner that traditional public schools. The board's actions also passed muster, though did not set standards, in regards to the Administrative Procedures Act. The case was remanded to the lower court for review, with the opportunity of amendments to the application.

Shenango Valley Regional Charter School v. Hermitage School District, 756 A.2d 1191 (Pa. Cmwlth. 2000).

In July 2000, a Pennsylvania court affirmed the State Charter School Appeal Board's decision to uphold a district's denial of a charter school application. The potential charter school petitioned for review of the Board's order on two grounds. First, the Board had refused to accept additional evidence from the school, finding it insubstantial. The charter petitioners also argued that the Board did not deliver its decision within the statutorily stipulated time frame. The court read the Charter School Law as clearly sustaining the Board's actions. The judges agreed with the Board and the district that the school's application failed to address the requirements of the law concerning curriculum, school operations, financial planning, and student enrollment.

Souderton Area Sch. Dist. v. Souderton Charter Sch. Collaborative, 764 A.2d 688 (Pa. Cmwlth. Ct. 2000).

In December 2000, a Commonwealth Court of Pennsylvania affirmed the State Charter School Appeal Board's reversal of a district's denial of a charter. The district had denied the charter on the grounds that the proposed school failed to add any new dimension to the district or to have adequate standards or facilities. The school appealed to the state board, which reversed the decision and, after the district still failed to sign the charter, signed the charter through the pen of a state board member. The district appealed to the court, questioning the board's procedures. The court found the Board's actions comported with the Charter School Law. First, the court accepted the timing of the charter school's appeal as suitable under the law. As well, the judges did not read the law's instructions, directing the state board to pay "due consideration" to a district's judgments, as requiring any particular standard of review. Finally, the court dismissed a range of objections by the district to the Board's operating procedures, only pausing in judgment over one argument concerning facilities. The court affirmed the Board's directive to the district to grant the charter and its denial of the district's motion to dismiss.

St. Clair Education v. St, Clair Intermediate, 630 N.W.2d 909 (Mich.App. 2001).

In May 2001, the Court of Appeals of Michigan upheld the Michigan Employment Relations Commission's decisions regarding union charges of unfair labor practices against a school district. In agreeing with the commission, the court found that the school had interfered with a nurse's right to attempt to join the union by threatening to eliminate her position, but that the district was clear of the charge of refusing to bargain collectively with the union, and that the commission did not err in refusing to reopen the proceedings in response to new evidence from the union, as it was insufficient to effect the decision. The district and a manufacturing group had set up a public school academy (Michigan's term for a charter school). The union objected to the contract between the district and the academy, in that it allowed the academy to hire "at-will" employees to carry out the services it was providing for the district. When the district transferred a program to the academy, in an arrangement that retained some control, the union viewed the "transferred" employee as jointly employed by the academy and the district, and thus subject to the district's collective bargaining agreement. The teacher had been laid off from his position in the district and hired at the academy in a similar position. The court found the level of the district's control over the employee, in the new academy position, insufficient to make the district a joint employer. Nor did it find any conflict between the Michigan and state labor law regarding joint employers. The court did not adopt the union's perspective, which viewed the academy as a charade constructed to avoid bargaining with the union and that, potentially, the entire school operations could be transferred beyond the reach of unionization.

Thompson v. Board of the Special School District No. 1, 144 F.3d 574 (8th Cir. 1998).

In a case brought under the Individuals with Disabilities Education Act (IDEA), the court held that when a child enrolled in a charter school, he could no longer file a complaint against his previous district as the charter school became responsible for providing FAPE upon his enrollment there.

Utah School Boards Association v. Utah State Board of Education, 17 P.3d 1125 (Utah 2001).

In January 2001, the Supreme Court of Utah affirmed a lower court decision finding the powers given to the State Board of Education in the Charter Schools Act constitutional. The state's school boards association had sued on the grounds that the state constitution only gave an overall supervisory control to the Board and not the power to control local schools, as would be required to establish charter schools. The court saw the general control granted the Board as inclusive of any lesser powers needed to grant charters. As well, the court pointed to a list of other legislation that gave particularized authority to the Board allowing it to administer specific school programs. The court saw no logic in the plaintiff's assertion that the Board's actions must be uniform across schools and suggested that extending such unreasonable thinking would require the Board to establish the same requirements for kindergartens and high schools. The court saw no limitations in the constitution that required such an ineffectual approach or that barred legislators from granting the Board the authority needed to grant charters.

Village Charter Sch. v. Chester Upland Sch. Dist., 813 A.2d 20 (Pa. Cmwlth. Ct. 2002).

A charter school challenged a school district over its failure to provide funding for students enrolled there under Pennsylvania's charter school law. The school had not availed itself of administrative remedies with the state department of education to resolve its grievance and instead argued that administrative remedies were inadequate to settle the issue in a timely fashion. The court determined that the charter school was required to exhaust administrative remedies prior to bringing suit on the issue and rejected the argument that such remedies were inadequate in this instance.

West Chester Area School District v. Collegium Charter School, 812 A.2d 1172 (Penn. 2002).

In December 2002, the Pennsylvania Supreme Court affirmed a lower court's determination that the State Charter School Appeal Board's (CAB) decision to reverse a school district's denial of a charter was proper. In the consolidated appeal, by the school district and taxpayers, the court ruled on several issues related to Pennsylvania's Charter School Law. It began by determining that the CAB was authorized to engage in a *de novo* review of any matter before it. It also determined that when the CAB vote was communicated to the board, the school district had ten days to act on that vote by approving the contested charter school application. The judges also agreed with the state board's interpretation of the statutes as not requiring a school to apply for a regional charter unless it was located in more than one district, and not, as the petitioners argued, when it drew students from beyond its home district. The court also concluded that the proposed contract between the charter school and a for-profit management company did not violate the charter school law. The court agreed with the CAB's determination that the non-profit corporation running the school had suitable independence from the for-profit organization hired to operate parts of the school and the non-profit charter school was ultimately in control, despite the for-profit company's involvement in the original application by the school. Finally, the court found the state board to be well within its authority in overriding a district's decision and in denying taxpayers' petition to intervene. The taxpayers' claims of harm, to the finances of their school districts and to public interest, were seen by the court as speculative and too far removed.

Wilson v. State Board of Education, 89 Cal.Rptr.2d 745 (Ct. App. 1999).

In October 1999, a California Court of Appeal, in affirming a lower court decision, found the state's Charter Schools Act constitutional. The court rejected all of the challenges brought by residents and taxpayers in their petition for a court order to stop the Board of Education from granting charters or from funding charter schools. The court found the plaintiff's reading of the law shortsighted and mired in future hypothetical situations. Under a standard of review that presumes the constitutionality of legislative actions, the court saw the law as tailored to fit the intent of the legislators, which was to bring innovation and choice to public schools. Given these goals, the court found the delegation of authority to charter schools reasonable and properly balanced with procedural safeguards. The court found the legislature had properly exercised its power, as charter schools were created as part of the public school system and remained under the control of public officers, even while controlling their own educational functions, such as those of curriculum, textbook selection, methodology, etc. The details of those functions were not prescribed in the state constitution and were not the responsibilities of the legislators, but rather were commonly the prerogative of districts and thus could be for charter schools. Adequate control remained in state hands by way of the application-approval process, regulations, funding, and through ongoing oversight with the possibility of charter revocation. This control remained adequate when schools were operated by nonprofit organizations and was sufficient to address the plaintiff's concern that religious groups would receive charters.

Appendix E

Charter School Statutes

State	Statutory Reference	Web Site Availability
Alaska	Alaska Stat. § 14, ch. 3	http://www.eed.state.ak.us/Alaskan_Schools/charter/
Arizona	Ariz. Rev. Stat. § 15, art. 8	http://www.ade.state.az.us/charter schools/info/
Arkansas	Ark. Code Ann. ch. 6, § 23	http://arkedu.state.ar.us/schools/schools_charterschools_p2.html# Waivers
California	Cal. Educ. Code § 47600 *et seq.*	http://www.cde.ca.gov/charter/
Colorado	Colo. Rev. Stat. § 22-30.5 *et seq.*	http://www.cde.state.co.us/index_charter.htm
Connecticut	Conn. Gen. Stat. § 10-66ee	http://www.state.ct.us/sde/charter.htm
Delaware	Del. Code Ann. tit. 14, ch. 5	http://www.doe.state.de.us/Charter Schools/charter_schools.htm
District of Columbia	D.C. Code Ann. § 31-2853	http://www.dcpubliccharter.com/
Florida	Fla. Stat. ch. 228.056	http://www.firn.edu/doe/choice/charter.html
Georgia	Ga. Code. Ann. § 20-2-2060 *et seq.*	http://www.doe.k12.ga.us/charterschools/cs_act_1998.pdf
Hawaii	Haw. Rev. Stat. § 302A-1182	http://www.uhh.hawaii.edu/%7Echarter/HawaiiStat.htm
Idaho	Idaho Code § 33-5200 *et seq.*	http://www.sde.state.id.us/instruct/charter/law.htm
Illinois	Ill. Comp. Stat. 5/27A *et seq.*	http://www.isbe.state.il.us/charter/
Indiana	Ind. Code § 20-5.5 *et seq.*	http://www.in.gov/legislative/ic/code/title20/
Iowa	Iowa Stat. § 256F	http://www.state.ia.us/educate/index.html
Kansas	Kan. Stat. Ann. § 72-1900 *et seq.*	http://www.ksde.org/charter/chartindex.html
Louisiana	La. Rev. Stat. Ann., tit. 17, ch. 42.	http://www.doe.state.la.us/DOE/asps/home.asp?I=CHARTER

Maryland	Md. Educ. Code § 6-401 *et.seq.*	http://www.msde.state.md.us/programs/charterquestions.html
Massachusetts	Mass. Gen. Laws ch. 71, § 89	http://www.doe.mass.edu/lawsregs/ch71s89.html
Michigan	Mich. Comp. Laws, part 6A, ch. 380,n§ 500	http://www.michigan.gov/mde/1,1607, 7-140-6525—,00.html
Minnesota	Minn. Stat. § 124D	http://cfl.state.mn.us/charter/
Mississippi	Miss. Code Ann. § 37-28	http://www.mde.k12.ms.us/
Missouri	Mo. Rev. Stat. § 160.400 *et seq*	http://www.dese.state.mo.us/divimprove/charterschools/index.html
Nevada	Nev. Rev. Stat. § 336	http://www.nde.state.nv.us/sca/standards/index.html
New Hampshire	N.H. Rev. Stat. Ann. § 194-B	http://www.ed.state.nh.us/about/departme.htm
New Jersey	N.J. Stat. Ann. § 18A:36A	http://www.state.nj.us/njded/chartsch/regs.htm
New Mexico	N.M. Stat. Ann. §§ 22-8B & 22-8C	http://www.sde.state.nm.us/
New York	N.Y. Educ. Law § 2850 *et seq*	http://www.nycharterschools.org/
N. Carolina	N.C. Gen. Stat. § 115C-238	http://www.dpi.state.nc.us/charter_schools/maincharter.html
Ohio	Ohio Rev. Code Ann. § 3314	http://www.ode.state.or.us/supportservices/laws/index.htm
Oklahoma	Okla. Stat. § 70-3-130 *et seq.*	http://sde.state.ok.us/home/defaultns.html　(click on site map, law book)
Oregon	Or. Rev. Stat. § 338	http://www.ode.state.or.us/supportservices/laws/index.htm
Pennsylvania	1997 Pa. Laws 22	http://www.psba.org/
Puerto Rico	0P.R. Laws Ann. Tit. 111 § 18	
Rhode Island	R.I. Gen. Laws § 16-77	http://www.ridoe.net/legis_legal/default.htm
South Carolina	S.C. Code Ann. § 59-40	http://www.sde.state.sc.us/archive/parcomm/charts98.htm
Tennessee	Tenn. Code Ann. § 49-13	http://www.state.tn.us/education/ci/cichartersch/charterschmain.htm
Texas	Tex. Educ. Code Ann. § 12	http://www.tea.state.tx.us/charter/hb6.htm
Utah	Utah Code Ann. § 53A-1a-500 *et seq*	http://www.usoe.k12.ut.us/charterschools/

Virginia	Va. Code Ann. § 22-1-212	http://www.pen.k12.va.us/VDOE/PolicyPub/vacharter.html
Wisconsin	Wis. Stat. § 118.40	http://www.dpi.state.wi.us/dpi/dfm/sms/csindex.html
Wyoming	Wyo. Stat. Ann. § 21-2-300 *et seq*	http://www.k12.wy.us/schoolimprov/alted/charter.html

Appendix F

Charter School Law and Policy Links

US Charter Schools	http://www.uscharterschools.org/pub/uscs_docs/home.htm
National Charter Schools Institute	http://www.nationalcharterschools.org/charter.nsf
National Association of Charter School Authorizers	http://www.charterauthorizers.org/
Charter Friends National Network	http://www.charterfriends.org/
National Conference of State Legislatures	http://www.ncsl.org/programs/educ/c1schls.htm
CharterSchooLaw.com	http://www.charterschoolaw.com/
Center for Education Reform	http://www.edreform.com/charter_schools/
National Charter School Clearinghouse	http://www.ncsc.info/cgi-bin/link/first.asp

Index

Abbott v. Burke Implementing
  Regulations, 69–70
Accountability,
  contractual, 45–54
  federal standards of, 43–45
  parentally enforced, 34–56
  state standards of, 45
Adolescent Family Life Act, 170–172
Age Discrimination in Employment
  Act, 79
Agostini v. Felton, 169, 170, 173, 174,
  175, 176, 177, 179, 184
All Tribes American Indian Charter
  School, 117, 118
American Federation of Teachers, 1, 60
Americans with Disabilities Act, 79
  Title II, 145, 146–150
Arizona, 61, 68, 69, 157
Arkansas, 61, 72
Association of Recovery Schools, 194
Attention Deficit Hyperactivity
  Disorder, 147

Bagley v. Raymond School Depart-
  ment, 179
Beaufort County Board of Education
  v. Lighthouse Charter School, 28,
  30–31, 103–104, 105, 107–108
Berry v. School District of the City of
  Benton Harbor, 114
Bethel School District v. Fraser, 190
Blaine Amendments, 178
Board of Education of Independent
  School District No. 92 v. Earls, 195,
  196, 197
Board of Education of Kiryas Joel v.
  Grumet, 172, 176
Board of Education of Roosevelt
  Union Free School District v. Board
  of Trustees of SUNY, 18, 63, 65
Board of Education of School District
  No. 1 v. Booth, 36
Boston Renaissance Charter School,
  147, 148
Bowen v. Kendrick, 170, 171, 172
Boyertown Area School District v.
  Department of Education, 66

Brackbill v. Ron Brown Charter
  School, 24–25
Brighter Choice Charter Schools, 128,
  136, 138, 139
Brown v. Board of Education, 101, 110,
  117
Budde, Ray, 1
Bureau of Indian Affairs, 68
Butler Area School District v. Einstein
  Academy, 25

California, 22, 32–33, 35, 61–62, 71,
  114, 133, 167, 178, 180, 200
Canady v. Bossier Parish School
  Board, 190, 191
Case summaries, 247–262
Center for Education Reform, 43
Charter schools,
  accountability of; see Accountability
  appeal of denial of petition for, 26–29
  authorizers of, 159–161
  background of, 1–5
  benefits of, 2
  boards of education and, 35–36
  definition of, 1, 206–209
  discipline codes in, 189–202
  discriminatory treatment of, 67–71
  distribution of assets upon closure
    of, 72
  economic effect on school districts
    of, 62–67
  employment in, 77–96, 124
  establishment of, 17–20
  financial mismanagement by, 60–62
  for-profit companies and, 24–26
  funding of, 59–60
  gender and, 123–141
  health and safety standards in, 30–31
  number of, 1
  race and, 101–119
  religion and, 165–186
  revocation or renewal of, 49–53
  school law and, 5–8
  state constitutional challenges to,
    31–36, 63–64, 69–70, 178–179
  state variations in; see State laws
  statutes for, 64–66, 166–169, 263–265

students with disabilities and, 145–161

teachers in; see Teachers

three types of, 17

tuition and, 29–30

Charter Schools Expansion Act, 145

Civil Rights Act of 1964,
Title VI, 79, 146
Title VII, 79, 124, 140, 141

Colorado, 36, 54, 64, 166

Comfort ex. rel. Newmeyer v. Lynn School Committee, 108, 110–111

Connecticut, 51

Council of Organizations about Parochaid v. Governor, 32, 35–36

Creationism, teaching, 182–183

Curriculum,
minority-based, 117–118

Cyber schools, 20–24

Daugherty v. Vanguard Charter School Academy, 180–182

Desegregation, court-ordered, 114–117

Education Amendments of 1972,
Title IX, 124–126, 129, 130, 133, 140, 141, 146

Educational Resources Information Center, 189

Edwards v. Aguillard, 183

Einstein Academy Charter School, 25, 51, 55–56

El-Hajj Malik El-Shabazz Academy, 117

Employment Division v. Smith, 192–193

Equal Protection Clause, 67–69, 73, 95–96, 198–200, 202
and gender, 123, 126, 128, 130, 131, 132, 133
and race, 101–102, 103, 104, 108, 112, 117, 118
and religion, 166, 179–180, 186

Establishment Clause, 165, 166, 169–178, 179, 180–186

Ethics and morality, teaching, 180–182

Excel Charter Academy, 182

Federal law, 29, 30, 86–88, 166–169; see also U.S. Department of Education; names of legislative acts

Federal Public Charter School Program, 167, 168

First Amendment, 95, 182, 185; see also names of clauses

Florida, 53

Fourteenth Amendment, 82, 94, 95, 129, 140, 145; see also Equal Protection Clause

Fourth Amendment, 194, 202

Francine Delany New School for Children v. Asheville City Board of Education, 66–67

Free Exercise Clause, 190, 201

Free Speech Clause, 190–191

Freedom of Association, 198–200

Frontiero v. Richardson, 129

Garrett v. Board of Education of Detroit, 131, 138

Gavett v. Alexander, 198–199

Georgia, 178–179

Good News Club v. Milford Central School, 184–185

Goss v. Lopez, 201

Grutter v. Bollinger, 106, 107–108

Hazelwood School District v. Kuhlmeier, 190

Hix v. Halifax County Board of Education, 193

Home schooling, 20–24

Hunt v. McNair, 173

Idaho, 190

Illinois, 28, 128, 179

Illinois ex rel. McCollum v. Board of Education of School District No. 71, 184

In re Complaints Filed by the Highland Park Board of Education , 64

In re Grant of the Charter School Application of Englewood on the Palisades Charter School, 33, 63, 65, 78

Individuals with Disabilities Education Act, 86–87, 145, 147, 150–157, 158, 159, 161

International High School v. Mills, 18

Iowa, 18, 51

IQ tests, 146

Keystone Central School District v. Sugar Valley Concerned Citizens, 63

Lemon v. Kurtzman, 169, 170, 171, 173, 176, 177, 181, 183, 184
Lewis Fox Middle School, 138
Littlefield v. Forney School District, 191, 193
Louisiana, 183, 190

Maine, 179
Maria Mitchell Elementary School, 137, 138
Massachusetts, 81, 108, 147
Meek v. Pittenger, 173–174
Michigan, 32, 35–36, 80, 90–91, 131, 180, 183
Milliken v. Bradley, 115
Mississippi University for Women v. Hogan, 130, 131
Mitchell v. Helms, 173

National Association for the Advancement of Single Sex Public Education, 127
National Commission of Excellence, 1
National School Boards Association, 88
Nevada, 149
New Jersey, 33, 62, 63, 64, 65, 69, 78, 177
New York, 18, 63, 65, 128, 172
No Child Left Behind Act, 29, 43–45, 87–88, 126, 133
Non–racial preferential admissions policies, 111–114
North Carolina, 66–67

Ohio, 94–95
Oregon, 80

Parents,
    involvement contracts with, 197–200
    rights of, 189–202
Pennsylvania, 21–22, 24–26, 28, 51, 55–56, 61, 65, 66, 80–81, 207
Personnel Administrator of Massachusetts v. Feeney, 113, 118
Peter W. v. San Francisco Unified School District, 54–55
Porta v. Klagholz, 177
Private schools,
    charter schools considered as, 31–34
    conversion into charter schools of, 19–20, 176

Public schools,
    conversion into charter schools of, 17–19
    limits on variability of, 34
    single-sex schools and, 126–128

Racial balancing, 102–111
Regents of the University of California v. Bakke, 104, 107, 109
Rehabilitation Act of 1973,
    section 504, 145, 146–150, 158, 161
Religious instruction,
    after-school, 184–185
    released time for, 183–184
Robert Coleman Elementary School, 138
Rufo v. Inmates of Suffolk County Jail, 115–117

Salt River Pima-Maricopa Indian Community School v. Arizona, 66, 69
San Antonio Independent School District v. Rodriguez, 67–68, 69
School District of the City of Grand Rapids v. Ball, 170, 174, 175
School District of the City of York v. Lincoln-Edison Charter School, 25–26, 80–81
Shanker, Albert, 1
Shelby School v. Arizona State Board of Education, 27, 68–69
Shenango Valley Regional Charter School v. Hermitage School District, 61
Single-sex schools, 126–140
South Carolina, 28, 30–31, 64, 104, 106, 173
Special education. See Students with disabilities
State laws; see also state names
    admissions preferences and, 111–
    appeals processes and, 26–27
    chemical dependency and, 194
    collective bargaining and, 89
    conversion of private schools and, 19–21
    court-ordered desegregation and, 114
    employment and, 79
    establishment of charter schools and, 2–5, 206

for-profit management and, 24
funding and, 31, 60
local educational agencies and, 151–156
miscellaneous provisions of, 95
nonrenewal standards and, 51–53
public schools and, 34
racial balancing and, 102–103
religion and, 167
retirement programs and, 91–92
revocation and, 49–50
statutory requirements and, 46–48, 166–169, 263–265
teacher assignment and, 84
teacher certification and, 85–86
teacher termination and, 93
teachers' development role and, 77–78
teachers' leave of absence and, 82–83, 93
tenure and, 92
tuition and, 29
Students,
at-risk, 71, 128, 138
with disabilities, 70–71, 145–161
rights of, 189–202

Tannahill ex rel. Tannahill v. Lockney Independent School, 195, 196, 197
Teachers,
assignment of, 83–84
certification of, 84–88
collective bargaining by, 81–82, 88–91, 93
development role of, 77–78
leave of absence for, 82–83, 92–93
retirement funds for, 91–92
tenure for, 92–96
termination of, 93–95
Texas, 71, 148, 157, 191–192
Thurgood Marshall Elementary School, 138
Tilton v. Richardson, 173
Tinker v. Des Moines Independent Community School District, 190
TOVAS Charter School, 148
Tuttle v. Arlington County School Board, 105

Uniforms, mandatory, 189–193
United States v. O'Brien, 190–191

United States v. Virginia, 131–132, 136, 138, 139–140
U.S. Department of Education,
accountability standards of, 43–45
guidelines for local educational agencies, 133–135, 156
guidelines for school-community partnerships, 177
nonregulatory guidance, 168, 211–220, 239–245
Office for Civil Rights, 125, 130, 147–148, 151, 221–237
Office of Special Education Programs, 158
and single-sex schools, 139
Title I, 87–88, 175, 239–245
Urinalysis tests, mandatory, 194–197
Utah, 166
Utah School Board Association v. Utah State Board of Education, 36

Vernonia School District No. 47J v. Acton, 194, 195, 196, 197
Village of Arlington Heights v. Metropolitan Housing Development Corporation, 112
Vorchheimer v. School District of Philadelphia, 130

Washington v. Davis, 112
Web sites, 263–265, 267
Wessman v. Gittens, 109
West Chester Area School District v. Collegium Charter School, 24, 28, 65
Wilson v. State Board of Education, 32–33, 35, 113–114, 178
Wisconsin, 6, 23, 29–30, 112, 113, 179
Wisconsin v. Yoder, 192, 193
Wright v. Council of the City of Emporia, 115, 117

Young Women's Leadership Charter School, 128, 136

Zelman v. Simmons-Harris, 165
Zorach v. Clauson, 183–184

About the Authors

   Preston Green is an associate professor in the Department of Education Policy Studies at the Pennsylvania State University. He received a J. D. from Columbia University in 1992 and an Ed.D. from Columbia University, Teachers College in 1995. His research focuses on the legal and policy issues related to school choice and educational access. He has published articles in Wests Education Law Reporter, Texas Forum on Civil Liberties and Civil Rights, Journal of Education Finance, Brigham Young University Journal of Law and Education, Journal of Negro Education, Educational Measurement: Issues and Practice, Journal of Special Education Leadership, Journal of International Educational Reform, Equity and Excellence in Education, and Southern University Law Review. Additionally, he is co-author of Financing Education Systems, with Craig Richards and Bruce Baker, which will be published by Merrill/Prentice-Hall in 2004.

Julie Fisher Mead is an associate professor in the Department of Educational Administration at the University of Wisconsin at Madison. She received her doctorate from the University of Wisconsin in 1994. Dr. Mead researches and writes about topics related to the legal aspects of education. Her research centers on issues related to special education and various forms of school choice. She is co-author with Julie Underwood of Legal Aspects of Special Education and Pupil Services published by Allyn & Bacon. She has also published articles in the Educational Administration Quarterly, West's Education Law Reporter, the Boston University Public Interest Law Journal, the Michigan Journal of Race and Law, the Harvard Journal on Legislation, the Journal of Law and Education, Brigham Young Journal of Law and Education, Educational Considerations, and School Business Affairs. She has makes regular presentations at the annual meetings of the Education Law Association (ELA), the American Educational Research Association (AERA), and the University Council of Educational Administration (UCEA). Dr. Mead teaches courses on the legal aspects of educational administration and the legal aspects of special education and pupil services. She has experience as a teacher of hearing impaired students and as a special education administrator.